DATE DUE

Photo courtesy of I. DeVore.

AGGRESSION

IN MAN AND ANIMALS

ROGER N. JOHNSON
RAMAPO COLLEGE

W. B. SAUNDERS COMPANY · PHILADELPHIA · LONDON · TORONTO

W. B. Saunders Company: West Washington Square
Philadelpha, Pa.   19105

12 Dyott Street
London, WC1A 1DB

833 Oxford Street
Toronto 18, Ontario

Aggression in Man and Animals   ISBN 0-7216-5160-7

Print No: 9   8   7   6   5   4   3   2

TO LORI

PREFACE

Seldom does an author attempt a project so broad that it covers everything from cannibalism in termites to the massacre at My Lai. Such breadth is at once both a strength and a weakness, for it is obvious that no one is competent to master and integrate the vast literature of so many fields. Unfortunately, this difficulty has led many talented writers to confine their thoughts to their own specialty without attempting to consider what research is taking place in other areas. As a result, one of the barriers to the understanding of aggressive behavior has been the lack of "cross-fertilization" among disciplines.

One assumption of this book is that no field has a monopoly of truth or interest in the subject of aggression, and that each discipline contributes in some way. Knowledge obtained in one area cannot always be directly applied to another, as is often the case when considering both animal and human aggression. But aggression is not a unitary phenomenon, and a variety of approaches can contribute insights into how to conceptualize the problem, a contribution which is no small feat. For inspiration I have drawn from ethology, behavioral biology, genetics, neurophysiology, endocrinology, psychiatry, anthropology, sociology, criminology, political science, and, last but not least, all areas of psychology. The behavioral sciences have much to learn from each other, and I hope this book will help stimulate interdisciplinary interest in a problem which possesses both scientific interest and social significance.

I must acknowledge with thanks the valuable criticisms of many of my colleagues, including Michael DeSisto, Colby College; Frank Ervin, Massachusetts General Hospital; Seymour Feshbach, University of California at Los Angeles; David Hamburg, Stanford University Medical School; Harry Kaufmann, City College of New York; John Paul Scott, Bowling Green State University; Robert Singer, University of California at Riverside; and Marvin Wolfgang, University of Pennsylvania. I hasten to add that I did not adopt every suggestion, and therefore I alone am responsible for the views contained in this volume. Finally, I would like to thank my wife, Lori, who patiently aided and encouraged me from the beginning.

ROGER N. JOHNSON

CONTENTS

1 THE CONCEPT OF AGGRESSION

Man has more than a detached, scholarly interest in aggression. His difficulty in living harmoniously with nature and with his fellow man now threatens all forms of life, and his own future may depend on his ability to understand and control aggressive behavior. The long path of evolution has led to the point where man is the only animal consciously able to influence his own future, but whether this privilege leads to his preservation or to his downfall remains to be seen. Among baboons, the animal society that most closely resembles human society, destructive fighting is almost unknown in a stable ecological setting (Hall, 1964). Evolution, of course, will have the last word, and it may turn out that other animals will survive while *Homo sapiens* goes down as a dazzling but unsuccessful twig on the phylogenetic tree. As a species, man must confess to unspeakable violence and brutality, yet he is also distinguished by altruistic behavior and a remarkable capacity to learn and to adapt. We are not yet forced to conclude that man is hopelessly doomed, but at the same time we find it difficult to explain our turbulent and precarious existence. If man intends not merely to survive but to improve the quality of life, it is abundantly clear that there is an urgent need for a clearer understanding of all aspects of aggressive phenomena.

The study of aggression invariably begins where it should end—namely, with speculation about the "true nature" of man. Such speculation is as old as man himself, and more often than not philosophers and theologians have stressed man's innate depravity and capacity for evil. Many great religions are based on assumptions of original sin, inherent evil, and man's inability to exist without a benevolent guiding force to save him. These views may be the result of civilization's endless preoccupation with power and conquest, whether they be in the form of tribal wars, holy wars, or cold wars. Throughout history many great societies have

1

attempted to exterminate entire segments of humanity and to embroil in combat as much of the world as technologically feasible. This ominous trend has continued into the 20th century, and as societies have become more "civilized" they have also become more destructive. In a recent six-year period human beings spent over one trillion dollars on weapons of war (Smith, 1970). The values and priorities of modern society are further reflected by the fact that throughout the world $7800 is spent every year to train and to equip each soldier but only $200 is budgeted to educate each child. With the equivalent of 15 tons of TNT stockpiled for every man, woman, and child (Weinraub, 1970), and a violent crime occurring in the United States every 48 seconds (Uniform Crime Reports, 1969), one cannot help but be concerned about the future of man.

But we are not the first to worry about our future: history records that even the ancient Egyptians were troubled by crime in the streets (Gardner, 1963). It is dubious consolation to know that in fact nearly every era of recorded history has been accompanied by social violence (Hofstadter & Wallace, 1971), and what distinguishes contemporary social conflict is not the sudden emergence of evil but the technological capacity to engage efficiently in massive forms of destruction. Because man's tradition of violence and turmoil is an ancient one, many authors have offered it as proof to help explain our behavior. Scientists, on the other hand, tend to feel that this history is more a description of the problem than an explanation. Through an understanding of the dynamics of individiual behavior we may gain insights about institutional and social violence, but the opposite is not necessarily true. The difficulty in studying forms of violence such as war, racism, or inequities in criminal justice is that complex historical, political, and economic considerations may be more relevant than individual motivation. Wars, for example, are not caused by soldiers who desire to kill, and understanding the motivation of those who fight will not explain war. It turns out that most soldiers fight only because they are ordered to do so, and if given a choice most would prefer safety well behind the front lines. As Rapoport (1966) notes, international warfare has little to do with the aggressiveness of individuals, but rather is more related to culture and human institutions.

It is not surprising, therefore, that scientists have concentrated on aggression as a behavioral process. Unfortunately, scientists often do not agree any more than philosophers or theologians. Some theorists have relied more on ethical beliefs, political attitudes, or crime statistics than on scientific facts. As a result, some of the most popular notions about aggression are fundamentally myths without any scientific foundation. An example is Freud's concept of an instinct for death and destruction, which he dramatically labeled *thanatos* after the ancient Greek personification of death. More recently there have been theories which are curious mixtures of science and social philosophy. Notable are those expressed by Ardrey (1961, 1966, 1971) and Lorenz (1965, 1966), which rely heavily on extrapolations from animals. These writers popularized the view that aggression is a kind of inherited "instinct" found in man as well as other animals which has to be released. While their views continue to enjoy popularity with the laymen, they have been generally rejected by the academic community both for well-founded scientific reasons and for ill-founded emotional reasons (see Montagu, 1968). Another approach is represented by some psychologists (e.g., Kaufmann, 1970) who emphasize the role of social and learned factors while leaving only a minimal role for genetic and physiological variables. Sociologists and criminologists go even further and concentrate almost exclusively on cultural and environmental influences.

One of the difficulties with many theories of aggression is that their proponents tend to concentrate on their own discipline and ignore contributions from neighboring disciplines. It is not surprising that the result is an abundance of oversimplified, sweeping generalizations, of which the following are examples: (a) aggression is a universal instinct; (b) aggression is a single underlying motivational process; (c) aggression has some single antecedent or cause, such as pain or frustration; (d) all aggression is bad; (e) killing members of the same species always involves aggression while killing between species does not; (f) humans are by far the most aggressive of all animals; (g) the study of aggression in animals contributes little toward the understanding of human aggression. All of these statements are totally or partially false, as we shall see.

The range of speculation about aggressive behavior is unusually intense and diverse, and this is probably an indication both of our ignorance and of our concern. Fortunately we are not forced to choose between total plasticity and inherited impulses, for modern science has succeeded in destroying some of the age-old myths while also synthesizing many new facts. This has been accomplished largely through a recognition that there is no single discipline or scientific approach which has a monopoly of "truth" about aggression. We have come to recognize that important contributions come from many fields, including biology, medicine, psychology, sociology, criminology, anthropology, and political science. The study of aggressive behavior involves problem-oriented research rather than discipline-oriented research, and one of the major obstacles is to persuade scientists to look beyond the sheltered world of their own specialty. The nature of the problem demands an interdisciplinary approach, both in conceptualization and in research. There are inherent limitations to treating aggression as a narrow and unitary concept, and these limitations become quickly apparent when one attempts to define the term aggression.

CAN AGGRESSION BE DEFINED?

While it is convenient to conceive of aggression as a behavioral process, it remains difficult to analyze and to isolate from other forms of motivated behavior. Like so many psychological terms, it is a colorful concept loaded with surplus meaning, and as a result it receives almost indiscriminate usage in every day language. Aggression may be applied to a specific response such as killing. It may be used to refer to a host of emotional and attitudinal states such as anger or hate. It may be conceived of as a personality trait, a learned habit, a stereotyped reflex, or an underlying biological process. It may refer to motivation or intention without regard to consequences, or to the consequences (e.g., injury) without regard to motivation. In addition to all of these, there is the usual dictionary definition which is concerned mainly with the moral justification or legitimization of an act. Some of the complexities become apparent if we consider a few examples (see also Kaufmann, 1970):

1. A boy swats at a hornet and gets stung.
2. A cat kills a mouse, parades around with it, and then discards it.
3. A wolf kills and devours a stray sheep.
4. A farmer beheads a chicken and prepares it for Sunday dinner.
5. A hunter kills an animal and mounts it as a trophy.
6. A dog snarls at the mailman, but never bites him.
7. A doctor gives a flu shot to a screaming child.
8. A tennis player smashes his racket after missing a volley.
9. A boxer gives his opponent a bloody nose.
10. A Boy Scout tries to assist an old lady, but trips her by accident.
11. A small boy daydreams of beating up the neighborhood bully.
12. A woman nags and criticizes her husband, and he ignores her in return.

13. A firing squad executes a prisoner.

14. A bombardier presses a button and hundreds below are killed.

15. A bank robber is shot in the back while attempting to escape.

16. A politician evades legislation which might help clear up a crime-ridden slum.

17. A man commits suicide.

18. An assassin misses his target.

19. The President asks Congress for more money for the Department of Defense.

20. A man dislikes all Negroes, Jews, and college students with long hair.

21. Two friends get into a heated quarrel after drinking too much.

These examples have almost nothing in common, except that it might be convenient to label most of the behavior as having something to do with aggression. If we base a definition of aggression on whether or not physical injury takes place, then the hornet, the farmer, the doctor, the bombardier, and the police, among others, are being aggressive. The snarling dog, the daydreaming boy, and the assassin are not aggressive because they failed to cause any injury. The tennis player injures an inanimate object and the man committing suicide injures himself. If we liberalize the meaning to connote "psychological injury" as well as physical injury, then we can include the nagging wife, the bigot, and the quarreling friends. We can also include the frightened mailman, or the target of an assassination, and even the suicide which may have been carried out in revenge against others. But is psychological or even physical injury always possible to specify? The politician who tolerates slums will insist that he has hurt no one, and the silent husband knows that refusing to argue can be most devastating. The President will argue that he is really saving lives, and the bombardier feels he is only doing his job.

If aggressive behavior is defined in terms of anger and emotional involvement it has to be pointed out that many individuals get extremely angry without ever attacking or injuring anyone. Conversely, some individuals are capable of committing hideous brutality without any emotional involvement. If aggressive behavior is defined in terms of certain acts, such as killing or injuring, such a definition is unsatisfactory unless we know the intentions of the attacker and how the behavior is perceived by others. A high proportion of all killing which takes place among animals involves predation or food-getting behavior, and such killing has little to do with aggression. The farmer is not angry at his chickens and has no desire to see them suffer. Like the wolf, he is merely hungry. The doctor may hurt a child with his injection, but he intends no harm and, in fact intends to prevent harm. The same is true of the Boy Scout who trips the old lady by accident. As for the silence of the hen-pecked husband, it may be perceived either as a gesture of appeasement or as a provocation. Whether the nagging wife considers silence as an aggressive response depends on her perceptions of her husband's intentions. The problem of anchoring a definition on intentions is that it immediately brings in mentalistic and teleological perplexities which may obscure rather than clarify the concept. But as Feshbach (1971) points out, a functional analysis based on goals may reveal that the same behavior can have entirely different dynamics. For example, an individual may engage in aggressive behavior which is instrumental in achieving a nonaggressive goal. Thus, a robber may use force to get money, but his goal is getting money rather than injuring his victim. But if one individual attacks another because he wants to see his victim injured, this involves an aggressive drive that is clearly different from instrumental aggression. In the case of aggressive drive, the goal is the injury; in instrumental aggression, injury is the means rather than the end. In Freud's theorizing all aggression falls into the aggressive drive category.

The above examples serve to illustrate that it is difficult if not impossible to isolate the necessary and sufficient conditions to produce a satisfactory definition. In spite of the many difficulties, some authors continue to offer hard and fast definitions. Buss (1971) for example, states that aggression is the attempt of one individual to deliver noxious stimuli to another. This definition may have some merits for human aggression but it is particularly poor in accounting for animal aggression (in spite of the fact that Buss considers animal aggression to be physical, direct, and relatively easy to define). Killing certainly involves the delivery of noxious stimuli, yet as already mentioned most killing in animals is unrelated to aggression.

Most animal aggression is also neither physical nor direct, for it is usually carried out at a distance through ceremonies which involve no contact. Furthermore, if actual fighting does break out it is usually ritualized to the point where little attempt is made to injure the opponent. Sometimes the "delivery of noxious stimuli" involves nothing more than looking, as in the case of baboons and macaque monkeys, who may threaten an opponent simply by staring at him. Thus, aggression may be defined in a manner that sounds exact and specific, but upon closer examination such definitions must be interpreted very broadly and even then they are often vague and incorrect.

Aggression as a Multidimensional Concept

The difficulty in agreeing on a precise and accurate definition of aggression may reveal something about its nature. Perhaps the inability to settle on a unitary definition indicates that we are not dealing with a unitary process, or a single set of antecedents or consequents. Feshbach (1964; 1970; 1971) has pointed out that distinctions should be made between descriptive definitions of aggression and those based on some underlying process or theoretical construct. For example, an individual may be said to be aggressive, thus hypothesizing an underlying personality trait or motivational state, but his aggressive behavior may be expressed in many different ways, all of which reflect the same process. Alternatively, a particular behavior, such as killing, may be found in many individuals, but need not be the result of similar processes. Aggressive individuals are not always aggressive, even in similar situations; nor are nonaggressive individuals always peaceful. And not all members of an aggressive species will behave aggressively.

Another important problem which clouds a definition is the issue of legitimization, for as Buss (1971) points out, injurious attacks may not be considered aggressive if they occur in the context of a socially accepted role. A parent punishing his child usually has no aggressive motivation, nor does a teacher when he gives a bad grade. A judge regularly doles out punishment to individuals, yet he is only fulfilling the requirements of his occupation. But it is easy to see how just "doing your job" or "carrying out orders" can be distorted to sanction brutality and violence. Evaluating the social context inevitably involves moral judgments, and such subjective judgments may be crucial in interpreting an act as legitimate or illegitimate. Feshbach (1971) notes:

> ... the moral evaluation of a violent act is a function of the lawful status of the act, the extent of personal versus social motivation and the degree of personal responsibility as reflected in the role of authority, the options available to the individual, the defensive or initiated basis of the violence, the degree of emotional disturbance, the amount of force employed, and the intentionality of the act. To these criteria must be added normative considerations of fair play, the degree and manner of the violence, the age and sex of the victim, and more generally, the appropriateness of the target. Last to be mentioned, but probably most important, is one's attitude toward the objectives of the violence.

Such are the difficulties in trying to pinpoint satisfactory usages, and this seemingly futile task may offer more rewards to the semanticist than to the scientist. Any narrow and precise definition is easily embarrassed, and more comprehensive concepts are so general that they are of little use. The term aggression has so many meanings and connotations that in effect it has lost its meaning. But happily this is not a serious problem, for the real task is not to frame some pithy definition of aggression, but to understand the dynamics of aggressive behavior. The fact that the term is so difficult to define may not be because of a lack of intelligent thought, or of inadequacies in our language, but simply because it is not a simple, unitary concept and therefore cannot be defined as such. There is no single kind of behavior which can be called "aggressive" nor is there any single process which represents "aggression". Perhaps this is the most important thing which can be said about defining aggression, for it suggests that aggression must be understood and analyzed at many levels. The primitive Murngin of Australia recognize six separate kinds of conflict (Warner, 1930), and hopefully we can be at least as flexible and inventive.

The legitimate definitional problems with aggression need not force us to avoid the word, but simply to recognize that it is a casual term, not a technical term. As such, it has considerable communicative value, for most people have little trouble recognizing aggression when they see it. Definitions become more critical in the laboratory, where aggression must be carefully measured and controlled as a dependent or independent variable, and in this case only rigorous operational definitions will suffice (e.g., latency of attack, intensity of delivered electric shock, score on a standardized test, etc.). Where only modest levels of precision are necessary, it may be useful to adopt the term *agonistic behavior* as a desirable alternative to "aggressive behavior." The term agonistic behavior benefits from the fact that it is widely used by scientists but not laymen and therefore carries with it considerably less surplus meaning. It refers simply to fighting and competitive behavior, usually in animals, and includes threats and offensive attacks as well as defensive fighting.

In summary, there are many different kinds of aggressive behavior, and as a result there can be no single, satisfactory definition. As Washburn and Hamburg (1968) point out, initial tentative definitions may help identify the general nature of the problem, but accurate definitions may be expected only at the conclusion of research. The important challenge is to sort out the different behavioral processes involved and the many interacting factors which influence them.

EVOLUTION AND AGGRESSION

We know that the contemporary behavior of man is partly the result of the long and selective process of evolution. For many years it was fashionable to stress the uniqueness and great antiquity of the human lineage, but it is now almost certain that man shared a long period of common ancestry with the apes, particularly the African apes (Washburn and Harding, 1970; Washburn, 1971). Recent advances in molecular biology, including DNA hybridization experiments and studies of the immunological characteristics of cells, indicate that physiologically man is closer to the chimpanzee than sheep are to goats or dogs are to foxes. In many respects gorillas are more distantly related to chimps than we are, and such differences can be precisely compared with respect to cell structure and function. (Washburn has reviewed a number of studies which compare such factors as DNA, albumin, transferrin, fibrinopeptides, and carbonic anhydrase.) In any case, human behavior is difficult to understand without some evolutionary perspective, and a logical start is to ask how and why aggressive behavior evolved in the first place. For centuries philosophers have debated the "problem of evil" and asked why life on earth has been accompanied by so much violence and suffering. Why could it not have been otherwise? Why have most organisms evolved with the capacity to fight and kill, and what beneficial functions have resulted from this ceaseless strife? On the face of it, one wonders why all the aggressive species did not kill each other off, and why peaceful and cooperative animals did not inherit the earth.

Such questions are worth pondering, but there are no easy answers (other than postulating the existence of a Devil). The key must be found in the process of evolution, which was, and still is, a struggle for survival, a struggle made necessary by a physically changing environment. Evolution has been an almost automatic consequence of a changing world, for without change there would be no need for evolution. In a uniformly constant universe, organisms could survive without adaptation, but in a changing environment failure to adapt spells death. Evolution is the process by which generations of organisms gradually adapt to a changing world through genetic mutations which lead to the alterations in behavior or physical structure that become necessary for survival.

Intimately related to this struggle is constant competition with members of the same species (conspecifics) and with other species (nonconspecifics). Since no two individuals are exactly alike, useful individual differences have been those which favored survival. For example, mammals with weak sucking reflexes at birth have been less likely to survive than those with strong sucking reflexes, and sucking has become a specialized adaptation with great survival value.

But what survival value is there to fighting and killing? It is not obvious that aggressive behavior is categorically maladaptive, for if it were it would have become extinct eons ago. Perhaps there were organisms that fought indiscriminately; if so, they have disappeared into oblivion. Because of the competition for survival, animals which were skilled at securing and defending the necessities of life tended to be successful. But those that survived were not necessarily the most aggressive, for evolution most likely favored species which were selective in their aggressive behavior. This can be illustrated by the evolution of the canine complex in primates (Washburn and Hamburg, 1968). At one time large canine teeth and powerful jaws provided a distinct advantage, and many of our relatives, such as the baboon (see Frontispiece and Figure 7) still possess such features. Biting attack is a well-developed skill in primates, largely because of years of infant play in which biting is relatively harmless. But in late adolescence the canine teeth erupt and the temporal muscles more than double in size, and a single bite now may lead to swift death. In the evolution of early man such destructive weapons may have been maladaptive so that selective pressures operated toward the reduction in the size of the dangerous canine teeth. This reduction in canine teeth was completed several million years ago and reflects a general shift away from savage fighting toward the reliance on tools and language.

Thus the proto-hominid (the earliest form of man) may not have been particularly aggressive, at least until he had to compete with other species for food. Not being unusually strong or fast, and possessing no deadly horns or hooves, man adapted by developing tools and weapons which allowed him to attack at a distance, thus gaining some advantage over his competitors. This is not a particularly unusual evolutionary step, for many animals even today use tools to assist their predatory behavior. For example, Van Lawick-Goodall (1968a) carefully describes how Egyptian vultures gather stones and sling them at ostrich eggs to crack the shell. We might conclude that evolution tended to favor the best hunters and killers, just as long as killing was selective and limited to nonconspecifics. While such deadliness may have had advantages, certainly it was not the only nor even the best path to survival.

Specialized Adaptation for Defensive Behavior

Many organisms survived the struggle for existence by out-fighting their opponents, but a great many others competed success-fully by doing just the opposite: avoiding conflict. Behavioral adap-tations which have proved useful include speedy withdrawal, ability to hide, or tonic immobility ("playing possum"). Distraction is also another effective defense, as in the case of many snakes which possess a tail closely resembling their head. When threatened they hide their vulnerable head and wag their tail (Maier and Maier, 1970). Another kind of distraction is that of *autotomy*, in which part of the body is shed to confuse opponents and aid escape (e.g., a lizard dropping its tail). Autotomy is normally associated with withdrawal, but in some cases it may be combined with an attack to strengthen defensive behavior (Robinson, Abele, and Robinson, 1970). In such attack autotomy, crabs may pinch their adversary and then autotomize (detach) the cheliped, leaving it attached to their opponent. While the attacker battles the autot-omized cheliped, the crab slips away.

Another adaptation which favors survival without fighting is chemical adaptation. It is no accident that the beautiful monarch butterfly thrives on plants such as milkweeds which are poisonous to predators like the blue jay. If a blue jay attempts to eat this butterfly, he will find it tastes unpalatable and causes him to vomit (Brower, 1969). Even though the sickness does not immediately follow the ingestion, the blue jay will never again touch the monarch butterfly. This kind of learning of bait-shyness with long delays of negative reinforcement seems to defy traditional laws of learning but such rapid adaptation is now well established (Garcia, Ervin, and Koelling, 1966; Revusky and Garcia, 1970). A by-product of such chemical defense for other species is that of protective mimicry. In the case of butterflies, the tasty North American *Limenitis archippus* has thrived simply because it has come to look like the unpalatable monarch. Another case in point is the foul-tasting tiger beetle, *Tricondyla*, a native of Malaysia. Because it is so unsavory, insectivores rarely molest it, and this also favors the survival of the flavorful katydid, which looks like the tiger beetle (Ross, 1965).

Other animals, including skunks, snakes, and many insects depend heavily on chemicals which repel or kill opponents (Whittaker and Feeny, 1971). Skunks treat their opponents to butyl mercaptan, and bombardier beetles squirt quinone secre-tions. Minute quantities of neurotoxins and cardiotoxins secreted from animals such as snakes and wasps quickly kill or paralyze their opponents. Such adaptations may not be without significance in the evolution of man, for it has been suggested that early man survived, not because of his strength or cunning, but simply because carnivores judged him to be foul-tasting (Leakey, 1967). Few wild animals attempt to prey on man, and the folklore about savage, man-eating beasts is mostly a myth. While "brave" safari hunters boast of their narrow escapes, most animals will attack man only when cornered, provoked, and threatened. Although "man-eating" tigers, lions, and leopards have killed people, it is almost unknown for them to eat human flesh. Many years ago some African tribes left their dead to be eaten by hyenas, but the hyenas would not touch fresh human flesh and waited several days until decay overpowered that horrible human smell. Perhaps modern man, like his ancestors, remains unpalatable.

Equally impressive are structural adaptations which favor survival. Animals as widely separated as the sea urchin and the porcupine do not need great offensive strength because they are well-protected by spiny projections. But protective coverings need not be menacing, as turtles and clams have discovered, and they need not be physically protective. Coloration alone provides a valuable defense for many species from insects to zebras. Dis-

Figure 1.   *Which is the head and which is the tail? The fulgorid fools most humans, not to mention other bugs. The menacing eyes and beak frighten some opponents, and those who do attack do little damage anyway, because these organs are fake. The real head is hidden at the left.*

guises based on color and structure are perhaps most successfully utilized by insects. Often they blend in with the background or resort to fake appendages that confuse and scare opponents. For example, the hornworm of India retracts its vulnerable head when threatened and exposes a pair of enormous but fake red and black "eyes" which make it appear large and dangerous. Thailand's two-faced fulgorid bug fools opponents into believing that its tail is its head with the aid of dark spots and projections on the tips of its wings (Fig. 1). When the harmless wings are folded behind, they mesh to form fake eyes, antennae, and a menacing-looking beak (Ross, 1965). If evolutionary success is measured by sheer numbers and proliferation, then insects are by far the most successful form of animal life. There are almost a million known separate species of insects, and in fact there are more types of weevils than all vertebrates combined (MacSwain, 1966).

Behavioral Adaptations

Behavioral adaptations other than fighting have also paved a path to survival with success accompanying the capacity for climbing, flying, swimming, burrowing, crawling, walking, grasping, seeing at night, and so on. The catfish *Hassar orestis* (Steindachner) survives attacks by piranha fish, not by fleeing or fighting back, but by following his opponent. The catfish swims under the piranha and duplicates every movement of his dangerous rival and thereby avoids being bitten (Markl, 1969). Some moths emit high pitched clicks when touched or exposed to ultrasonic pulses of bats, their main predators, and these clicks are aversive enough to repel some of their enemies (Dunning, 1968).

More complex adaptations have also taken place in social behavior, particularly cooperative social behavior. In a troop of baboons, for example, a small group of adult males will stand together and fight a common opponent while the rest of the troop flees to safety. This cooperative behavior will lead to the defeat of a dangerous opponent such as a leopard which could easily overpower an isolated baboon (Hall and DeVore, 1965). Antelopes cooperate by displaying a white rump to warn other members of their herd of impending danger (Etkin and Freedman, 1964). Equally impressive is the schooling behavior of fish and the mobbing behavior of birds. Birds such as starlings or chaffinches will flock together when danger threatens, and the distress call of a single member adds a margin of safety to the entire group (Hinde, 1954). While this kind of social behavior has obvious survival value, the exact reasons for it remain unknown. It may be that there is safety in numbers because a distress call can warn the entire group, or it may be that individuals congregate in mobs so that others will be eaten first (Goss-Custard, 1970). Sometimes social cues are utilized for "selfish" rather than "altruistic" reasons. Arctic foxes have been observed to make fake warning calls to frighten away other foxes (even their own cubs) so they don't have to share a tasty meal (Rüppell, 1969).

In short, it is not necessary to assume that the process of evolution automatically favored the development of aggressive behavior, for fighting ability is only one of many routes to survival. Sometimes it is suggested that more "advanced" species relied on aggressive ability while more primitive forms of life survived because of defensive rather than offensive adaptations. But this, too, is probably an oversimplification, and may reflect nothing more than the lack of scientific research on the social behavior of simpler organisms. Not too long ago it was stated that rats had relatively little social behavior (Munn, 1950), an observation which we now know to be grossly erroneous. Even seemingly peaceful animals such as frogs and box turtles defend territories and form social hierarchies (Test, 1954; Emlen, 1968; Boice, 1970a). Crickets are unusually aggressive insects with much fighting taking place between adult males. Agonistic encounters begin with lashing of the antennae and kicking followed by ramming, biting, and attempts to flip an opponent on his back (Cloudsley-Thompson, 1965). Marine rag worms will bite the posterior of another worm if the intruder tries to enter its dwelling. No doubt future research will uncover many new facets of aggressive behavior throughout the animal kingdom, from army ants and fighting fish all the way to humans.

Inhibitions Against Killing

One of the few generalizations which might be drawn is that while not all animals evolved as fighters, those which can fight do fight (Scott, 1958a). Specialized weapons for fighting, such as teeth, claws, or horns evolved because of their adaptive survival value. But this leads to a puzzle: some animals have developed dangerous weapons, but often fail to use them. Snakes, for example, possess deadly fangs and poison with which they can kill almost instantly, but when fighting other snakes they never use them. Instead they engage in a kind of Indian wrestling in an attempt to force an opponent to the ground (Eibl-Eibesfeldt, 1961). Lorenz

Figure 2. *Rattlesnakes could quickly kill each other with their deadly fangs. But evolution has favored mechanisms which inhibit intraspecific killing, and hence they are content to merely "put down" an opponent by Indian wrestling. (From The Fighting Behavior of Animals, by I. Eibl-Eibesfeldt. Copyright © 1961 by Scientific American, Inc. All rights reserved.)*

(1966) has noted that animals with deadly specializations generally developed controls to limit their use, for those which killed indiscriminately probably killed each other and became extinct. Those which were able to assert superiority *without* fighting have been the most successful, and it is not surprising that destructive intraspecific fighting (i.e., between animals of the same species) is the exception rather than the rule. Nearly all animals are content to dominate or to banish conspecific rivals; only man, it seems, has a desire to injure his opponents and gain vengeance on them. It is not necessary, however, to assume that other animals are bestowed with more mercy and compassion than man, but simply that they act out of self-preservation. Unlike humans, they have not developed the capacity to injure at selected spatial and temporal distances, and describing their behavior in terms of human motivation (e.g., "bravery" or "cowardice") can be misleading.

Are there any lessons to be learned for our own aggressive behavior? Man has no deadly specializations, and a naked human would be an easy meal for most other animals of similar size. Without weapons, humans would also find it difficult to inflict serious injury or death on other humans. Lorenz has argued that because man did not evolve with deadly specializations, he also did not develop elaborate inhibitions and controls about when *not* to kill. But man began to use his brain to construct tools and weapons, and although at first they were simple and crude, within a few thousand years they became unspeakably deadly. The slow course of evolution could not keep pace with man's talents for designing new weapons, and hence man's acquired deadliness was not matched by appropriate inhibitions. Today, the art of weaponry has "progressed" to the point where the suicidal behavior of a few individuals may exterminate the bulk of all life—where, as Nikita Khrushchev said, the living will envy the dead. If the past is a model for the future, we might reasonably expect that natural selection will eventually eliminate organisms such as man who have failed to develop strong inhibitions against killing their own kind.

This line of reasoning sounds both compelling and alarming, but fortunately it need not be accepted. There is no reason to conclude that as a species man has no inhibitions against killing simply because some men kill each other. Nor should it be assumed that all other animals have perfected the control of their own aggressive behavior. Above all, the Lorenzian argument overlooks the fact that our rituals have become just as sophisticated as our weapons. Man does not have to wait around for millions of years to perfect gestures of threat or appeasement, nor does he have to rely on the slow process of evolution to correct miscalculations about the intentions of opponents. The main feature which distinguishes man from all other animals is his development of a complex and symbolic language, and this language gives him the opportunity to communicate rapidly and precisely almost anything. In addition to a sophisticated language, humans also have an unusually long socialization process which provides them with a marvelous opportunity to learn and to profit from the experience of their predecessors. Presumably our brains are not limited to constructing deadly weapons, but also may be used to communicate with each other and to develop mutually beneficial moral values. These moral values, if well ingrained, are far superior to any kind of stereotyped ritual. When we lost our canines, we may have lost our inhibitions against savage, biting attacks, but we also gained a language which has become the most effective ritual ever devised.

Perhaps the main lesson to be learned from the study of evolution is that increased aggressiveness is neither the only nor the best path to survival, and it is certainly not the inevitable result of natural selection. But species which became more social and profited from cooperative behavior also found themselves exposed to more opportunities for conflict. It therefore became of paramount importance to be able to discriminate fellow conspecifics from potential prey. The ability to have deadly force and to use it only when necessary may be one of the keys to the understanding of how aggression evolved. Either using force too often or not using it often enough would be detrimental to survival, and ideally an organism would quickly recognize situations where it should or should not be used. However, given variable conditions in a changing environment, an infallible control system is unlikely to evolve, and most organisms are likely to make both kinds of errors. Evolution would seem to favor surplus aggression rather than surplus caution, for animals that failed to fight when it was essential probably fared worse than those that fought when it wasn't necessary. The net result might be a tendency to err on the high side and resort to aggressive behavior too often rather than not often enough.

It might be argued that ideally there should be no aggressive behavior at all, but this reasoning is based on the assumption that all conflict is intrinsically bad and without adaptive value. As we shall see in later sections, agonistic behavior may be either constructive or destructive; it is mainly destructive fighting which is maladaptive. In the long run, agonistic behavior helps assure social stability and *prevents* serious destructive behavior. A total lack of agonistic behavior would be valuable only in an unchanging world where there were no competition for survival.

PREDATION AND AGGRESSION

In attempting to define aggression, it was pointed out that one of the difficulties is that aggression may be situationally determined so that a particular behavior may be considered aggressive in one instance and not in another. An example of this is that whether killing constitutes aggression depends in part on who the victim is. Killing is widespread in nature, however most of it is interspecific, that is, between members of different species. Usually such killing is characterized as predation or feeding behavior, and it is generally agreed that predation should not be confused with aggression (Carthy and Ebling, 1964). Food-getting behavior can be described as a complex chain or web involving many animals and plants which get killed in the process of supporting other animals. Sometimes the chain may run full circle, particularly when interfering with one segment may lead to widespread ecological disturbances. For example, industrial wastes, including poisonous mercury, are pumped into rivers and oceans where they settle to the bottom. But small and primitive forms of marine life absorb such wastes, and they are eaten by small fish which in turn are preyed upon by larger fish which get caught and eaten by man. The larger organisms may die, or their wastes may be returned to the smaller organisms. Thus the first step is usually composed of plant life, and a total food chain may involve three to five major links. Going through the food chain, the size of the predator increases, but the number decreases. A kind of pyramid is formed in which a vast number of small animals at the bottom support comparatively few large animals at the top (Cloudsley-Thompson, 1965).

In general, interspecific killing is related to food chains and predation, although animals may be part of a food chain without being killed. This is the case in parasitism, in which an animal may feed off of its host without killing it. Of more concern to students of aggression is intraspecific killing, a phenomenon which is relatively rare in nature. But we all know that humans kill each other, and sometimes it is declared that humans are the only species to kill their own kind. Richardson (1960) estimated that, between 1820 and 1945, 59 million humans were killed by other humans in wars or in peacetime crimes. Pessimists of human nature are quick to cite such statistics and then leap to the conclusion that only humans are grossly deviant in their social behavior. In order to properly evaluate such a proposition it would be necessary to analyze statistically the incidences of intra- and interspecific aggression in many species.

We do not have such information, so we can only guess how humans might compare with other animals. In a small town, a homicide may occur only once in a decade while each year there are probably tens of millions of peaceful social interactions. In a large city like Boston, Massachusetts, there were 137 reported cases of murder and non-negligent manslaughter in 1969 out of a population of over three and a quarter million people. It is likely that for every murder there were probably billions or trillions of peaceful interactions. If a baboon came to Boston disguised as an anthropologist he might prowl the city for several months without ever seeing a single killing. He might then go back to Africa and report that humans are unusually peaceful and rarely kill each other. If we consider wars, only a small fraction of the population actually participates in the armed services and a large proportion of the men in uniform never see any combat. Andreski (1964) estimated that for the three centuries before 1914 Britain was involved in dozens of wars, yet soldiers comprised less than one per cent of the population. Such estimates are not meant to deny that humans kill each other, but rather to put the proportion of killings into some overall perspective.

Unfortunately, no one keeps accurate "crime" statistics for other animal societies, and we know only that intraspecific killing is not commonly observed. Perhaps this is partially because individual animals sometimes disappear from a group after being killed in combat which was not conveniently arranged for photographers. If a comparison were made, it is likely that intraspecific killing occurs with about the same statistical frequency in man and other animals. For example, Schaller (1969) tagged about 150 lions and attempted to keep track of their activities over a three-year period in Tanzania. Fighting is common among both male and female lions, and while intraspecific killing is relatively rare, it does occur as is shown in Schaller's photographs. In one case, a male fought until he was killed while attempting to defend a lioness in heat and a zebra carcass. Later, two adult males killed three cubs, eating one of them, leaving another behind, and carrying off the body of the third as if it were a trophy. Schenkel (1966) documents other observations of lions killing each other.

The social behavior of nonhuman primates has often been romanticized to the point of overlooking the fact that serious and destructive fights actually take place. Our nearest relative, the chimpanzee, is generally peaceful, but individuals occasionally brutally beat one another to the point where wounds and deformities are easily seen. In her study of the wild chimpanzee, Van Lawick-Goodall (1968b) counted 284 attacks of which about 10 per cent could be classified as violent. She also observed a fight between two baboons in which one was killed. Klingel (1967) observed destructive fighting between zebra stallions which involved biting and kicking resulting in serious injuries. In such fights submissive gestures were rarely observed and death was probably avoided only because of the limited offensive capability of the zebra. In studies of African wildebeests (Fig. 3) Estes (1969) noted that about one out of fifty adult males had one or both horns broken and some had their eyes put out. During serious fights goring from the side was seen, and observers were convinced that the animals would kill each other if possible. Serious injuries were prevented more by their tough hide than by any inhibitions.

Many other examples of intraspecific killing can be found, although in some cases it is better understood in terms of defensive behavior. For example, worker bees which return to the wrong hive are quickly smelled out and killed or dismembered. The same fate may befall an insect which accidentally picks up a foreign odor and then attempts to gain entry into his home colony (Cloudsley-Thompson, 1965). Lizards, elephants, and rodents sometimes fight to the death (Lorenz, 1964), and hippopotamuses have been observed to do the same, particularly when overcrowding occurs (Matthews, 1964). The ferociousness of the piranha

Figure 3. In the African wildebeest, serious injury and death is prevented more by a tough hide than by any inhibitions. (Photo courtesy of R. D. Estes.)

fish of South America is probably highly exaggerated, at least in its attacks on man and other large mammals (Zahl, 1970). But its razor-sharp teeth may be used against other piranhas, for if one is hooked on a line the others will attack and kill it within seconds. Termites will quickly kill and eat a colony member that is wounded or crippled, and female spiders often kill the males they have just finished mating with (Cloudsley-Thompson, 1965). The female European hamster (*Cricetus frumentarius*) frequently kills a male attempting to court her (Hediger, 1965).

In general, destructive intraspecific fighting and killing takes place in many species including man, but in relative terms serious conflicts are rare in all species. Non-predatory fighting may also take place between different species, as in the case of chimps and baboons squabbling over bananas. Interspecific fighting can also result from defensive behavior, as has been reported with wasps (Lin, 1963). Wasps tend to guard their home sites and aggressively chase all intruders including butterflies, beetles, dragonflies, grasshoppers, small boys or other wasps. They will even attack pebbles thrown at them. Some fish (Johnson and Johnson, 1970) and mice (L. Baenninger, 1971) are known to attack nonconspecifics as well as conspecifics. Interspecific rivalry over territory can be found between different species of birds such as the blackcaps (*Sylvia atricapilla*) and the whitethroats (*Sylvia communis*) (Wynne-Edwards, 1962).

The above examples serve to illustrate that, while aggression and predation should not be confused, it is not always possible to make simplistic distinctions between the two. Animals may adopt entirely different modes of behavior for feeding as opposed to fighting, but sometimes feeding behavior is derived from fighting behavior (Eibl-Eibesfeldt, 1970; Wickler, 1962). Distinctions cannot always be made on the basis of whether the opponent is a conspecific or a nonconspecific, for some *inter*specific killing involves aggression as well as predation, and some *intra*specific killing involves predation rather than aggression. An example of the latter is cannibalism.

Cannibalism

When animals kill and eat other members of their own species we usually refer to it as cannibalism. Abhorrent as it may seem, the practice is quite common in nature, particularly with some birds, fish, mammals, and insects which eat their own eggs or babies. In a bumblebee colony, some workers develop ovaries and lay eggs. The queen promptly eats these eggs and lays her own eggs, whereupon the workers try to eat some of the queen's eggs (Free, Weinberg, and Whiten, 1970). In Schaller's (1969) study of African lions, he observed a mother eating one of her cubs (although the cub was killed by another lion). Sometimes babies feed on each other, as is the case with the sand tiger shark (Kenney, 1968). Shark eggs hatch within the uterus, and the first-born survive by devouring their younger and weaker brothers and sisters. Because there are two separate uteri, only two baby sharks finally survive. Newborn ladybugs also eat their brethren (Hagen, 1970). In some mammals, such as rats and dogs, the mother may mistakenly kill and eat her babies in the process of chewing off the umbilical cord. Such cannibalism occurs more often in captivity than in the wild, and it may be related to hormonal disturbances, dietary deficiencies (particularly protein), and psychological stress (Cloudsley-Thompson, 1965; Fox, 1968).

Cannibalism sometimes occurs during courtship, as Roeder

Figure 4. A male praying mantis (left) is about to be eaten head first by
the female he is trying to court. (Photo courtesy of K. Roeder.)

(1967) has shown with the praying mantis (Fig. 4). Since the male
is smaller than the female, his courtship is more like a sneak attack.
A male may stalk a female for hours, freezing whenever she moves,
until at last he gets within a body length. He then takes a flying
leap and flagellates her head with his long antennae while he
probes her ovipositor and begins to make copulatory movements.
After copulation has begun the female may bite his head off, particularly if she is hungry. The male's copulatory movements are
reflexive in character and continue even after he is decapitated
(in fact, experiments have shown that experimental decapitation
of the male appears to facilitate sexual behavior). Spiders sometimes engage in cannibalism, during both courtship and disputes
over territory. Spiders threaten each other by spreading their
chelicerae and fangs while vibrating their abdomen (Fig. 5).
After a fight, the winner may eat the loser (Rovner, 1968).

It should be observed that the term cannibalism does not
properly distinguish between killing for food on one hand and eating the dead on the other. Rats seldom kill each other, but when
one dies the others feed on it, often eating only the brain. The word
cannibal comes from the Latinized name of the Caribs of the West
Indies, who were thought to eat human flesh. Historians as far back
as Herodotus and Marco Polo described tribes which practiced
cannibalism, including some which killed and ate old people.
Until relatively recently, cannibalism was known to be practiced
on every continent in the world, and at one time human flesh was
sold regularly in the markets of West Africa (Cloudsley-Thompson,
1965). Cannibalism was practiced both for ceremonial rites and

Figure 5.   *Spiders threaten each other by spreading their chelicerae and vibrating their abdomen. The loser may end up as a meal for the winner. (Photo courtesy of J. Rovner.)*

because of food shortages; however, these two factors may be closely related. Religious rites stressed the magical benefits of eating human flesh, and such benefits in fact often occurred, presumably because of the supplementation of poor diets rather than the ingestion of spirits of the devoured. Even this may be open to question, for recent and somewhat unflattering analyses of human flesh indicate that it is not as nutritious as we might have supposed (Garn and Block, 1970).

Most people are understandably revolted by cannibalism in any species, but cannibalism is clearly a part of nature, not necessarily a sin against it, and aversion to it must be weighed against its biologically adaptive value. As for the moral value, the following story (Delgado, 1967) offers food for thought.

> A missionary was trying to convince a savage that cannibalism is evil. The savage pointed out that white men did the same thing, for they engaged in war and killing. The missionary admitted that this was indeed true, but in a morally superior tone he added that at least white men did not *eat* their victims. To this the cannibal replied, "Then why kill? What a waste!"

RITUALIZED AGGRESSION

The great complexity of aggressive behavior makes it desirable to introduce appropriate distinctions wherever possible, but the previous sections have indicated how distinctions can be misleading if pushed too far. It is true that much *inter*specific killing involves predation, but some does not. *Intra*specific killing does take place in many species, and while such behavior usually involves aggression it sometimes more closely resembles predation. Even more fundamental is the fact that the majority of aggressive encounters in both man and animals involves no fighting, violence, injury, or physical contact. This is because agonistic behavior is highly ritualized and most conflicts are settled by means of social signals which eliminate the need for overt fighting.

The preponderance of ritualized combat over physical combat is illustrated by a recent study of agonistic behavior among elephant seals living off the coast of California (LeBoeuf and Peterson, 1969). It was reported that for every actual fight there were 67 aggressive encounters which never went beyond ritualistic threats.

Figure 6.   Both pictures are of the same bird. At the right, the Squacco heron ruffles its feathers in a display. (Photo by E. Hosking, in Welty, J. C. *The Life of Birds.* Philadelphia, W. B. Saunders, 1962.)

Figure 7. *It is easy to see why a large male baboon usually gets his way without having to fight. The exposed canine teeth and the erected fur around the shoulders make the head appear much larger than it actually is. The white eyelids cover the eyes momentarily, which further amplifies the ferocity of the threat display. (Photo courtesy of I. DeVore.)*

A considerable amount of fighting in primates involves bluffing an opponent into intimidation. Kummer (1968) reports that baboons often threaten to bite their opponents on the neck, but hundreds of such threats result in only a few actual bites. The display of threatening or submissive social signals without actual fighting is by far the most common form of agonistic behavior, and most animals quickly recognize and respond to such gestures. It is because these rituals are so effective that overt fighting becomes unnecessary.

Such aggressive behavior has become so ritualized that it often has the appearance of a ceremony rather than a confrontation. Aggressive displays and gestures are easy to recognize because they generally involve marked physical changes which make the combatants appear larger and more threatening. A cat arches its back, raises its fur, bares its teeth, and extends its claws. Birds may fluff their feathers and spread their wings (Fig. 6). A baboon displays its large canine teeth (see Frontispiece and Figure 7)

25

and erects the fur around its shoulder, which instantly gives it a gorilla-sized appearance. Some fish intensify their color, swish their tail, and extend their fins to maximum size. The agonistic behavior of the Hawaiian coral reef fish (*Pomacentrus jenkinsi*) consists almost entirely of displays, and fights are won and lost by visual cues alone (Rasa, 1969). The normally yellow eye changes to a greyish-black to indicate aggressive motivation, and the raising of a dorsal fin is correlated with fear. In many animals threat displays are accompanied by menacing vocalizations such as hisses, snarls, screeches, or shrieks. Even fish have been found to grunt in an effort to amplify their threats (Brawn, 1961). Gestures may also be used to signal submission as well as threat. Figure 8 shows two male iguanas fighting over territory until one drops to his belly indicating submission.

Figure 8. Two marine iguanas butt heads and push at each other (top). One finally gives in and signals his submission by dropping his belly to the ground (bottom). (From The Fighting Behavior of Animals, by I. Eibl-Eibesfeldt. Copyright © 1961 by Scientific American, Inc. All rights reserved.)

Primate Rituals

The complex social signals involved in ritualized aggression are well-illustrated by Jane Van Lawick-Goodall's (1968) classic study of wild chimpanzees in the Gombe Stream Reserve in Tanzania. Chimps are relatively peaceful, but order is maintained by the threats of high ranking males. There is no single stereotyped threat gesture, but rather a number of rituals which may be employed in varying combinations, including the following:

1. Glaring or staring an opponent into submission.
2. Tipping or jerking the head.
3. Raising an arm high above the head or hunching the shoulders.
4. Arm waving while running bipedally.
5. Swaggering back and forth from foot to foot.
6. Stamping the ground with the feet.
7. Branching, a practice which consists of grabbing a small tree and vigorously shaking it, possibly even uprooting it and dragging it around.
8. Aimed throwing of rocks at an opponent.
9. Hair erection.
10. Hooting and screaming.

Opponents usually flee, but if they do not a fight may erupt which consists of rolling on the ground with an opponent and pounding him with both feet and hands while also biting, slapping, and pulling hair. In some cases fights may take place instantly without warning as if it were the result of a previous quarrel.

In order to head off an attack, a threatened chimp may adopt one of several possible submissive postures: (1) sexual presenting (raising rump toward opponent); (2) whimpering or screaming with an open mouth with lips retracted exposing the teeth and gums; (3) bowing, bobbing, or crouching; (4) kissing on the lips or groin; (5) reaching out to be touched; (6) submissive mounting and pelvic thrusting, regardless of the sex of the combatants; this may be accompanied by a grasping of the scrotum if the dominant individual is a male. Another set of gestures, sometimes called reassurance gestures, are used by a dominant individual to indicate he will not harm a subordinate. They include: patting on the head, touching the subordinate with a finger or hand, inspection or touching of the genitals, hand holding, embracing, mounting the submissive individual, rump-turning, and kissing. If a dominant individual withholds reassurance, the subordinate may become very upset and have a "temper tantrum". Sometimes a subordinate female may attempt to calm a dominant male who has just been in a squabble by touching him, grooming his fur, or fondling his scrotum. In summary, there are a number of gestures and rituals, and their precise meanings are partly contextually determined. For example, mounting and thrusting in a non-sexual situation may be an expression of either dominance or submission depending on the context. It should also be pointed out that squabbles are often peacefully settled through elaborate gestures, but sometimes these rituals fail and a subordinate chimp may take a merciless beating. An example of a typical encounter is the following, described by Van Lawick-Goodall:

> An adolescent male (Pepe) approached a mature male (Goliath) who was feeding on bananas. Pepe crouched and whimpered, looking at Goliath, and meekly extended his hand. Goliath patted Pepe, and Pepe slowly reached for a banana, but pulled back screaming in fear. Goliath patted him again and finally Pepe gathered a few bananas and hastily retreated.

Social rituals are obviously an important part of animal behavior, and it is fair to ask what part they play in human behavior. Morris (1967) has pointed out that humans have a great many gestures, many of them expressions of affection, hostility, friendliness, or appeasement. We shake hands, smile, frown, yawn, stand up, kneel, box, kiss, wave, nod, spit, blush, and roll our eyeballs. Expressions of emotion are generally quite obvious to others, even when we want to remain inscrutable. Everyone recognizes pupil dilation, flushing or blanching, furtive glances, shortness of breath, forced smiles, grinding teeth, tensed muscles, and beads of sweat. Facial expressions are of utmost importance in humans, but visual signals and expressions are important in many other animals as well (Vine, 1970). It has been pointed out that the facial muscles of apes are just as complex as those of man, and in fact chimps have a wider variety of expressions than man (Washburn and Hamburg, 1968).

One gesture that man has in common with many other non-human primates is that of the stare, which is considered threatening in monkeys and apes and rude in humans. Several studies have been carried out using staring in humans as a measure of aggressiveness (Moore and Gilliland, 1921; Gilliland, 1926) and dominance (Strongman and Champness, 1968). The Moore and Gilliland study is both interesting and amusing because the investigators were able to get the entire faculty of Dartmouth College to submit to the registrar letter grades evaluating 1480 students for their aggressiveness, reliability, and personality. In addition, they were also able to persuade students to rate each other, and after all this work they finally selected the 13 most aggressive and the 13 least aggressive students. The most aggressive individuals included the president of the senior class, the quarterback of the football team, the track manager, and even the president-elect of the outing club. The 13 students in the low aggression group were, according to the authors, "decidedly without prominence." Having independently established the character of each group, the experimenters then did an eye control task based on the assumption that "the shifty eye is generally a sure sign of personal weakness, if not downright dishonesty."

The subjects were directed to perform mental arithmetic problems while staring at the experimenter. They found that the low aggression group shifted their gaze a mean of 5.5 times while the high aggression group did so with a mean of only 0.5 times. The experimenters then predicted that fear would more easily distract nonaggressive persons from completing the solution of mental problems. This was put to a test by measuring problem solving ability while (a) having a professor stare at the subjects; (b) shocking subjects with 75 volts; (c) compelling subjects to look at a dead snake. They discovered that the low aggression group performed more poorly than did the high aggression group, thus confirming the hypothesis. In general, these experiments indicate (a) experimental psychology has come a long way in the past 50 years, and (b) so has college life.

In spite of such experiments, it is probably safe to say that much human aggression is ritualized through visual and other signals, the most important of which is language. We use language to express everything from sarcasm to obscenities, and even silence can be devastating. Most people have been infuriated more than once by a well-placed yawn. Humans also have a wealth of more impersonal rituals to draw from, such as writing nasty letters to the editor, spreading rumors, defacing billboards, and using bumper stickers. Other human rituals and gestures are less subtle. For example, throughout much of human culture and history the penis has been used as a symbol of power and protection. Phallic guardians are carved into some Romanesque churches, and genital amulets are still used (Fig. 9) to ward off evil spirits and protect the bearer from danger (Eibl-Eibesfeldt, 1970; Eibl-Eibesfeldt and Wickler, 1968; Wickler, 1966). Among many other primates, males often wag an erect penis at strangers to warn them (Fig. 10).

Whatever the form of ritualized threats, opponents easily recognize them and are forced to respond. Failure to recognize a threat and respond with a gesture of submission may be inter-

Figure 9.   In modern Japan, amulets containing an erect penis (top) are carried to ward off evil spirits and to protect the holder from car accidents. Female amulets (bottom) offer appeasement through sexual presentation. (Courtesy of I. Eibl-Eibesfeldt.)

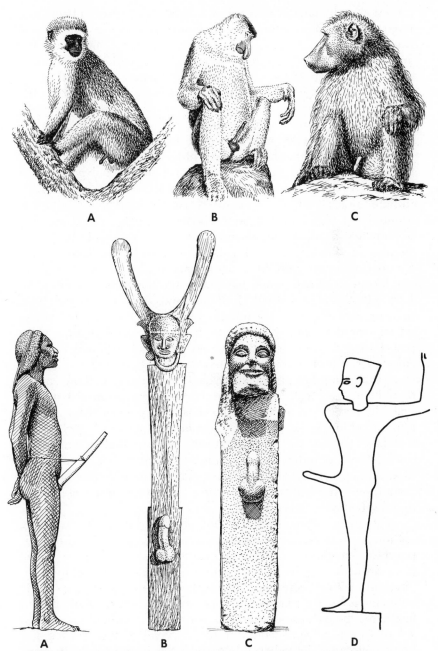

Figure 10. Top: Genital displays are used by the (A) male vervet monkey, (B) proboscis monkey, and (C) baboon to warn strangers. Bottom: (A) Some Papuan tribesmen from New Guinea emphasize their strength and masculinity by artificial means. (B) Natives on the island of Nias use this statue as a house guardian. (C) The Greeks and (D) the Egyptians also made use of phallic guardians. (Courtesy of I. Eibl-Eibesfeldt and W. Wickler.)

preted as a challenge and result in a fight. But gestures of appeasement will usually inhibit attack, and such gestures become almost
routine greeting rituals. Appeasement gestures are often the
antithesis of threat gestures (Darwin, 1872), and they consist of
a crouched, cowering, head-lowering posture rather than an
extended and dominating upright position. Morris (1967) has
speculated that some contemporary rituals, such as bowing,
bending over when being spanked, and lowering the head in
prayer, may be related to primitive gestures of submission.

The very fact that hostile encounters do not immediately lead
to fighting indicates the complexity of agonistic behavior, for if
only aggression were involved, individuals would immediately
initiate attacks without making threats. Tinbergen (1951) has
pointed out that such encounters usually involve the conflicting
tendencies of attack and escape, and it is fear counterbalancing
aggression which leads to threats rather than to immediate attack.
Conflicting motivation in a dangerous situation may lead to a
displacement of aggression to some neutral activity. For example,
Estes (1969) noted that wild bull antelopes often interrupted their
fighting and initiated grazing side by side. Sometimes the antag-
onists would lie down next to each other, and following a short
pause they whirled into combat position and resumed fighting.
Another result of conflicting motivation may be redirected aggression. If a chimp has just been attacked by a higher ranking chimp,
or if he is unable to eat because of the presence of a dominant
male, he may prowl nervously and chase, threaten, or attack a lower
ranking chimp or a member of another species (Van Lawick-
Goodall, 1968b). Some cichlid fish become highly aggressive
during their reproductive phase, and if no other fish are available
to attack, aggression may be turned against the breeding partners.
Sometimes this overaggressiveness becomes channeled into
digging behavior (Rasa, 1969).

Ritualized aggression has the obvious benefit of asserting
authority or possession without having to resort to fighting. It
provides an important communicative function without being
physically destructive, and it permits animals to live in close
proximity without constant conflicts. In the long run, such agonistic
behavior is highly adaptive because it spaces out populations and
facilitates the defense of the necessities of life without great risks.
All of this is advantageous for the survival of the species and
helps maintain relatively stable populations in spite of fluctuations
in the environment.

REFLEXIVE FIGHTING AND STEREOTYPED AGGRESSION

The fact that much of the aggressive behavior in animals is highly ritualized tempts some theorists to conceive of aggression as a relatively simple and stereotyped process. To a human observer, ritualized fighting often seems to be characterized by stereotypy, almost as if it were a reflex triggered by a specific stimulus. If the observer chooses to emphasize the simplicity and rigidity of such behavior, he may want to compare it to simple unlearned reflexes like the knee-jerk. In a previous section it was noted that the male praying mantis continues its copulatory behavior even after its head has been eaten, which shows that some behavioral sequences are preprogrammed. The fact that some forms of behavior are genetically determined, particularly in simpler organisms, leads us to ask whether it is useful to conceptualize aggression as some kind of stereotyped or reflexive process. It may be useful to analyze a complex process into simpler components, but this is done at the risk of oversimplification which can be misleading. Two examples, one with fish and the other with rats, may help illustrate this problem.

Siamese Fighting Fish

One of the most popular tropical fish for hobbyists is the fresh water *Betta splendens* which earned (and deserves) its popular name, fighting fish. Bettas come in many vivid shades of red, blue, and green, and because they are so pugnacious they must be kept in individual containers. Without provocation, bettas will quickly attack any other male conspecific at any time and at any place, almost as if it were pure, senseless aggression. This fighting may last for hours and can lead to serious injury (although rarely death); it also takes place between females, but to a lesser extent (Braddock and Braddock, 1955).

Why do fighting fish fight? It is not necessarily to defend a territory or nest, and it is not related to monopolizing food or mates. Because of its intensity and universality, some observers have concluded that it is an innate, stereotyped response triggered by particular stimuli. As soon as a fighting fish sees another betta or even his own image in a mirror he will immediately mobilize for a fight. Bettas can learn to swim through a hoop in order to see another fish or a mirror image of themselves (Thompson, 1963), which suggests that these fish actively seek out aggressive encounters and find them rewarding.

The aggressive behavior itself is quite dramatic, for fighting fish put on a colorful threat display which has been described in much detail (Simpson, 1968). At the first sight of another betta the gill covers are extended perpendicular to the body, the large medial fins and tail erect to maximum size, and the color intensifies. Both combatants beat their tails vigorously and alternate lateral fin displays with frontal assaults in which the erected gill covers make them appear much larger and more menacing (Fig. 11). If allowed to continue fighting they will ram each other and engage in fin-tearing until one is finally defeated.

The stereotyped nature of these aggressive encounters is quite impressive, but simply watching them provides few clues to the factors governing their behavior. Although the threat display is quick to appear initially, repeated exposure will cause it to weaken and habituate and finally disappear completely (Clayton and Hinde, 1968). The display is not an all-or-none response, and often there are partial displays involving partial fin erection or gill cover extension without fin erection and vice versa. Different com-

Figure 11. The male Siamese fighting fish (Betta splendens) engages in a vigorous threat display in which the medial fins, tail, and gill covers are extended while color intensity brightens. (Courtesy of T. Thompson.)

ponents of the display will habituate at different rates (Peeke and Peeke, 1970), and there are many individual differences among fighting fish as to the quality and intensity of their threat display. This may be related to previous experience, since bettas which have been victorious in the past are more likely to seek out another encounter than similar fish which have experienced defeat (Baenninger, 1970). Previous social experience of any kind, or the lack of it, has also been emphasized in experiments where bettas are raised in isolation (Braddock and Braddock, 1958).

That the fighting response is modifiable has also been demonstrated in conditioning experiments. The threat display can be classically conditioned so that it can be elicited by an arbitrary stimulus chosen by the experimenter, and it can be eliminated by using electric shock as punishment (Adler and Hogan, 1963). The particular effect of electric shock depends on its intensity, for a milder shock may have the opposite effect and strengthen aggressive displays (Melvin and Anson, 1969).

If the aggressive behavior of the fighting fish is "released" by a specific "sign" stimulus, such a stimulus has yet to be discovered. Releasing stimuli have been described in the widely quoted work of Tinbergen (1951), who reported that a red belly on either fish or models of fish triggered an aggressive attack in male three-spined stickleback fish, and that the intensity of the attack depended on the amount of coloring and the location of the color. More recent experiments, however, report that the intensity of aggressive behavior is related to the number of previous presentations, while the amount of coloring appears to have little differential effect on aggressive behavior (Peeke, Wyers, and Herz, 1969).

In the case of the fighting fish, color does not appear to be a critical stimulus. Fighting fish will display at live bettas and to crude models no matter how much they vary in color and brightness (Grabowski and Thompson, 1968; Simpson, 1968), although the effect of color may interact with the color of the betta being tested (Thompson and Sturm, 1965). Fighting fish will also display and fight with a variety of other fish which bear little resemblance to other bettas (Lissman, 1932; Johnson and Johnson, 1970). An observer may find it difficult to distinguish the response of a fighting fish to a conspecific from the response to some nonconspecifics, particularly if a blind technique is used so that the observer has no knowledge of what the fighting fish is looking at. More important than the visual characteristics of the opponent is the social behavior of the opponent. For example, a fighting fish will soon ignore the relatively shy and peaceful giant gourami (*Colisa fasciata*), but it will engage in extended battles with the similar-appearing (but smaller) dwarf gourami (*Colisa lalia*), which is much more aggressive in its behavior.

Does the fighting fish seek out other males because of aggressive motivation? A recent experiment (Johnson and Johnson, 1972) questions this assumption using a kind of Butler Box for fish. Butler (1954) enclosed monkeys in a chamber which had small windows that could be opened for one minute allowing the monkey to view a variety of stimuli, such as another monkey, a bowl of fruit, an electric train, and an empty room. He found that monkeys would repeatedly perform a response to open the windows, and that satisfying their "curiosity" acted as a strong reward. In the Butler Box for fish, swimming through a small hoop opened a door and allowed the fish to look outside for 30 seconds before the door automatically closed. By recording the number of responses made during an experimental period when the door opened as well as the number of responses made in a control period

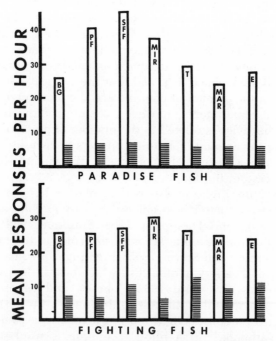

Figure 12. Both paradise fish and Siamese fighting fish will swim through a hoop in order to see a variety of visual stimuli, including a blue gourami (BG), paradise fish (PF), Siamese fighting fish (SFF), a mirror (MIR), a turtle (T), a marble (MAR), or an empty chamber (E). The response rate for all stimuli is significantly higher when compared to a control condition (striped bar), which suggests that they are motivated more by "curiosity" than by aggression. (After Johnson and Johnson, 1972.)

when the door remained shut, it was possible to compare preference for a variety of visual stimuli. The visual stimuli in this case included another conspecific male, several nonconspecific fish, a mirror, a turtle, a marble, and even an empty chamber. The subjects were fighting fish and paradise fish (*Macropodus opercularis*), and it was discovered that both species made about four times as many responses per hour when the door opened, regardless of what the stimulus was (Fig. 12). It therefore appears that what has been assumed to be aggressive motivation may be part of a more general tendency to visually explore the environment, for visually-guided behavior plays an important role in the natural behavior of fish.

It seems fair to conclude that the social and aggressive behavior of fighting fish is characterized neither by rigid, stereotyped responses nor by complete plasticity. Like most other animals, their aggressive behavior is relatively complex, and oversimplified explanations do little justice to what is actually happening and can mislead us about the underlying causes of aggressive behavior.

Shock-Induced Aggression

Few animals are as spontaneously aggressive as the fighting fish, and by comparison, the common laboratory rat is relatively peaceful. It is difficult to study aggressive behavior in a peaceful animal, so experimenters who want to work with the rat have developed artificial means of provoking this beast. Some years ago it was discovered that if two seemingly friendly rats were subjected to painful electric shock they began to fight defensively (O'Kelly and Steckel, 1939). In recent years this technique has been used in a great many detailed studies of what is often called reflexive or stereotyped fighting (Ulrich and Azrin, 1962). The term reflexive fighting was chosen because shocked rats adopt what looks like a stereotyped fighting posture and continue to attack each other as long as they are subjected to pain.

The number of attacks counted by observers depends on such things as the intensity of the shock, the size of the chamber, the length of the session, and the age of the animals (Ulrich, 1966). Even if another rat is not present, attacks may be directed at inanimate objects. Azrin, Hutchinson, and Sallery (1964) restrained monkeys in front of a tennis ball and applied extremely painful electric shocks to their tails. The harnessed monkeys responded by biting the tennis ball whenever the shock was administered; such findings are often cited as evidence that some aggression is reflexive in nature and that pain is a major cause of aggression.

These experiments demonstrate that electric shock can disrupt behavior, but it is not clear what general conclusions should be drawn about aggression. First of all, no species is adapted to deal with an artificial threat like electric shock because in the course of evolution this was never necessary. That abnormal behavior results in this unusual situation should not be surprising, and whatever is learned about how rats respond to shock, no matter how detailed and systematic, may be of little importance outside the laboratory.

Second, it is fair to question whether the elicited behavior should even be considered as aggression. Rats have no single stereotyped fighting response, but rather a sequence which involves many different types of attack and defense (Barnett, 1963; Eibl-Eibesfeldt, 1961). Typically, fighting begins with the chattering of the teeth, erection of the fur, and arching of the back, all of which serve as threat gestures. Before fighting, the two rats will each present their flank toward their opponent, and both will move along on all fours side by side, jostling each other. If fighting erupts, the next stage involves a fury of leaping, kicking, biting, and wrestling on the ground (Fig. 13). During lulls in this overt fighting, rats may stand on their hind legs and adopt a defensive "boxing" posture. It is significant that electric shock tends to elicit only this defensive boxing and not the other components of normal fighting. Perhaps the boxing stance indicates an attempt to minimize contact with the electrified grid floor rather than a desire to fight.

It may be correct to say that the response to shock is stereo-

Figure 13. Serious fighting in rats usually involves biting, kicking, and wrestling on the ground. Such behavior is rarely elicited by electric shock. (From The Fighting Behavior of Animals, by I. Eibl-Eibesfeldt. Copyright © 1961 by Scientific American, Inc. All rights reserved.)

typed, but it is less certain that aggression or even social behavior is involved. For example, rats in the shock box do not "box" as much if they happen to be separated or are not facing each other when the shock comes on (Ulrich and Azrin, 1962). Furthermore, they stop fighting shortly after the shock is terminated and often ignore each other between shocks (and sometimes even while the shock is on). If a rat is shocked by himself, and another rat is introduced a few seconds after the shock is terminated, little fighting takes place (Roediger and Stevens, 1970). If only one member of a pair is shocked, escape and avoidance responses will take priority over attack (Knutson, 1971). All this serves to demonstrate that the behavior is neither highly directed nor persistent and may be considered "motivated" or "social" behavior only in a very superficial sense. It may be possible to learn a great deal about how rats respond to shock while learning very little about aggression.

It should also be pointed out that attacks may be directed against anything handy, including inanimate objects, and that rats may attempt to escape rather than to attack (Galef, 1970b). Sometimes rats minimize the pain by trying to stand on their opponent, but such scuffles involve no biting or attempts to injure (Baenninger and Ulm, 1970). If the shock is delivered through the tail they may try to do the logical thing and bite the electrode rather than the other rat (Scott, 1966). With regard to interspecific aggression, rats which normally do not kill mice cannot be made into killers by shocking the rat in the presence of a mouse (Karli, 1956; Myer and Baenninger, 1966).

As to whether shock-induced behavior is "reflexive," recent experiments have revealed the following: (a) Previous experience with shock modifies the effect (Powell and Creer, 1969). (b) Whether or not shock leads to attack depends partly on the target. Wild rats are unlikely to attack familiar objects, even when shocked, so the effect of shock can hardly be described as a reflex (Galef, 1970b). Discrimination does take place even while the shock is on, for domesticated rats which normally kill mice will discriminate between mice and baby rats, attacking the former but not the latter (Myer and Baenninger, 1966). Electric shock may cause young rats to attack each other, but in similar circumstances they will not attack their mother (Johnson, Sachs, and Boitano, 1971). (c) Most reflexes, such as an eye blink, are relatively easy to condition, but shock-elicited boxing is not. Vernon and Ulrich (1966) paired a conditional stimulus (a tone) with an unconditional stimulus (painful shock) in the hopes of getting a classically conditioned response to the tone alone. But even after thousands of pairings, boxing was elicited by the tone on less than half of the test trials. Other experimenters have had more success using somewhat different procedures (Lyons and Ozolins, 1970).

Finally, such fighting may not reflect the general effect of pain as it is sometimes assumed (i.e., "pain-elicited aggression"). When other noxious stimuli are used, such as heat, cold, or loud noises, fighting is much less pronounced (Ulrich and Azrin, 1962). Shock-elicited aggression may also interact with drive states, increasing aggressiveness in the case of hunger (Cahoon et al., 1971) and, oddly enough, decreasing it in the case of thirst (Hamby and Cahoon, 1971). Other experimenters (Baenninger and Ulm, 1970) have proposed that "reflexive aggression" may be due to generalized arousal.

Before going on, it should be noted that electric shock has no unitary effect, for it may either magnify or suppress fighting depending on the experimental contingencies. If "reflexive" aggression is elicited in pairs of rats by tail-pinching, electric shock contingent on this aggression will suppress, not augment, the fighting (Baenninger and Grossman, 1969). If the shock is low in intensity but high in frequency, attacks will decrease across sessions. But if the shock is high in intensity and low in frequency, the opposite result is obtained (Hutchinson, Renfrew, and Young, 1971). If strong shock is applied to fighting fish when they are engaging in a threat display, the shock will act as punishment and aggressive behavior will be suppressed (Adler and Hogan, 1963; Grabowski and Thompson, 1968). On the other hand, if the shock is of moderate intensity it may have the opposite effect and increase the vigor of the display (Melvin and Anson, 1969). Shock intensity appears to have a similar effect on interspecific aggression in rats (Baenninger and Ulm, 1970) as well as many additional complexities. Myer and Baenninger (1966), as mentioned previously, showed that painful electric shock applied to rats which normally do not kill mice did not induce them to kill. But for rats which naturally kill mice, shock could be used to suppress killing. In addition, killer rats whose killing had been suppressed could be induced to kill again by shocking them in the presence of a mouse. The termination of shock as well as the onset of shock may also be used to control behavior. Miller (1948a) found that he could train peaceful rats to fight each other by withdrawing a negative reinforcer (shock) whenever they began fighting. It should be added that painful shock may instigate other kinds of responses, including copulatory behavior, even in castrated rats (Barfield and Sachs, 1968, 1970; Caggiula and Eibergen, 1969).

CONCLUSION

This extended discussion of stereotyped fighting should serve as a caution against emphasizing the simplicity and rigidity of aggression. The agonistic behavior of the Siamese fighting fish may appear stereotyped, but its dynamics are actually quite complex and modifiable. The defensive behavior of rats subjected to electric shock may look reflexive, but small variations in experimental procedures produce marked variations in behavior. These examples illustrate the theme of this chapter: aggression is a complex rather than a unitary process, and it is under multifactored control. Predation and defensive fighting may both lead to killing, but these are separate processes which are controlled by different factors. These factors may be internal motivational factors, such as hunger, or external stimulus factors, such as the species of the opponent. Aggression may be influenced by both genetic and learned factors, or it may be instrumental behavior, with the attack being incidental to other goals. Because of such complex dynamics, the term aggression defies simple definitions and sweeping generalizations, and requires analysis on many levels from different points of view. Aggression is not an accident of nature, an invention of the Devil, or a product of the 20th century. It represents behavior which has adapted through the process of evolution to the needs of survival. Not surprisingly, it has adapted differently for different species and different situations. The following chapters will attempt to illuminate some of these differences.

2 BIOLOGICAL FACTORS I

TERRITORY, SOCIAL DOMINANCE, AND ECOLOGY

With the exception of man, nearly all animal aggression is instrumental in character. Fighting is not an end in itself, but rather it is part of the competition for home sites, breeding ground, mates, food supplies, and other necessities of life. Animals show little inclination to see their opponents injured or humiliated, and generally they manage to assert their rights through rituals which avoid dangerous fighting. Meaningless fights are rare, and a defeated animal does not hesitate to give up and flee. This point was made many years ago by Craig (1928), when he stated:

> Fundamentally among animals fighting is not sought nor valued for its own sake; it is resorted to rather as a means of defending the agent's interest.... Even when an animal does fight he aims not to destroy the enemy but only to get rid of his presence and interference.

This chapter will attempt to describe agonistic behavior related to competition for social and environmental privileges.

TERRITORIAL DEFENSE

The earth's environment is characterized by heterogeneity, and accordingly there are great variations in climate, vegetation, altitude, natural shelter, and food supply. All of this is of great biological significance because most animals have evolved adaptations enabling them to survive in only limited segments of this heterogeneous habitat. Favorable surroundings are an important key to survival and this has naturally led to competition over the use of space. If animals simply multiplied without regard to the ability of the environment to sustain life, overpopulation, suffering, death, and extinction would result. Where space is at a premium, many species have limited their growth and favored their survival by marking off discrete living spaces or territories. There are many definitions of territory, but usually it simply refers to any defended space. Just how territorial behavior evolved is still a mystery, for it could have been an adaptation to population pressures, or evolution could have favored those animals which restricted their aggressive behavior to places of feeding and nesting. Whatever its origins, territorial behavior also had an effect on evolution, for spatial isolation contributed to the development of small, random mutations which eventually led to division of populations (Klopfer, 1969). As a result, territoriality is well-established in many (but not all) animal societies, and the dynamics of securing and defending territory has a central place in the study of animal social behavior.

Territorial behavior, particularly in songbirds, has been known for centuries, but it is only recently that careful observations have been made on a wide variety of species. How are territories established? Close observation of a community aquarium will show that some fish do not simply swim around in a random fashion. Individual fish frequently stake out some particular portion of their habitat, perhaps a corner or around a plant, and will confine most of their swimming to this region. They endlessly patrol arbitrary boundaries and challenge any intruding fish, thereby staking out a territory. At the same time they probe the territory of their neighbors until recognized boundaries are established. Such arbitrary boundaries have an important effect on social behavior, for individual fish will defend their own territory so fiercely that they generally win any fights on home ground. Intruding fish, even if they are larger, are usually driven off.

A more familiar example is that of the common dog. Man's best friend may be the owner's best friend, but to the delivery man the same pet is a vicious menace. On home territory the dog may attack strangers or at least threaten them with growls and barks, hence their value as watch dogs. If the same dog strays into a neighbor's yard he is easily shooed away. In the African wildebeest (*Connochaetes taurinus* Burchell) (see Figure 3) most intraspecific conflict is related to territory, partly because owning territory is a prerequisite for reproduction (Estes, 1969). Elaborate challenge rituals lasting about 45 minutes take place every day, and in this way the territorial status quo is maintained. Thomson's gazelles (Fig. 14) fight over territory by dueling with their horns (Estes, 1967). Because the horns are close together and curved away from the body, they are relatively harmless and more adapted

Figure 14. Gazelles frequently engage in territorial battles, but serious injury is rare, partly due to the shape of the horns, which are better suited to banging than to stabbing. (Photo courtesy of R. Estes.)

to banging than to stabbing. Perhaps because of this, gazelles are quick to fight, but rarely injure each other.

Pheromones and Fighting

How are territories established and discriminated? In animals with highly developed olfactory systems, scents play an important role in territorial behavior. Odorous glandular substances called *pheromones* are secreted by most mammals from special scent glands located on the cheeks, ribs, groin, and other strategic places so that rubbing against anything leaves a distinctive odor. A good example is the territorial marking behavior of rabbits (Mykytowycz, 1968). Certain species of rabbits live in small colonies of about eight animals with a central burrow or warren from which many interconnecting paths radiate (Fig. 15). The outermost path defines the territorial boundary, and by constantly patrolling these paths and rubbing their bodies as they go, colony odors saturate the region and aid identification of colony members

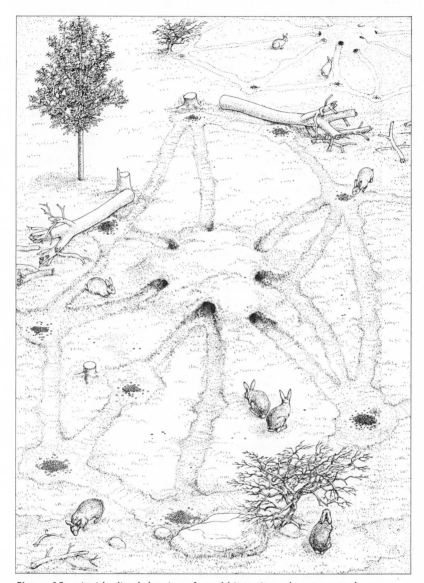

Figure 15. An idealized drawing of a rabbit territory shows a central warren and radiating paths. Mounds of fecal pellets warn other rabbits that the territory is occupied. (From Territorial Marking by Rabbits, by R. Mykytowycz. Copyright © 1968 by Scientific American, Inc. All rights reserved.)

while also warning others that they are intruding. Feces are carefully deposited in key locations, and in this case the odor comes from pheromones of the anal scent gland rather than the feces themselves. Inside their own territory, individual rabbits will wander freely, but when they venture outside they appear tense and alert. Even a strong fighter will quickly retreat when challenged on unfamiliar territory.

The importance of pheromones in territory defense and fighting in general is easily demonstrated by eliminating distinctive odors. In one experiment, mice which were shown to be highly aggressive in fighting contests were sprayed with Dior perfume. When allowed to fight again, few did (Ropartz, 1968). In another experiment (Lee, 1970), mice deliberately trained to be aggressive were allowed to attack male mice sprayed with Man Power, a deodorant, or non-deodorized controls. The fighting mice preferred to attack the controls. They were then matched with normal female mice or females sprayed with Pristeen, a feminine hygiene deodorant. The fighters attacked both groups with about the same intensity but were more sexually attracted to the non-deodorized females. Other recent experiments have uncovered several odors produced in mice which appear to increase aggressiveness in conspecifics (Mugford and Nowell, 1971).

In hamsters, removal of the olfactory bulbs of the brain (an operation called a bulbectomy) greatly diminishes many kinds of social behavior, including territorial marking, fighting, and sexual behavior (Baran and Glickman, 1970; Murphy and Schneider, 1970). Normal hamsters greet each other in an upright posture and then proceed to investigate scent glands and the genital regions of each other, after which they are likely to fight. In contrast, bulbectomized hamsters show normal eating, sleeping, grooming, and hoarding but display little social responsiveness to other hamsters. Bulbectomies do not always have a clear-cut unitary effect on aggressive behavior (Myer, 1964; Bernstein and Moyer, 1970), but in general social behavior is altered.

It should be pointed out that other sensory modalities can have important functions in animal social behavior. To give only one example, experimentally deafened turkeys are likely to kill their own chicks, thus suggesting that maternal protective behavior is partly dependent on hearing the chicks (Schleidt, Schleidt, and Magg, 1960). Olfaction has been emphasized because of its importance in territorial behavior; however, scent marking is used for purposes other than territorial marking, including alarm signals, individual or group recognition, indications of social status, and as sexual attractants (Ralls, 1971). Some silk moths can chemically detect a mate over distances of several miles, and in the cockroach only 30 molecules of sexual attractant will elicit copulatory behavior in the male (Hall, 1966). Primates do not rely so heavily on olfaction for social communication (Marler, 1965); however, scientists have recently isolated vaginal secretions in the rhesus monkey which serve as sexual attractants to males (Michael, Keverne, and Bonsall, 1971). It may be that humans also give off such odors, although we generally are not aware of it. Anecdotes from primate laboratories suggest that some male monkeys get sexually excited when in the presence of human females who are having their monthly period. In humans there are considerable cultural differences with respect to whether odors are attractants or repellants. The strong, musky odors prized by Middle-easterners are often considered offensive to Americans, who tend to prefer the bland smells of deodorants and toothpaste.

Territorial conflict appears to be quite widespread in nature and has been documented in frogs, lizards, worms, insects, mollusks, and many mammals (Denny and Ratner, 1970). But it is by no means universal. There is no evidence for territoriality in zebras (Klingel, 1968) and most primates, with the exception of gibbons, do not defend territories. Some primates, such as howler monkeys, will defend wherever they happen to be but will not fight for a specific location. Of two closely related African gazelles, Thomson's gazelles are vigorously territorial, while Grant's gazelles are not (Estes, 1967). Among certain cichlid fishes, nonterritorial males fight more than territorial males (Albrecht, 1968), and some birds are territorial only during breeding season (Marler, 1971). In addition, there may be different kinds of territorial behavior, such as only for mating, only for roosting, for mating and roosting but not for feeding, or for all three (Klopfer, 1969). Some herding animals such as mountain goats or deer do not defend individual territories but rather occupy larger areas called home ranges.

Human Territoriality and Personal Space

It is always hazardous to generalize from one species to another, particularly when extrapolations are made to humans. (It is even dangerous to generalize from one human culture to another.) But the importance and pervasiveness of territorial behavior in animal societies has provided an irresistible temptation for speculation as to whether some forms of human social behavior, and particularly aggressive behavior, might be complex manifestations of the same underlying process. Humans strive to acquire property, carefully divide it, and establish strict ownership of most material goods. In a more general sense, people tend to get attached to their loved ones, their home, their ethnic group, their school, their political party, their favorite football team or TV program, or whatever. Any probing of such boundaries quickly reveals elaborate defenses, and misunderstandings over rights of possession often lead to conflicts, even among friends.

Such analogies are interesting, but prove little. The idea that humans or any other animals are motivated by primitive, ancestral territorial instincts is unfortunately little more than a romantic myth cultivated by popular writers such as Ardrey (1966). Certainly there is no basis for believing that a territorial motive is the basis of human aggression. As previously mentioned, there are many kinds of territorial behavior, and not all animals are territorial. Even some human cultures are known to reject ownership and possession of goods (Benedict, 1934). But it is not necessary to subscribe to territorial instinct theories in order to give due recognition to the fact that humans often have disputes over space and ownership, whether over the location of a fence or over the establishment of an international boundary. It is possible to discuss the use of space by humans without any assumptions about underlying mechanisms, and particularly without assuming the behavior reflects mechanisms found in animals. Good examples of human "territorial" fighting may be found right in the heart of almost any large city. For example, crime in metropolitan areas is usually structured around recognized divisions. Gangsters may divide the "rights" to the city into clear sections, or they may agree that one gang will monopolize gambling while another will stick to narcotics. If these codes are broken, gang warfare may result.

Among teenagers in the cities, street gangs are often established on the basis of territory or "turf," and violence between rival gangs may be the result of territorial infringements (Fig. 16). Such gang fights are not new, for Henry Adams noticed them in the 1840s and wrote about it in his *Education*. At that time there was a continual rivalry between Bostonians living on the North Side and those living on the South Side (there still is), and frequently people would meet on neutral territory in the Boston Common to slug it out.

A more contemporary conflict over turf is illustrated by the following quote of a member of a street gang (Yablonsky, 1966):

> The Balkans were busted up into block communities, so many members to a block. They know who was on their block, who belongs to the Balkans.... Like if a fight came up tomorrow, they'd get in touch with the sector commander. The first sector which is Manhattan between 110 St. and 125 St. could

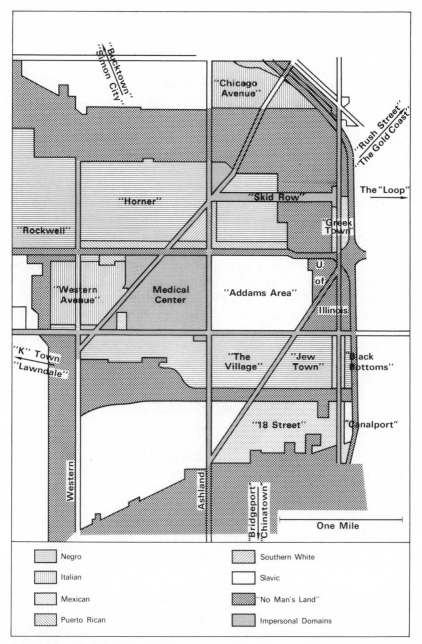

Figure 16. The West Side of Chicago, once the territory of Al Capone, is now sociologically divided into a number of smaller territories or turf occupied by rival street gangs. (Courtesy of G. Suttles and the University of Chicago Press.)

raise 400 guys.... You have a certain piece of land, so another
club wants to take over your land, in order to have more space,
and so forth. They'll fight you for it. If you win, you got your
land; if you don't win, they get your land. The person that loses
is gonna get up another group, to help out, and then it starts
all over again. Fight for the land again.

The concept of turf does not, of course, prove that humans are
territorial or have a territorial instinct. Most of the time anyone is
free to enter or leave such areas, and gangs defend their "rights"
only under certain conditions. General Motors and the Roman
Catholic Church also defend their rights, although this behavior
is only remotely associated with any concept of territory. Perhaps
a more fruitful approach is to examine the use of space in both
man and other animals. Quelea birds, for example, may perch
peacefully side by side, but they carefully space themselves.
Their gregariousness is balanced by a tendency to observe certain
minimums of individual spacing, and if one bird gets too close
the neighboring one may leave or threaten the intruder (Crook
and Butterfield, 1970). When these birds sleep they usually move
closer together, but upon awakening they become startled by the
closeness of their neighbors and immediately engage in agonistic
squabbles. Another example can be seen in Figure 17, which
shows congregations of sea birds in which each individual is
carefully spaced.

Human beings also tend to be selective in their use of space.
Sommer (1967) and Hall (1966) have attempted to analyze such
behavior, and out of their work has emerged new concepts about
small group ecology and personal space. The term personal space
is used to refer to the feeling of immediate psychological control
over a surrounding area and is hypothesized to operate like a
buffer zone in interpersonal relationships (Dosey and Meisels,
1969). Humans make large-scale use of fences, walls, and gates
and develop elaborate rules to insure privacy. In the suburbs
we find "snob zoning" restrictions and NO TRESPASSING signs;
in the cities the signs say DO NOT ENTER, KEEP OUT, and
RESERVED. Tailgating on the highway is usually considered
rude because it violates tendencies to observe spatial separation.
In athletic contests the home team is usually assumed to have a
slight advantage over the visiting team. For example, over the past
decade the best basketball teams in the NBA (National Basketball
Association) have won 78.5 per cent of their home games but only
57.1 per cent of their away games (Koppett, 1972). Sommer (1969)
points out that many individuals have a favorite chair, or if presented with a novel seating arrangement they may have a marked
preference for one chair over another. In many public places such
as airports or hotels furniture is usually arranged to minimize con-

Figure 17. *These sea birds may seem randomly congregated, but closer observation shows that they are actually carefully spaced with respect to individual distance. (Photo courtesy of E. Hosking. In Welty, J. C. The Life of Birds. Philadelphia, W. B. Saunders, 1962.)*

tact between people. In others, such as bars, furniture is intimately arranged to increase socializing (and drinking). We also find cultural differences in the use of space. Hall (1966) notes how Frenchmen often carry on conversations at very close range with perhaps only 18 inches separating the individuals. Americans regard such closeness as being threatening and tend to feel uncomfortable.

A number of experimental studies have attempted to test the common observation that people tend to seek well-defined territories or spaces and dislike intrusions. Felipe and Sommer (1966) systematically watched patients on the lawn of a mental hospital and noted that they sought out private benches. When someone else approached and sat on the same bench, one-third departed within two minutes, and two-thirds within 20 minutes. This apparently has little to do with their mental condition, for college students reveal a similar pattern of behavior. Coeds studying alone at large library tables were approached by a female accomplice of the experimenter who sat down next to them. More than half of those studying picked up their books and left within 10 minutes. If the intruder sat across the table or several chairs away, the victimized subject was less likely to leave.

In public spaces, people sometimes attempt to "mark" territory by leaving behind a possession such as books or a coat, and others usually tend to respect such boundaries (Sommer and Becker, 1969). Another method of establishing possession of space is to make contact with a stranger in the hope that he will defend the territory against intruders while the acquaintance is temporarily absent. Sommer's experiments indicate that this method is surprisingly ineffective as most people seldom strongly defend the space of strangers.

DOMINANCE AND SOCIAL STATUS

Establishing and defending territory is the cause of much conflict in many animal societies, but in the long run it contributes to social organization. Another factor which operates the same way is social dominance. A considerable amount of fighting takes place in order to gain or maintain social status, but once established, social hierarchies help preserve order. Dominance relationships may be established between different species occupying the same habitat, as is the case with chimps which dominate baboons, leopards which dominate cheetahs, and walruses which are dominant over seals (Cloudsley-Thompson, 1965). But more important are the dominance hierarchies established by members of the same species.

Peck Orders

Social rank may be established in many ways, but usually relationships are established through force or threats of force. A good example is the well-known peck order found among chickens (Guhl, 1956). In any flock of hens there is usually one (sometimes referred to as the *alpha* animal) which is dominant and pecks freely at any of the other hens. They accept this insult and rarely fight back. The alpha hen struts about with her head erect and feathers fluffed, which serves to indicate her high status. Subordinate hens communicate their submission by meekly lowering their heads whenever there is an encounter with a higher ranking hen. Following the highest ranking hen is number two in rank (the *beta* animal) who pecks at all the hens except number one. This dominance hierarchy continues down the line with the weakest and most submissive hen (the *omega*) at the bottom of the order with no one to peck at. The omega individual, however, is usually simply ignored rather than constantly picked on. Males also have their own peck order and only rarely do they peck at females.

Peck orders are established gradually in young chickens, and rankings are determined by a series of round-robin fights in which individuals come to recognize each other as being dominant or subordinate. Once the hierarchy is established, fighting declines and the flock thrives in relative peace. If a new chicken is introduced into the flock it will have to fight each member to establish its status. If two flocks of birds are joined together, social disorganization results, with an increase in fighting and a decrease in egg laying until a new hierarchy is formed.

Other examples may be found among nonhuman primates. In chimps, the large adult males dominate the rest of the chimps; Van Lawick-Goodall (1968b) reported that such males initiated four and a half times as many attacks as adolescent males and five times as many attacks as females (although she also observed an adult male named David who was relatively peaceful but still maintained a high rank.) As adolescents grow older they begin to fight adult females and eventually become dominant over them (except for their own mother, whom they never really dominate). Since infants and juveniles are rarely attacked, it is the adult females which are the most frequent targets of aggression. Family ties are also important in determining social rank, for the status of the mother may be as important as fighting ability in determining the rank of offspring. Young males tend to be more belligerent if they are in close proximity to older brothers who will back them up. The importance of dominance relationships in monkeys and apes can be seen in feeding and courtship behavior. In the presence of the alpha male, others are reluctant to mate or press for food.

What are the advantages of trying to obtain high social rank? In general, dominant animals are larger, stronger, and older than their subordinates, and they take first priority in the choice of food, mates, and resting places. Dominant hens, for example, eat to their heart's content at feeding time and select the choicest roosting places at night. Lower ranking hens eat what is left over after their superiors have finished and roost in any place they can find. In animals such as baboons, which show cooperative social behavior, the high ranking males exert leadership in defending the troop and in directing terrestrial wanderings for food and shelter.

Dominance struggles may consist almost entirely of chases and threats with little fighting, as in the case of Canadian geese (Raveling, 1970), or they may end in death to the rival, particularly if the victim cannot escape. Chaffinches and doves may gradually peck their rivals to death, and subordinate fish may be pestered and hounded until they eventually die. But some of the most ferocious stag fights which take place with deer, buffaloes, antelopes, and goats rarely result in injury, mainly because the dangerous horns are never used for goring an opponent. Giraffes have sharp hooves, but when fighting with other giraffes they spar with their long necks and do not use their hooves (Cloudsley-Thompson, 1965). The same type of phenomenon has already been noted in snakes, which use their fangs only against prey or predators. Such examples help illustrate the fact that predatory killing is entirely different, both in function and in form, from dominance or territorial quarrels. Similarities can be seen in some human cultures such as the Indians or Eskimos, where hunters are skilled in the use of deadly weapons yet in-group fighting is rare.

Dominance hierarchies are an important part of social organization, and reliable rankings are found in both domestic and wild animals (Candland and Bloomquist, 1965). Among domesticated species we find social dominance in puppies (Scott, 1958b), dairy cattle (Schein and Fohrman, 1956), and laboratory rats (Grant and Chance, 1958; Baenninger, 1966). In Baenninger's study, dominance orders were established early and remained stable throughout life.

Among wild animals, dominance orders have been described in chaffinches (Marler, 1955), wolves (Scott, 1958b), wasps (Lin, 1963) turtles (Boice, 1970a), baboons (Washburn and DeVore, 1961) and electric fish (Westby and Box, 1970). In the electric fish *Gymnotus carapo* dominance orders can be reliably predicted by the electrical characteristics of the interacting fish. Wolves may cooperate in killing prey, but they observe status by the order in which they eat what they have killed. Lions also show cooperation in hunting but not in feeding (Schaller, 1969). Baboons have a more complex mode of social dominance, with several high-ranking males joining forces to dominate the rest of the troop. The ruling coalition sticks together if possible, but if they are separated, individuals from the coalition may lose their dominance (hence, they usually stick together). The dominance relationship between individual baboons is often expressed by mounting behavior in a nonsexual situation (Fig. 18). The dominant baboon may approach from the rear and give a quick, perfunctory mount while the submissive baboon displays his rump and adopts the female sexual

Figure 18. A male baboon mounts another male to assert his dominance. Such gestures in a nonsexual situation reduce overt conflict. Sometimes it is the submissive male which does the mounting. (Photo courtesy of I. DeVore.)

posture (Simonds, 1965). The roles are sometimes reversed, however, and the submissive baboon may perform the mounting.

Social dominance may appear to be a kind of "law of the jungle" in which the stronger subdue the weaker. In rhesus monkeys, for example, it is possible simply to record the number of fights and their outcomes and show a linear relationship between number of wins and social rank (Sade, 1967). But sometimes macaque social orders show complexities such as the formation of alliances in which a low ranking individual may improve his stature by being associated with a high ranking individual who will back him up (Varley and Symmes, 1966). In addition, dominance relationships do not hold for every kind of behavior. Dairy cattle, for example, may have a milking order, a leader-follower order, and another dominance order for other kinds of social relationships (Dickson, Barr, and Wieckert, 1967). Feeding hierarchies in frogs do not necessarily correspond to aggressiveness in nonfeeding situations (Boice, 1970b). There is also some evidence that intraspecific dominance is not always related to interspecific aggressiveness. If one observes caged rats attacking nonconspecifics, there is usually only one rat which does the killing (DeSisto and

Huston, 1971), but the "killer" rat is not always the most dominant rat (Johnson, Reich, and DeSisto, 1972). Further evidence for this comes from reports that rats which kill mice do not differ significantly in social rank from non–mouse-killers (Baenninger and Baenninger, 1970). No doubt there are many species differences, for in baboons the dominant males appear to do almost everything: they defend the troop against predators, they occasionally kill prey, they lead the group during the day time, and they maintain order within the group.

Status Seeking in Humans

Because dominance relationships are so prevalent in nature, and particularly in other primates, it is inevitable to attempt comparisons. Most modern democracies claim to be classless societies, but of course they are not. We no longer encounter royal blood, nobility, and slaves, but we certainly have upper, middle, and lower classes (in spite of the fact that nearly everyone pictures himself as a member of the middle class). On an individual level we find status seeking, social climbing, struggles for political power or patronage, desire for financial wealth, and striving for prestige. Whether it is a promotion, a husband, a home in suburbia, membership in the country club, entrance to an Ivy League college, a key to the executive washroom, a low-numbered license plate, a red Ferrari, or skiing at Sugarbush, humans are unquestionably status-oriented. In cultures other than our own status may be reflected by the number of cows, wives, or servants. While this struggle for prestige seldom leads to overt fighting, others may be crushed or exploited on the road to the top, and violence is not avoided but made indirect. Humans have invented almost unbelievable rituals in an effort to get ahead or to make themselves feel that they are already ahead. For many, status is the main goal in life. Whether the concept of dominance can be applied to human society remains a matter of open speculation. The fact that many animals, including primates, show strong dominance hierarchies does not mean that it is a necessary or fundamental part of human behavior. Human social behavior is distinctive because of its governance by many complex factors, not the least of which are culture and tradition. There are so many dimensions upon which humans could be scaled that a simple unidimensional concept like dominance would seem to be of little use.

One may wonder why dominance relationships exist in any species, for it seems like a constant source of strife. But this overlooks its adaptive significance, which makes it fundamental to many kinds of social organization. A considerable amount of energy is devoted to marking and defending territories or setting up social hierarchies, but once they are established, relative stability is achieved which minimizes destructive fighting. Thus, in the long run territory and status probably *prevent* more violence than they produce. There are a number of benefits to such social organization, for it frees individuals to live in close proximity without fear of having to fight every other individual. Any fighting which does take place is usually reduced to a ritual or ceremony which minimizes the possibility of injury. There are also important implications for reproductive success and gene flow: in many species dominant males mate much more frequently, and in a number of birds females are sexually unresponsive to males who do not have territory (Howard, 1948). In addition, individuals are optimally spaced out to prevent overpopulation, which tends to foster orderly growth. As a result, individuals can enjoy relative tranquillity and devote their energies to food gathering, pursuit of mates, care of young, or play.

Social Darwinism

There are also disadvantages of tight social organization, ones we tend to overlook in animals but not in man. What may be adaptive to the survival of a species as a whole may be achieved at the expense of those individuals of low status unable to acquire and defend "territory." Since human beings are nowadays supposedly concerned with equality and justice, the natural selection of Mother Nature is not good enough, for it leads to the exploitation of the poor by the rich. In the late 19th century it was fashionable to apply the biological principles of natural selection to human society in a movement called Social Darwinism. This philosophy became a convenient apology for ruthless businessmen and unprincipled politicians who felt that only the fittest should survive and that those who lost out deserved to get trampled. Fortunately, Social Darwinism disappeared as a conscious philosophy by the 1920's, but it never completely died. Many wealthy and powerful people attribute their position to Horatio Alger-like hard work and keen motivation, while at the same time dismissing the less fortunate as being lazy and irresponsible. No one can seriously maintain this simple-minded philosophy in today's world, for wealth is often achieved by inheritance, powerful friends, a good lawyer, or nothing more than luck. If one is born in a coal mining town or in a black ghetto, all the hard work in the world may lead to nothing. Hard work led to an annual salary of $790,000 for James M. Roche, former board chairman of General Motors, but many waitresses, shoe shine boys, farm hands, and bartenders work just as hard. Certainly it is difficult to justify why one man should earn more in a couple of days than most people do in an entire year, particularly when the average man is paying Mr. Roche's wages by buying his Chevrolets. Richard Hofstadter (1955) offers the following conclusions regarding Social Darwinism and survival of the fittest:

> ... The life of man in society, while it is incidentally a bio-
> logical fact, has characteristics that are not reducible to biology
> and must be explained in the distinctive terms of a cultural
> analysis; that the physical well-being of men is a result of their
> social organization and not vice-versa; that social improvement
> is a product of advances in technology and social organization,
> not of breeding or selective elimination; that judgments as to
> the value of competition between men or enterprises or nations
> must be based upon social and not allegedly biological conse-
> quences; and finally, that there is nothing in nature or a natural-
> istic philosophy of life to make impossible the acceptance of
> moral sanctions that can be employed for the common good.

ECOLOGICAL FACTORS IN AGGRESSION

Both territory and dominance play an important role in animal behavior, but there is a certain danger in viewing such factors as keys to social organization. Crook (1970) has pointed out that in many primates it is difficult to understand social behavior in terms of simple concepts like dominance, and that dominance rankings should not be treated as the universal behavioral basis of group structure. Ecological factors may influence social behavior, and Crook suggests that climatic changes may have had an important effect on the social evolution of man, particularly in the origins of family patterns and male control. When climatic changes forced apes out of the dense forests into a savanna (grassy plain) habitat, loose social groupings were replaced with more tightly knit organizations which favored the development of monogamous family-type patterns. Crook and Gartlan (1966) have described a model (Fig. 19) which relates primate social organization to such ecological factors as the availability of food and sleeping sites and predator pressures. For example, food supply may directly affect population size and dispersion, which in turn affects the social structure and social dynamics of the group. Or, to take another example, if nesting sites are accessible to predators, populations become more dispersed and group cohesion is reduced. Jay (1965)

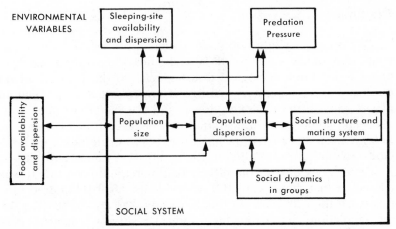

Figure 19. The social system adopted by primates is partly determined by ecological variables. This hypothesis is depicted above in a drawing adapted from Crook and Gartlan (1966) and Crook (1970).

has summarized how ecological factors help determine the natural behavior of many primates.

The importance of habitat and ecological pressures can be illustrated by an experiment involving two sympatric (occupying the same area) rodents, the meadow vole and the collared lemming (Banks and Fox, 1968). Ordinarily the voles are less aggressive than the lemmings, but if voles from optimal habitats are matched with lemmings from suboptimal habitats, the reverse is true. In another experiment, wild rhesus monkeys were put in captivity and subjected to food reduction, a limitation of space, and changes in group membership. Food reduction led to decreases in aggressive behavior, whereas the other two variables caused increases (Southwick, 1967). Southwick (1969) has also reported that rhesus monkeys living in forests are less aggressive than those residing in Indian villages and temple areas.

Just what happens when the ecological balance is upset can be seen in a case involving wild deer living near the Grand Canyon many years ago (Bourlière, 1954). A stable population of about 4000 deer cohabited a plateau along with wolves, coyotes, and other predators. The weak and sick deer were regularly preyed upon, and this had the net effect of keeping the predator population healthy which in turn kept the deer population from expanding. Then humans came along and decided to eliminate the wolves and coyotes, and as a result the deer population skyrocketed. It went to 40,000 by 1920 and to a peak of 100,000 in 1924. The habitat could not support such a large population, and in the next 15 years of massive starvation the population sank back to 10,000.

The Effects of Crowding

What occurs when populations increase in size is a matter of great importance in a world already heavily overpopulated in many areas. From ecological disasters such as the Grand Canyon deer and from laboratory studies it appears that overcrowding places unusual stress on individuals and may lead to various forms of social pathology. An illustration may be taken from experiments in which scientists tried to find a way to eliminate rats from large cities. In one project (Calhoun, 1948), rats were caught and marked in a one block area in the city of Baltimore, and from this it was estimated that there were 168 rat-residents. Over a hundred new rats were then let loose in this block, thus greatly increasing the rat population. But before long, human residents began noticing unusual numbers of dead rats. Most of the dead were the new or foreign rats, but some of those killed included the old-timers. In short, what happened was that the social disorganization caused by the introduction of foreign rats led to fighting and killing and the net result was an overall decrease from the previous population level.

Thus, carefully regulated social behavior may be upset by disorganization caused by overcrowding. Calhoun and Webb (1953) systematically captured field mice in a marked location and were surprised to find that as time went on they began trapping more rather than fewer mice. It turned out that the population pressures had induced mice from neighboring areas to migrate into the vacuum. Such population pressures may vary from year to year depending on the abundance of food and space, and the result may be cyclical patterns of socially destructive behavior. Probably the most frequently cited example of this is the story of periodic migrations of the Norway lemmings, which are said to push forward in suicidal waves until they finally reach the sea and plunge to their death. This quaint story is unfortunately clouded by much romantic folklore (Archer, 1970). Although migrations do take place, they are probably directed at taking advantage of seasonal changes in food supplies. Lemmings often migrate individually rather than in hordes, and they do not simply rush in any direction over any obstacle until they fall into the sea. With regard to their aggressiveness, there may be more threats and displays as population density increases, but actual fighting tends to decrease (Kock, Stoddart, and Kacher, 1969).

Drastic fluctuations in populations are the exception rather than the rule, for most animal societies limit their own population growth. It has been calculated that a single pair of aphids could produce a pile of insects as high as Mt. Everest in a single season (Cloudsley-Thompson, 1965). Fortunately, there are factors such as the availability of food and the presence of predators which prevent such disasters. But there are also important internal limitations, for crowding limits endocrine function (Thiessen and Rodgers, 1961), which has a marked effect on health and behavior. Continued stress in the competition for food, space, and mates overworks the adrenal glands (Christian, 1955), which adversely affects body growth, ability to fight diseases, and reproductive and maternal behavior.

As part of the Baltimore experiments Calhoun (1950) showed that introducing wild rats to a large protected area with an unlimited food supply did not result in uncontrolled population growth. The 10,000 square feet used in these experiments might have sustained as many as 5000 rats, but after two years the rat population was only about 150. The main factor which limited growth was the territorial and dominance behavior of rats living near the food supply. Other rats forced to the periphery were less successful in surviving, and high mortality rates were found among their offspring.

Calhoun (1962) also conducted a series of experiments with domesticated albino rats confined to a 10- by 14-foot room for 16 months. This room was partitioned into four sections, with weanling litter-mates growing up in each section. At 45 days of age the mothers were removed and ramps were installed to provide limited connections among the four areas. With food and water readily available the entire room could support about 48 rats comfortably; the population, however, rapidly grew to 80, at which point it was stabilized by removing animals. What happens when animals are forced to live in such crowded conditions? For one thing, the rats did not distribute themselves equally among the four pens, but tended to gravitate toward one of them, which led Calhoun to label it a "behavioral sink." The two pens which had only one entrance tended to be monopolized by strong males who fought off all others except a small harem of females. Most eating became concentrated in the crowded "sink," although such congregations were mainly the result of a food dispenser which required the rats to engage in lengthy feeding bouts to get enough to eat. Most interesting was the social pathology which developed in this crowded environment. Males became pansexual and attempted to mount any rat regardless of age, sex, or receptivity. Fighting increased in both frequency and intensity to the point where there were many scratches, gashes, and tail severances. Female mortality was 3.5 times that of males, partly because of difficulties in giving birth. For those which did have babies, maternal behavior was so disorganized and inadequate that most of the pups died.

One major problem with Calhoun's experiment is that he may have started with a disorganized population to begin with, for the original rats were strangers to one another. An experiment with mice (Brown, 1953) compared fighting in a relatively stable population of mice (begun from the mating of a single pair) with fighting in a disorganized population composed of wild mice who were strangers to each other. The stable group reproduced and thrived with a minimum of fighting whereas the disorganized group was characterized by more aggressive behavior, including that of some females who attacked and killed males. Similar results have been reported for rats (Wolfe and Summerlin, 1968), although after a short period a dominance hierarchy was formed which contributed to stability. In this case experimenters trapped groups of wild cotton rats which either (a) knew each other, or (b) were unfamiliar to each other. The rats were housed in group cages while observers noted the frequency of agonistic encounters. It was found that the social structure established in the wild rats was transferred to captivity, so that familiar rats fought less than strange rats. But after one day the unfamiliar rats formed a dominance hierarchy and displayed social organization which reduced their fighting to the level of the other group. It should be stressed that population pressure resulting from laboratory confinement may lead to unusually aggressive behavior, and in wild rodent populations it is much more difficult to find simple relationships between population density and aggressive behavior (Archer, 1970).

It is tempting to suggest analogies to human social organization. Animals engage in agonistic behavior to establish territory and rank, and this relatively mild form of aggression usually prevents overcrowding and accompanying large-scale disasters. Overcrowding, of course, is only one of many possible causes of social disorganization, and increased aggressiveness is not the inevitable result of crowding. But population pressure clearly has disruptive and negative effects on any society, and one needs only to look at any major city to see how it affects humans. We cannot assume that because rats form a pathological behavioral sink under the stress of crowding that humans will do the same. But if humans are so clever and adaptable, why have they allowed their cities to degenerate into breeding grounds for crime and violence? We know that every major city contains crowded slums in which a disproportionate amount of crime takes place. A report to the President's Commission on the Causes and Prevention of Violence (Violent Crime, 1967) asserts that the connection between violent crime and slums is "one of the most fully documented facts about crime." In cities with populations above a quarter of a million the rate of major violent offenses is 11 times higher than it is in rural areas. It should be noted, however, that population density alone may have complicated effects, and just what happens may depend on who is being crowded and the situation in which crowding occurs (Erlich and Freedman, 1971). New York City, for example, is much more densely populated than Los Angeles (26,000 people per square mile in New York compared to 5500 in L.A.), yet Los Angeles has a higher crime rate. Some laboratory experiments on how people react to crowded rooms indicate that there may be sex differences: men tend to become more competitive and hostile while women respond more positively. Interestingly enough, mixing sexes appears to negate the effects of crowding, at least in the laboratory. In the long run, it may be that crowding *per se* is less of a factor than the quality of crowding and the kinds of interactions dictated by the crowding. For example, many people can be "crowded" into luxury apartments and be perfectly happy, while those similarly crowded into ghettos may not. Thus, crowding may be only indirectly responsible for the problems of our cities, for it leads to urban decay and other factors which may be more directly involved.

Historical and sociological explanations have also been offered to explain the problems of cities. Faris (1955) points out that the rapid expansion of the American frontier led to fast population growth which may have contributed to lawlessness. In the East, cities rapidly increased both their size and their problems with the sudden influx and mixing of racial and ethnic groups. Crowding is relative to the amount of food as well as the amount of space, which can be seen from cases of prolonged malnutrition and semi-starvation. For example, in the German blockade of Leningrad during the harsh winter of 1941–1942, food supplies were cut off and severe rationing resulted. Within a month semi-starvation was evident and many citizens were reduced to 75 per cent of their normal body weight. The psychological deteriorations reported included widespread apathy, dulling of the emotions, narrowing of intellectual interests, and a general leveling of individual differences (Keys, et al., 1950). In the Minnesota starvation experiments carried out with 36 volunteer conscientious objectors during World War II (Keys, et al., 1950), semi-starvation was imposed for six months. Participants soon altered their social behavior and became more independent, irritable, and slovenly.

The effects of crowding may also be found within individual families. Viel (1971) examined infanticides among South American children and found that the larger the family the more the likelihood of infantile deaths not due to biological (e.g., disease) factors. For example, the death rate of children in families with 10 or more children is five times as high as for families with only one child.

Human societies differ from other animal societies in that we have acquired the technological capacity to nullify natural limitations in our reproductive behavior. With improved medical care people are more likely to survive crises and live longer. Through either donated or mechanical organs our lives may be extended even longer, and some individuals have even been frozen shortly after "death" in the hopes of being thawed out and revived in another century. Reproductive technology has become so sophisticated that in the not too distant future we may have perfected artificial wombs, embryo transplants, genetic engineering, asexual reproduction, and duplication of living organisms from their own tissues. Many of these "engineering" feats have already been demonstrated on laboratory animals (Francoeur, 1970), and they raise the possibility that future generations may have an almost infinite power to create as many offspring as they choose while also specifying their physical and psychological characteristics.

The days of unlimited and unregulated conception are obviously numbered, but as frightening as that sounds it may be much more humanitarian than the chaos created by overpopulation. It took 4.5 billion years for the human population to reach one billion in 1830, and in the next hundred years it doubled. By 1960 it reached three billion and by 1975 it will be four billion (Lerner, 1968). Every day the world's population increases by 220,000, and already 60 per cent eats less than the average human requirement of 2200 calories a day. The approximately 15 million people who died in World War II were replaced in only three and a half months. It has been calculated that if present reproductive practices were to continue, there would be one person per square foot in the United States within six or seven centuries (Coale, 1970). In 1500 years our descendants would weigh more than the earth itself, and it can be calculated that within a few thousand years this sphere of flesh would expand outward at speeds approaching the velocity of light. Of course, we need not worry about this because in only 900 years our accumulated body heat will be sufficient to roast everyone (Lerner, 1968). To achieve a stable population by voluntary and humane methods may take hundreds of years in some countries, and even radical methods may be only partially successful in others. In India, for example, a stable population of 657 million could be reached by 1991, provided that everyone over the age of 22 is sterilized. Some experts suggest the encouragement of homosexual behavior in an effort to avoid the disasters of overpopulation.

Obviously man cannot survive in an overpopulated world, nor would it be desirable to do so. There is no longer any question about whether man will change; the only question is whether change will result from self-imposed restraints or from catastrophic suffering. In many respects, the ecological problems are analogous to those of aggression in general. In the very near future, man may have the knowledge and means to control both, but is man prepared to make the psychological adjustments that such controls necessitate? The problems of ecology and the environment will be raised again in a more sociological context in Chapter 6.

3 BIOLOGICAL FACTORS II

PHYSIOLOGY, GENETICS, AND SEX

Ultimately, all behavior is controlled by the brain and central nervous system. While other chapters in this book emphasize the influence of external stimuli as well as social and developmental experience, the present chapter concentrates on internal biological processes and their relation to external behavior. In recent years this has been a particularly fruitful area of investigation, and scientific study of the brain, genes, hormones, and other physiological processes has greatly enhanced our understanding of aggressive behavior.

CHEMICAL AND HUMORAL FACTORS IN AGGRESSION

During an aggressive exchange with another person, the brain usually signals the adrenal glands to liberate epinephrine (also called adrenalin) into the bloodstream and we quickly notice an increase in physiological arousal and level of excitement. This can be demonstrated in the laboratory by insulting and provoking college students while monitoring vascular activity (Hokanson and Shetler, 1961; Hokanson and Burgess, 1962). The students may not respond to their tormentor, but they will show elevations in blood pressure and heart rate. More dramatic changes can be observed by studying the physiology of defeated animals. Bronson and Eleftheriou (1965) trained C57BL/6J mice as "gladiators" and then matched them with nontrained opponents, who were quickly defeated. Defeated mice were later given visual exposure to gladiator mice, and the stress response was compared to that of similar mice which had never experienced defeat. Stress was measured by sampling blood plasma and recording concentrations of unbound corticosterone, a circulating hormone which provides an index of adrenal activity. It was found that mice which had previously (but not recently) experienced defeat had more than three times ($p < .001$) as much circulating corticosterone in their blood compared to mice which had never been defeated. Thus, defeat caused a relatively permanent change in the physiology of the animal.

Such experiments demonstrate the interaction between external stimuli and internal physiology. This relationship can also be studied by directly manipulating physiological events and observing the effect on behavior. Alcohol, for example, makes some people more friendly and jovial while others become more hostile and aggressive. The exact effect may depend on the amount and type of liquor consumed as well as individual differences. The importance of the concentration of alcohol can be easily demonstrated in Siamese fighting fish. If placed in solutions containing low concentrations of alcohol, they emit more aggressive displays, but if immersed in more concentrated solutions threat displays decrease (Raynes, Ryback, and Ingle, 1968). The effect may also depend on the presence of particular flavoring congeners. For example, Old Crow bourbon decreases aggressiveness in fighting fish, while similar concentrations of alcohol without congeneric flavoring may increase aggressiveness (Raynes and Ryback, 1970). Fighting fish may also launch into aggressive displays in the absence of opponents if norepinephrine bitartrate is placed in the water (Marrone, Pray, and Bridges, 1966). Norepinephrine is a major adrenergic mediator released by the adrenal medulla, and it has been suggested (Funkenstein, 1955) that norepinephrine release is directly correlated with aggressive behavior.

In humans, epinephrine can be injected directly into the bloodstream, resulting in physiological arousal. But just how such experimentally induced arousal gets directed and cognitively labeled depends on the situation (Schachter and Singer, 1962; Schachter and Latané, 1964). In a pleasant surrounding, aroused subjects are likely to report euphoria (i.e., compared to controls who are injected with saline). In an anger-producing situation, injections of epinephrine may result in hostility.

More recently it has been reported that aggressiveness can be modified by changing the rate of metabolism of a number of central nervous system neurotransmitters, including norepinephrine, dopamine, and serotonin (Welch and Welch, 1969). Normal fighting in mice can be depressed by pharmacological interference with the biosynthesis of neuronal catecholamines and serotonin, or by accelerating the rate of release of these amines. Other kinds of chemical imbalances in the bloodstream and nervous system may contribute to aggressive behavior, including hypoglycemia (low blood sugar) and specific allergies. Moyer (1971) reports the case of a child who had violent temper tantrums every time he ate bananas. Of major significance is the role played by the sex hormones, a topic which will be considered separately toward the end of this chapter. A detailed consideration of other biochemical and endocrine functions is beyond the scope of this book; however, the reader may wish to consult Garattini and Sigg (1969) for several recent reviews of this literature. One important fact which does emerge from studying the biochemistry of the brain is that the neurotransmitters and biogenic amines (such as serotonin, norepinephrine, and dopamine) that appear to mediate aggressive behavior are found in high concentrations in the limbic system.

THE LIMBIC SYSTEM

The limbic system is composed of a series of structures in the upper brain stem and lower cerebrum which are intimately involved in the control and elaboration of most motivated behavior. The limbic system is sometimes called the "old brain" because it is earlier and more primitive, both in embryonic and phylogenetic development. Not too long ago it was also referred to as the "smell brain" or "nose brain" because of its involvement in olfactory functions so important to motivated behavior, particularly in more primitive vertebrates. To greatly oversimplify, the limbic system is the neural substrate for behavior related to motivation and emotion, but its action is partly regulated by the neocortex (new brain), which is extensively elaborated in man. The names of the structures within the limbic system come from ancient anatomists, who chose the term "limbus" because it means border and refers to those structures which outline the inner portion of each hemisphere (see Figure 20). Thus, the limbic system includes such structures as the thalamus (bridal chamber), the epithalamus (roof of the chamber), hypothalamus (floor of the chamber), hippocampus (seahorse, because of its curved shape), amygdala (almond, again because of its shape), cingulum (belt), and septal region (fence).

All of these areas have been implicated in the regulation of aggressive behavior. Almost a century ago researchers noted that

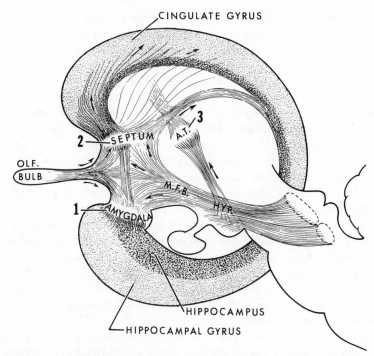

Figure 20.   *Just beneath the neocortex lies the more primitive limbic cortex (indicated by stippling), which has complex connections with other portions of the limbic system. Important pathways lead from the hypothalamus (HYP.) through the medial forebrain bundle (M.F.B.) and feed into the limbic cortex through the amygdala (1) and the septum (2). Connections from the olfactory bulb also join at these points. Other pathways (3) bypass this area and go directly to the limbic cortex through the anterior thalamic nuclei (A.T.). The entire limbic system integrates and elaborates the expression of emotional and aggressive behavior. (Courtesy of P. MacLean.)*

lesions in the amygdala and hippocampus made monkeys unusually tame; however, the significance of these crude experiments was not realized until the classic work of Kluver and Bucy (1937), who made bilateral lesions in the temporal lobes (including the amygdala and hippocampus) of wild monkeys. After recovery, the monkeys were no longer aggressive and in fact became playful, hypersexual, and visually stupid (i.e., putting strange objects in their mouths). More recently, temporal lobe lesions in squirrel monkeys have been shown to cause animals to lose rank in their dominance hierarchy (Plotnik, 1968). Experiments have also been conducted with wild rhesus monkeys in their natural habitat that indicate that such lesions impair many social behaviors, including aggressive threats and submissive gestures (Dicks,

Myers, and Kling, 1969). In this experiment portions of the amygdala were removed which may have had a direct effect on emotionality or an indirect effect through disruption of olfactory capacity.

Along with the hypothalamus, a small but important forebrain structure located on the bottom surface of the mammalian brain, the amygdala, has received the most attention from experimenters interested in the neural substrate of aggression. The hypothalamus and amygdala are intimately connected, and it has been shown that stimulation of the amygdala can either facilitate or suppress attack depending on whether the hypothalamus is stimulated at the same time (Egger and Flynn, 1963). If areas of the amygdala which normally suppress attack are ablated, attack elicited by stimulation of the hypothalamus will be facilitated (Egger and Flynn, 1967). Some of the first experiments involving surgical lesions in the amygdala resulted in increased irritability and rage reactions in cats (Bard and Mountcastle, 1948); however, other researchers have reported the opposite, an increase in docility. For example, vicious wildcats have been tamed by amygdalectomies (Schreiner and Kling, 1956), and wild Norway rats lose not only their aggressiveness but their fear of novel objects (Galef, 1970). These findings are not necessarily discrepant, for the amygdala contains many nuclei, some of which have opposing functions.

Brain Stimulation and Elicited Attack

In recent years sophisticated techniques have been developed for selectively activating particular structures of the brain with electrical or chemical stimulation. This is accomplished by a relatively minor and painless operation in which animals are anesthetized and then situated on a stereotaxic instrument (designed to precisely position the animal's brain). This instrument is carefully placed with reference points on the animal's head, and in conjunction with a stereotaxic brain atlas it allows experimenters to estimate the exact location of a particular brain structure. A small hole is made in the head at just the right place, and a fine insulated wire or electrode is carefully lowered into the brain a distance specified according to the brain atlas and calibrations on the stereotaxic instrument. The electrode is then firmly and permanently anchored to the skull with mounting screws and cement, and the skin is sutured around the electrode. The animal recovers from the anesthesia in a few hours and is ready to test in a few days. By connecting the electrode to a stimulator, the experimenter is able to apply a few millionths of an ampere of electric current to neurons around its tip, and by using different stimulation parameters and by testing electrodes implanted in different locations of the brain it is possible to elicit a number of consummatory behaviors, such as eating, drinking, gnawing, and copulating. Using this method, violent attack and killing behavior can be elicited, particularly if the electrode tip is situated in parts of the hypothalamus (Fig. 21). As early as 1928 Hess reported that highly emotional rage reactions accompanied hypothalamic stimulation, and this behavior was often called "sham rage" because, unlike real rage, it disappeared quickly (as soon as the experimenter turned off the stimulator). Partly because this rage response could not be easily conditioned to a neutral stimulus, it was suggested (Masserman, 1941) that elicited rage was simply a motor automatism with no directed motivational properties.

This interpretation is no longer tenable because more recent research has identified relatively discrete portions of the hypothalamus which appear to mediate specifically directed killing behavior. Wasman and Flynn (1962) investigated elicited aggres-

Figure 21. The monkey on the cage floor grimaces fearfully as he is attacked by another monkey whose actions are controlled by radio telemetry. When the experimenter pushes a button, electric current flows from the battery package around the monkey's neck through a cable to electrodes surgically implanted in the brain. Depending on which electrodes the experimenter chooses to operate, the monkey can be made either to attack or to withdraw. (Courtesy of J. Delgado.)

sive behavior in cats by first selecting animals which normally behaved peacefully in the company of rats and then stereotaxically implanting their cats with chronic electrodes in the lateral hypothalamus. After recovery from the operation, the cats remained peaceful, but if electrically stimulated through the electrode their behavior changed. Low intensity stimulation would cause an alerting response and the cat would get to its feet and start to prowl around his cage ignoring the presence of a rat. At slightly higher stimulus intensities (above attack threshold), cats would pounce on the rat and viciously bite it on the back of the neck, usually killing it. Such attacks appear to be relatively selective and unemotional, and for this reason they have been called "stalking attacks," "directed attacks," or "quiet biting attacks" (Flynn, 1967). An indication of this selectivity can be seen when cats are given a choice of objects to attack (Levison and Flynn, 1965), such as real rats, dummy rats, anesthetized rats, toy dogs, and rubber blocks. In the case of the elicited stalking attack, most cats attack what most closely resembles a real rat and rarely do they attack such irrelevant objects as a rubber block or an experimenter. If given a choice between fresh horse meat and an anesthetized rat they will attack the rat (Flynn, et. al., 1970).

In contrast to this selective and directed attack, electrical stimulation of the nearby medial hypothalamus results in an "affective attack," which transforms the cat into a Frankenstein-like demon, lashing out at almost any handy object, including the experimenter (Egger and Flynn, 1963; Roberts and Kiess, 1964). In this affective attack the pupils dilate, the back arches, the hair stands on end, the claws are extended, and hissing and urination takes place. Affective and quiet-biting attack can also be behaviorally defined in the rat (Panksepp, 1971a). In normally non-aggressive rats, electrical stimulation causing affective attack elicits mouse-killing and biting attacks on other rats. During quiet-biting attack, rats bite live or dead mice but not other rats. Although killing can be facilitated (i.e., quicker attacks in natural killers) by posterior hypothalamic stimulation, it is only in the anterior and medial hypothalamus that stimulation causes killing in natural nonkillers (DeSisto, 1970; Vergnes and Karli, 1969; 1970). Directed attack by nonkillers has also been elicited from 53 points in the ventrolateral hypothalamus (Woodworth, 1971). In this case the specificity seems to be related to the size of the victim rather than the species, for stimulated rats tend to attack mice and rat pups but not adult rats or guinea pigs. In any event, it becomes clear that slight differences in electrode location may result in distinctly different kinds of aggressive behavior.

The extent to which aggressive behavior can be controlled by manipulating brain function is effectively demonstrated in a recent experiment which demonstrates that there are built-in killing mechanisms which are both chemically and anatomically specific (Smith, King, and Hoebel, 1970; see Bandler, 1969, for a similar experiment). Tiny tubes or cannulas about the size of a hypodermic needle were surgically implanted in the brains of anesthetized rats. The cannulas were positioned in both hemispheres and aimed at the lateral hypothalamus with the aid of a stereotaxic instrument. Subjects were previously screened as being spontaneous mouse-killers or nonkillers, and a chemical (either a potent drug or a neutral substance) was injected directly into the hypothalamus. It was found that: (a) carbachol, a drug which acts like acetylcholine and is therefore cholinergic in its action, induced killing in normally peaceful rats; (b) another drug (atropine methyl nitrate), which blocks cholinergic action, had the opposite effect of suppressing killing in rats which were spontaneous killers. Smith, King, and Hoebel also demonstrated both chemical specificity and anatomical specificity. The former was demonstrated by showing that the effect was limited to certain chemicals and that other neurohumors had no effect. The latter was demonstrated by injecting carbachol at various locations about 1 mm. from the lateral hypothalamus, resulting in no effect on aggressive behavior. To date, this experiment comes the closest to demonstrating specific neural mechanisms controlling aggressive behavior. It shows that pharmacological manipulation can arouse or suppress aggressive behavior regardless of the natural behavior or past history of the animal.

The fact that hypothalamic stimulation leads to aggressive attacks does not necessarily prove that this structure is an "aggression center." Hypothalamic stimulation also causes stimulus-bound eating and it may be that the attacks reflect some form of predatory behavior. For example, killing will be facilitated if an animal is hungry but will occur less often when he is satiated (DeSisto, 1970). In addition, the same lateral hypothalamic sites which elicit stalking attack can also elicit feeding (Hutchinson and Renfrew, 1966). But in the experiment of Hutchinson and Renfrew higher intensities of electrical stimulation had to be employed to obtain attack rather than feeding, and it may be that other neural pathways were activated by the stronger stimulation. Current spread at the electrode tip, however, cannot completely explain the difference between feeding and attack, for the authors report that increasing current had a similar effect at all electrode locations. More to the point is the fact that following an elicited attack cats rarely attempt to eat the carcass, which suggests that predation may not be involved. In addition, hungry cats in the process of eating will interrupt a meal when stimulated in order to attack a rat (Roberts and Kiess, 1964). Sometimes stimulation causes a cat to bite at food, but it is more like an attack than an eating response since he continues to prowl around with the food dripping out of his mouth (Wasman and Flynn, 1962). Finally, there are hypothalamic sites which readily elicit attack but fail to cause eating behavior no matter what the stimulation intensity (Flynn, et al., 1970).

Thus, there is no simple relation between elicited attack and predation. Another possible explanation is that elicited attack is a form of pain-induced aggression, for rats will perform a response to terminate the stimulation, which might indicate that it has aversive properties (King and Hoebel, 1968; Renfrew, 1969). It appears that this cannot be a complete explanation, for sites which facilitate killing or elicit quiet-biting attack in nonkillers also support self-stimulation; this indicates that it may have reinforcing properties (DeSisto, 1970; Panksepp, 1971a; Woodworth, 1971). The question of whether aggression itself is rewarding or "pleasurable" will be discussed in Chapter 5.

It is clear that there are many complexities which remain to be resolved, but before going on a few more need to be raised. While the stimulus-bound aspects of elicited attack may be impressive, many other factors influence the quality and intensity of such attacks, including sensory information, the presence of relevant external stimuli, and previous experience. In the cat, brain stimulation may initiate attack movements, but the exact topology is guided in part by peripheral sensory systems such as vision and touch (MacDonnell and Flynn, 1966a). Attack-inducing hypothalamic stimulation establishes sensory fields for reflexes related to biting and can facilitate sensory and motor components which help direct attack. Flynn and his associates (1970) have attempted to relate both central and peripheral influences into a general theory of neural mechanisms underlying the attack behavior of the cat.

Species-Typical Behavior and Neural Organization

Is elicited aggression merely a laboratory artifact or is it related to the natural behavior of animals? Animals which learn an escape response to painful tail shock can transfer this response and perform it in order to terminate aversive brain shock which elicits attack (Adams and Flynn, 1966). Stimulus-bound attack is obtained more easily in rats which naturally attack mice compared to those which are not spontaneous killers (Panksepp, 1971a). It appears that elicited attack, particularly selective and directed attack, resembles natural behavior, particularly if appropriate goal objects are present. Thus, the hypothalamus does not completely "control" attack behavior, for guidance may also come from sensory feedback, external stimuli, and previous experience. These factors interact to different degrees, depending on the type of behavior involved, and it is likely that there are a number of overlapping systems mediating many consummatory activities. For example, in the relatively primitive Virginia opossum, hypothalamic stimulation can elicit biting attack, defensive threats, escape, eating, grooming, copulating, yawning, and exploration (Roberts, Steinberg, and Means, 1967). Similar findings have been obtained with other mammals, indicating considerable phylogenetic continuity.

Attack is one kind of species-typical consummatory behavior, and it is characterized neither by total rigidity nor by complete plasticity. For example, quiet-biting attack may be elicited only if there is an appropriate victim available. Previous social experience may influence elicited attack, for cats with extensive social experience will engage in more vigorous and persistent attacks and will be more selective about their choice of victims (compared to cats raised in isolation). But aggressive attacks can be electrically elicited from animals isolated from birth, which demonstrates that social experience is not necessary in order to obtain coordinated and directed killing (Roberts and Berquist, 1968). Thus, the neural control of aggressive behavior is not unlike that of sexual behavior, for maternal behavior can be elicited from the hypothalamus of normal males, and male sexual behavior can be elicited in females (Roberts, 1971). The ordinary absence of such behaviors does not mean that the normal brain lacks the neural organization to direct such behavior.

There are a number of important conclusions which can be drawn from studies dealing with elicited aggression. First, the mammalian brain appears to possess some innate organization which gives every individual the potential to engage in destructive attacks no matter what he has previously learned or experienced. The fact that these mechanisms have a genetically predetermined organization does not tell us how often, *if ever,* the system will be used, nor does it preclude modification by experience. To put it more simply, every individual has the neural machinery to engage in coordinated violent aggressive behavior, but this in no way implies that such behavior is either natural or probable.

Second, there are qualitatively different kinds of aggressive behavior. How many "kinds" and just what they should be called is partly a semantic question, but it is clear that there is no single stereotyped response called "aggression." A number of attempts have been made to catalog aggressive behaviors into meaningful categories, and although none can be considered definitive, all rightly recognize the diversity of aggressive behavior. For example, Kaada (1967) differentiates among neural structures involved in attack, defense, and flight, and argues that each has separate but overlapping neural representations. Moyer (1968; 1969a; 1969b; 1969c; 1971) suggests a classification of seven overlapping kinds of aggressive behavior based on their neural and endocrine basis as well as the stimulus situations which provoke them. These classes of aggression are: predatory, intermale, fear-induced, irritable, territorial, maternal, and instrumental.

Finally, physiological studies of aggressive behavior reveal that there is no such thing as an "aggression center," and that destructive attacks and killing can be elicited from a number of widely separated portions of the mammalian brain. The concentration of research on the hypothalamus is perhaps because it is presently better understood, or at least more widely investigated, than other structures. After all the discussion about the hypothalamus, the reader may be crushed to learn that the hypothalamus can be neurally isolated from the rest of the brain without interfering with normal aggressive attacks (Ellison and Flynn, 1968). This is accomplished by inserting small surgical knives which can be rotated around the entire hypothalamus to isolate it completely. Cats treated in this manner continued to display normal affective arousal and visually-guided interspecific attacks. This should not be too surprising, for the hypothalamus is only one of many limbic system structures, all of which are important in emotional and aggressive behavior. As we shall see in the next section, most research done on the human brain is concentrated on the amygdala, partly because it is larger and more accessible than the hypothalamus.

Brain Disease and Human Violence

In laboratory animals, brain function can be studied by experimental lesions. Unhappily, similar effects can be observed in man because of the many cases of reported brain damage. Mark and Ervin (1970) estimate that 10 million Americans have obvious brain damage while another five million may be victims of less obvious brain disease. How does such brain damage occur?

Frequently it takes place before birth or at delivery, and can be caused by such things as maternal diseases during pregnancy, disproportions in size between the mother's pelvis and the baby's head, prolonged reduction in blood sugar level, Rh incompatibility, head damage during delivery, and overuse of pain-killing drugs at birth. Windle (1969) found that monkeys deprived of oxygen for only a few minutes at birth suffered permanent brain damage, damage which is often undetected by ordinary neurological examinations. Obvious behavior deficits may not show up for years, and the only sure way to detect brain damage is to remove and section the brain for histological examination.

Brain damage in normal children and adults is also caused by tumors, certain diseases, and trauma. Trauma commonly results from automobile accidents, gunshot or military wounds, athletic injuries, misuse of drugs, or simply by accidents involving head-banging that insults the brain. In the case of automobile accidents, about three million people are injured each year, and among those with head injury about a third involve physical damage to the brain (Kihlberg, 1966).

In many cases, brain damage goes unnoticed and behavior remains within the very broad "normal" range. This is not surprising because there is considerable redundancy and overlap in the brain, and in fact the brain is made up of two separate hemispheres which are structurally, but not functionally, alike. The exact effect of brain injury depends largely on the extent and location of the damage, and major behavioral effects (if any) may include impairment of sensory or perceptual abilities, muscular or motor coordination, speech, and memory. Of major concern is when damage takes place in the limbic system, in which case the effects are likely to be motivational.

A good example of how brain damage affects motivated behavior comes from the dreaded disease rabies, which has always been fatal to humans, at least until early 1971, when one boy bitten by a rabid bat survived following elaborate treatment. Rabies literally means "rage" and is caused by a viral infection which attacks the medial hippocampus of the limbic system. Rabies is more common in animals (i.e., the proverbial mad dog), but when contracted by humans it rapidly changes the most likable individual into one possessed with uncontrollable rage and violence. What is critical in the case of rabies is not how it is contracted, but the location of the brain which gets damaged. Similar damage produced by other means will have the same effect.

A case in point is the mass murders by Charles Whitman at the University of Texas in 1966. Whitman had spoken to psychiatrists about his periodic uncontrollable violent impulses, but to no avail. On the evening of July 31 he wrote:

> I don't quite understand what it is that compels me to type this letter. Perhaps it is to leave some vague reason for the actions I have recently performed. [At this point, Whitman had harmed no one; his wife and mother were elsewhere in the city, still alive.]
>
> I don't really understand myself these days. I am supposed to be an average, reasonable and intelligent young man. However, lately (I can't recall when it started) I have been a victim of many unusual and irrational thoughts. These thoughts constantly recur, and it requires a tremendous mental effort to concentrate on useful and progressive tasks. In March when my parents made a physical break I noticed a great deal of stress. I consulted a Dr. Cochrum at the University Health Center and asked him to recommend someone that I could consult with about some psychiatric disorders I felt I had. I talked with a Doctor once for about two hours and tried to convey to him my fears that I felt overcome [sic] by overwhelming violent impulses. After one session I never saw the Doctor again, and since then I have been fighting my mental turmoil alone, and seemingly to no avail. After my death I wish that an autopsy would be performed on me to see if there is any visible physical disorder. I have had some tremendous headaches in the past and have consumed two large bottles of Excedrin in the past three months.
>
> It was after much thought that I decided to kill my wife, Kathy, tonight after I pick her up from work.... I love her dearly, and she has been a fine wife to me as any man could ever hope to have. I cannot rationally pinpoint any specific reason for doing this. I don't know whether it is selfishness, or if I don't want her to have to face the embarrassment my actions would surely cause her. At this time though, the prominent reason in my mind is that I truly do not consider this world worth living in, and am prepared to die, and I do not want to leave her to suffer alone in it. I intend to kill her as painlessly as possible....

Later in the night he killed both his mother and wife, and then wrote:

> I imagine it appears that I brutally killed both of my loved ones. I was only trying to do a good thorough job.
>
> If my life insurance policy is valid please see that all the worthless checks I wrote this weekend are made good. Please pay off all my debts. I am 25 years old and have never been financially independent. Donate the rest anonymously to a mental health foundation. Maybe research can prevent further tragedies of this type.
>
> CHARLES J. WHITMAN

The next morning he barricaded himself on the observation deck at the top of the University tower with a high-powered hunting rifle equipped with a telescopic sight. For 90 minutes he shot at everything moving (he even hit an airplane), and by the time he was gunned down he had shot 38 people, killing 14. A post-mortem examination of his brain revealed a tumor the size of a walnut (a highly malignant type called glioblastoma multiforme) in the area of the amygdaloid nucleus (Sweet, Ervin, and Mark, 1969).

The Clinical Treatment of Brain-Damaged Patients

The Whitman case received much publicity because of its dreadful toll in human life, but his case is not rare. Like Whitman, many people who experience occasional episodes of rage also have some insight into their inability to control themselves, and often they can tell when an attack is about to occur. Case histories reveal that such people often go to the police or call a doctor before they commit a crime, but due to lack of facilities and a poor understanding of the potential seriousness, such individuals rarely receive any help. In one study, records were kept for an eight-month period at the Massachusetts General Hospital, during which 45 people showed up complaining of violent and destructive impulses (Lion, Bach-y-Rita, and Ervin, 1969). These self-referred patients related vague fears of aggressive feelings such as a desire to hurt themselves or someone else or to destroy something. A typical example is the following:

> A 28 year old married man presented in the emergency room with a chief complaint of going out of control and possibly injuring someone. That day, he had applied for a job and had abruptly left the employment office when the clerk questioned his past history. He then went to the police and asked to be locked up because he was afraid he would hurt someone. He was refused. He next drove to a distant state hospital and requested admission, but was encouraged to use the facility in his cachement area. The night before he had been stopped by state police for driving over 100 mph without his lights on. In the past, he had abused his wife and children, and lost many jobs because of altercations with employers. He had been assaultive on several occasions. Mental status revealed a paranoid individual who was quite agitated. Though not psychotic, he appeared to be on the verge of loss of control, and was hospitalized immediately.

Of the 45 self-referred patients, about a quarter had symptoms of neurological disorders. Thirteen had criminal histories, 11 owned deadly weapons, and many had been involved in reckless driving or assault under the influence of alcohol.

In a more complete survey, 83 self-referred violent patients and 80 inmates of a prison were given detailed psychiatric and neurological examinations (Mark and Ervin, 1970). Among the patients, about half had symptoms of epileptic-like phenomena and 10 turned out to have temporal lobe epilepsy. Half of the prisoners also showed epileptic symptoms. Three-quarters of the hospital patients had previously sought medical help for their impulsive violence, and half had tried to commit suicide. From an early age, many had a history of setting fires and being cruel to animals. Two-thirds owned guns or other lethal weapons and the majority said they often tried to work out their aggression on the highway. They freely admitted that they were dangerous drivers.

It is probably fair to assume that there is a significant number of individuals who suffer from this "dyscontrol syndrome" but never receive any treatment. Society expends relatively little effort to help or to understand such people, either before or after a crime, and communities often limit their involvement to providing jails and beefing up the police force. Criminals rarely receive any neurological examinations, and only a few years ago it was reported (Halleck, 1965) that fewer than 100 psychiatrists are deeply involved in the treatment of prisoners in the entire United States. One can only speculate about how much violence is a result of biological disease, the kind one would expect to find in the slums and ghettos where health care is poor. In a survey of 400 prisoners Mark and Ervin (1970) found that epilepsy was 10 times as common among criminals compared to noncriminals. Levy and Kennard (1953) found that abnormal EEG's (electroencephalograms) are much more common in prisoners compared to the normal population, particularly those prisoners who are repeated offenders. It is unfortunate that society tends to treat all violent offenders as responsible criminals. No doubt much innocent suffering by both law breakers and their victims could be prevented with a more enlightened approach to the problem.

Brain Surgery and the Control of Assaultive Behavior

Until recently, little could be done about violent behavior caused by brain disease. The most common kind of localized or focal brain disease associated with destructive behavior and dyscontrol is temporal lobe epilepsy. The violence is episodic rather than continuous, so relatively normal behavior is punctuated with occasional seizures or attacks. While the violent spells are obvious, it is somewhat more difficult to establish that they are indeed caused by abnormal brain activity. Sometimes clues come from EEG recordings, in which case distinctive 6- and 14-cycle spiking from the temporal lobe may indicate epilepsy (Sweet, Ervin, and Mark, 1969).

A case history may help illustrate the effects of focal brain damage (Mark and Ervin, 1970).

> Patient Jennie was a teenage girl reported to be a model child. When criticized for playing records too loudly, she suddenly had an episode of destruction. She smashed everything in her room and the police had to be summoned to restrain her. Subsequently her moods varied from "angelic" to "devilish," and she was finally institutionalized after smothering to death a baby whose crying annoyed her. Her brother had a history of epilepsy, which suggested to doctors that her violence might be caused by organic brain disease. She was referred to the Massachusetts General Hospital, where careful tests of her brain activity revealed abnormal electrical patterns in the hippocampus. Because she had managed to attack several other babies, an attempt was made to localize the diseased brain tissue by probing with surgically implanted electrodes. Electrical recordings of brain activity were made from these depth electrodes when the patient was (a) relatively relaxed, (b) angry, and (c) when she heard a baby crying. The EEG patterns (Fig. 22) proved useful in localizing the diseased brain tissue, for in these areas abnormal EEG's could be evoked by the sounds of a crying baby. Unfortunately, Jennie was not able to receive further medical attention because authorities removed her and sent her to a state institution.

In the past decade remarkable progress has been made in the development of stereotaxic surgery and its application to disorders in man. In principle the surgical procedures are similar to those described for research in animals, but naturally they are carried out only by skilled neurosurgeons (Fig. 23). For ethical reasons, such operations are carried out for therapeutic rather than experimental reasons, and they are generally a last resort when all other treatments have failed. By precisely locating small electrodes within the brain, electrical activity can be recorded, structures can be stimulated, and if necessary small lesions can be made (Heath, 1963; Schwab, et al., 1965; Delgado, 1969a). Such techniques have been successfully used to treat aggressive behavior, as is illustrated in the following case history (Narabayaski, et al., 1963):

> A one year old girl fell on a concrete road and suffered from brain damage. Until she was treated 10 years later she experienced convulsive attacks about three times daily. She had difficulty concentrating, her I.Q. was only 70, her moods were unstable, and her behavior was hyperaggressive. Stereotaxic amygdalotomy was

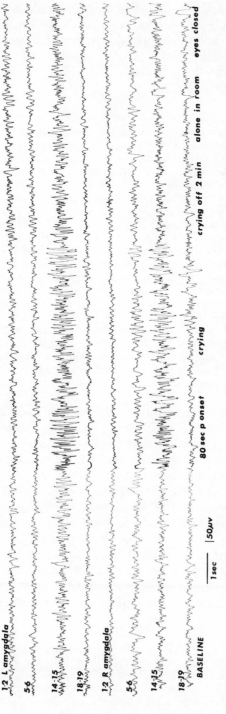

Figure 22. Patient Jennie smothered a baby to death after being enraged by its crying. Doctors suspected organic brain damage, and implanted electrodes through the temporal lobe into the left and right amygdala. First, normal baseline electrical activity was recorded from these electrodes; this is shown at the left. A tape of a baby crying was then played; the middle recordings show EEG activity from the same electrodes 80 seconds after the onset of the crying. It is apparent that most brain waves remained unchanged except for electrodes 14–15 in both hemispheres, which indicated localized seizure activity. At this point the patient was extremely angry. When the tape of the crying baby was turned off (right), the patient's EEG's and overt behavior returned to normal. (From Mark, V. H., and Ervin, F. R. Violence and the Brain. New York, Harper and Row, 1970. Courtesy of the Neuro-Research Foundation, Inc.)

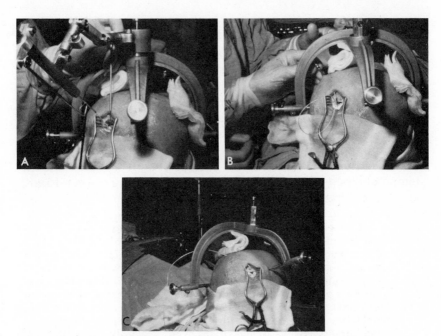

Figure 23. *Human stereotaxic surgery can now be done with great precision. The target area is first pinpointed with X-rays and EEG recordings, after which an electrode is lowered (A) through a small opening in the skull and locked into place. The electrode carrier is removed and the tail of the electrode is then brought out about 6 cm. from the wound (B and C) for external connections. The patient suffers no discomfort and the electrode connections are easily concealed with a wig. The electrodes can be removed if desired at a later time. (From Mark, V. H., and Ervin, F. R. Violence and the Brain. New York, Harper and Row, 1970. Courtesy of the Neuro-Research Foundation, Inc.)*

performed to destroy the left amygdaloid nucleus, and in conjunction with anticonvulsant medication the patient's mood and behavior changed dramatically. She was able to read and concentrate, lost her tendency toward violence, and resumed a normal life.

More recently, favorable results have been obtained by combining electrical stimulation with selective lesions. In some parts of the limbic system, such stimulation can relieve intense pain and cause relaxation and a state of euphoria which has been likened to the effect of several martinis (Ervin, Mark, and Stevens, 1969). Such treatment is of great benefit to terminal patients who are suffering from excruciating pain which cannot be alleviated by drugs or other means. Recent technological advances have made it possible to miniaturize electrical components and to establish remote communication with the brain by telemetry (Delgado,

1969a; 1969b). Through the use of a "stimoceiver," human patients can be stimulated from a distance and have their brain waves transmitted to a remote recording machine. In fact, they can learn to control their own brain waves if such waves are used as selective cues to determine when stimulation will be delivered. Devices are now being tested in which the entire assembly can be buried under the skin so that no one can tell from external appearance whether a patient is receiving brain stimulation or transmitting brain waves.

Such stereotaxic surgery has been used to treat severe cases of temporal lobe epilepsy and accompanying violence (Sweet, Ervin, and Mark, 1969):

> A generally reserved 34 year old man reported episodes of violence about once a week. Frequently they would be initiated by a petty remark made by his wife after which he would work himself into a fury and then physically beat and injure his wife and children. In an attempt to solve his problem he went to three different psychiatrists for a period of seven years, all to no avail. He was finally given EEG tests which revealed abnormal electrical activity in the temporal lobes. When antiseizure drugs failed, he volunteered for stereotaxic surgery. Banks of electrodes were surgically implanted bilaterally into the medial and lateral nuclei of the amygdala. Electrical stimulation through one of the electrodes in the medial area caused the patient to declare that he "felt" one of his fits coming on. Similar stimulation just 4 mm. lateral in another electrode caused the patient to completely relax and exclaim, "I feel like I'm floating on a cloud." By regular stimulation about once a day in the lateral amygdala, favorable moods continued and seizures were avoided. When such continued treatment became impractical, small portions of the medial amygdala were electrically lesioned with high levels of electrical current. Following this, the patient returned to normal life and experienced no further attacks.

Another case is that of Clara T. (Mark and Ervin, 1970), who suffered from brain damage for almost three decades until she was helped by stereotaxic surgery:

> At the age of 33, Clara T. slipped on a patch of ice and sustained a head injury which soon led to temporal lobe epileptic seizures. Despite anti-seizure medication the frequency and intensity of her seizures increased during the following 29 years. She became more physically assaultive, attacking her mother-in-law, her husband, and many visitors. After being hospitalized, she stabbed a nurse with a scissors during one violent episode. It took six people 45 minutes to subdue this 62 year old woman who weighed only 86 pounds.
>
> Neurological examinations showed that Clara had extensive damage in her temporal lobes, and stereotaxic surgery was performed in which a bank of 40 electrodes was implanted in and around the amygdala. The electrodes were kept in place for several

months during which extensive tests were carried out. Abnormal brain waves were discovered in recordings through certain electrodes, and when weak electrical stimulation was applied at these points Clara began having a seizure. Using radio frequency current, heat was then generated through these electrodes to destroy the cells around the electrode tips. The electrodes were then withdrawn and Clara's behavior was closely observed. She continued having epileptic seizures, but they were much milder and decreased in frequency. For six years following the operation there was a total absence of rage or unprovoked assaults, and once again she was able to resume her normal family and community life.

Stereotaxic surgery appears to have great potential for the treatment of certain kinds of violent and aggressive behavior which cannot be reduced through conventional means such as drugs or therapy. But it is still in the experimental stage and remains a long way from large-scale application. Above all it raises many important ethical questions about the control of the mind and behavior of other individuals. Once again science has given mankind awesome power before society has contemplated the consequences. Like atomic energy, the physical control of the mind is a two-edged sword, and hopefully man will use it for his own benefit. Philosophically the problem of external control over behavior is nothing new, for teachers, ministers, advertising executives, and therapists make a specialty out of trying to alter people. Perhaps biological manipulations make people pause only because they are so much more dramatic. Perhaps they are resisted because it forces upon us realization of our fragile and mechanical existence.

GENETICS AND AGGRESSION

Neurophysiology has given us many valuable clues about how the brain is constructed and how it operates, both in normal and abnormal behavior. Additional insights have come from the study of genetics. Today we know that hereditary factors are carried by complex organic molecules called genes which act on biological processes throughout life and may thereby affect behavior. Aggression itself is not an inherited trait, but factors which influence aggression may be transmitted genetically. For example, genes may influence growth patterns and thereby contribute to size or strength. They may also influence hormonal activity or thresholds of activation of brain structures. Such factors alone will not cause an individual to be aggressive, but if fighting begins, one may react more quickly, fight more fiercely, and if successful he may be more likely to fight in the future. As Scott (1958a) puts it, aggressiveness is produced by both genes and past experience, and aggressiveness plus environmental stimulation leads to aggression.

Laboratory studies have shown that individual strains of the same species may vary considerably in aggressive tendencies, although the exact reason for these differences are not precisely known. Ginsburg and Allee (1942) and Scott (1942) compared different strains of mice, each of which had been inbred for 20 or more generations. They both independently found that one strain (in this case C57BL) consistently outfought other strains. Other experimenters have used several strains in dominance tests (Lindzey, Winston, and Manosevitz, 1961) in which individual mice were first trained to run through a small tube to obtain food at the other end. When they had learned this response, mice were put at opposite ends of the tube to see which one forced the other one out. They reported that mice of certain strains were nearly always forced out by opponents of another strain. The losers in turn were nearly always dominant over an even weaker strain, thus indicating a transitive relationship among the three strains.

Perhaps a better example is that of different breeds of dogs, for as all dog lovers know, temperaments vary widely. Many years ago terriers were commonly used by hunters to bait game and drive them out of their holes. Today we still find terriers highly aggressive. The importance of genetic factors is illustrated in a laboratory experiment (James, 1951) in which litters of fox terriers and beagles were divided shortly after birth and raised as mixed litters. Even though the young terriers were smaller than the beagles, terriers monopolized not only the food but the females of the litter, and all puppies later born were sired by terriers. The role of developmental compared to genetic factors will be considered in more detail in Chapter 4; however, the James experiment clearly demonstrates the importance of hereditary influences on aggression.

Genetic factors are also partly responsible for the ferocious behavior of the Siamese fighting fish. For centuries the natives of Thailand have regarded fish fighting as something of a national pastime (Smith, 1945), and males of the species *Betta splendens* were often brought to the village marketplace to be matched in fighting contests, with spectators betting on the outcome. The winners were used for breeding while the losers were discarded, and today the descendants can be found in almost any tropical fish store. Partly because of such selective breeding for aggressiveness, male fighting fish always have to be kept in separate containers. One wonders if the "fighting fish" might have been called the "chicken fish" had only the losers been selected.

Deliberate attempts to breed emotionality and aggressiveness in rats have met with success in as few as 12 generations. Hall (1938) tested emotionality in rats by recording the frequency of urination and defecation when placed in an unfamiliar environment. By inbreeding the animals with high scores and those with low scores an emotional and a nonemotional strain were developed. In a later experiment, the emotional and nonemotional strains were tested for aggressiveness by pairing them off and observing fighting. It was found that rats from the nonemotional strain initiated almost five times as many attacks as those from the emotional strain (Hall and Klein, 1942). The relation between emotionality and aggressiveness will be discussed again in the following chapter. Suffice it to say here that animals can be selectively bred for aggressiveness whether they are fighting fish, fighting cocks, fighting bulls, hunting dogs, or laboratory rats.

Chromosome Abnormalities and Human Criminality

Genes, the units of heredity, are not randomly distributed throughout living cells but are arranged in ladder-like strands of DNA (deoxyribonucleic acid) called chromosomes. The characteristics of chromosomes can be determined by *karyotyping*, in which cells are stained at the stage of mitosis when the chromosomes are dividing and doubling in number. Modern cytogenetics permits rapid identification of the chromosomes by examining buccal smears from the mouth or by culturing lymphocytes of white blood cells. The number of chromosomes found in cells varies with each species; in humans there are normally 46 chromosomes or 23 pairs, with one-half of each pair coming from each parent. Twenty-two pairs are identical in males and females and are called autosomes. Only one pair, the sex chromosomes, differs for males and females: the female has a matching pair (XX) while the male has one chromosome resembling the female (X) but another (Y) which is different. The Y chromosome in the XY pair somehow affects the distribution of hormones which masculinize the sex organs and suppress female characteristics. Masculine characteristics may include not only superficial differences such as body hair but other factors, including physical size and strength, which may contribute to aggressiveness (Valentine, 1969; Turpin and Lejeune, 1969; Shah, 1970a; 1970b).

Unfortunately, cell division is not always normal and a disruption of the sequence of DNA, the composition of a chromosome, or the number of chromosomes may lead to a variety of physical and mental abnormalities or failure to survive at all. An example is mongolism, or Down's syndrome, involving the 21st pair of chromosomes. This abnormality occurs in about one out of every 700 births and accounts for 10 per cent of hospitalized cases of mental retardation in the United States (Shah, 1970b). Of particular interest are disorders of the sex chromosomes in which there are extra or missing chromosomes. In Turner's syndrome (XO) the Y chromosome is missing, usually resulting in physical anomalies. In Klinefelter's syndrome (XXY), there is an extra female (X) chromosome. Individuals with XXY patterns are usually (but not always) raised as males, for they have male genitals; however, the testes may be underdeveloped and breasts may appear in adolescence. While many XXY males are entirely normal, it is not uncommon to find cases associated with feminine behavior, mental retardation, emotional disturbance, and delinquency.

More recently, sex chromosome disorders of the XYY pattern or "supermale" syndrome have been reported along with speculation that the extra Y chromosome may increase aggressiveness and hence be related to criminality. Court-Brown (1967) examined inmates at institutions for the criminally insane and reported that such individuals are 20 times more likely than the general population to have XYY abnormalities. Price and Whatmore (1967) intensively studied nine XYY males and found that eight of the nine came from relatively normal family backgrounds and all tended to have records of antisocial behavior dating back to an early age (although none was considered psychotic). The importance of this is that antisocial behavior due to environmental influences would be expected to develop gradually and would not be expected in only one member of a family.

A number of other characteristics have been reported for XYY males, including unusual height, homosexual tendencies, and tendency to commit crimes against property. Daly (1969) describes the case history of a 25-year-old XYY male with a long history of behavior problems. From his earliest school years he received poor grades and had difficulty getting along with teachers. He was expelled from high school for stealing and later sentenced to prison for burglary. He recalled that from an early age he had many episodes of sudden anger in which he expressed fear of killing himself or someone else. His rage was often directed at animals and he admitted strangling, drowning, and shooting over 150 cats and dogs. He had latent homosexual tendencies and was considered to be of dull to normal intelligence.

Such findings are suggestive but not conclusive. Much remains to be learned about the behavioral effects, if any, of chromosomal abnormalities, and at present research is concentrated on three general objectives. First, what is the incidence of such abnormalities in the general population? Estimates vary widely and many projections have been made on the basis of relatively small samples. Until recently it was believed that XYY patterns could be found in one out of every 1500 to 2000 males; however, if the three largest studies are combined for a total of 6746 males, the incidence is one out of every 570 (Lubs and Ruddle, 1970). Lubs and Ruddle examined cells of 4500 babies in New Haven, Connecticut and reported that the incidence of all types of gross chromosomal abnormality is one in 200, with the figure being three times higher for babies born to mothers over 34 years of age. In general, it appears that the chance of an individual male having the XYY pattern is relatively small but is larger than previously estimated. A recent study by the National Institutes of Mental Health (Shah, 1970b) concludes that the best rough estimate is one chance out of 550 for having the XYY pattern. While this may seem small on an individual level, it could mean that there are hundreds of thousands of XYY males in the United States alone.

The second question is whether there is a causal link between XYY abnormalities and criminal behavior. The most thorough review to date (Shah 1970b) states that such a link remains unproved:

> The preponderant opinion among the Conference participants was that the behavioral aberrations implied or documented thus far do not indicate a direct cause and effect relationship with the XYY chromosome constitution. Thus, it would not be possible to say at the present time that the XYY complement is definitely or invariably associated with behavioral abnormalities.... Moreover, the widespread publicity notwithstanding, individuals with the XYY anomaly have *not* been found to be more aggressive than matched offenders with normal chromosome constitutions. In this respect, it appears that premature and incautious speculations may have led to XYY persons being falsely stigmatized as unusually aggressive and violent compared to other offenders.

The report does conclude that tallness appears to be a common characteristic of XYY males and does not discount the possibility that future research may reveal that XYY patterns, like some other chromosomal abnormalities, may be related to physical and behavioral deficiencies. It is possible that an XYY constitution may contribute to physical size, and that unusual aggressiveness may be the result of growing up larger and stronger than one's peers. Recent evidence, however, tends to dismiss this possibility (Hook and Kim, 1971).

The third question about chromosomal abnormalities is how they are caused and how they can be prevented. Although XYY patterns cannot be directly related to criminality at this time, genetic deficits in general unquestionably cause much suffering and hardship. Radiation has long been known to be a prime cause of genetic mutation; however, some authors have suggested that modern food habits and drug abuse (particularly LSD) are equally dangerous (Livingstone, 1967). Many years ago a study was made of 75 women who received X-ray treatment for tumors while pregnant. The result was that more than one-third of their babies had physical or mental abnormalities directly attributable to the radiation (Murphy, 1929; 1957). In Japan, children who were exposed to radiation before birth at Hiroshima and Nagasaki had a much higher incidence of mental retardation and physical abnormalities (Wood, et al., 1967; Plummer, 1952). There has long been fear that such abnormalities will be passed on from generation to generation, and as a result in modern Japan there is an entire caste of people who are rejected because they or their parents may have suffered genetic damage in 1945. Fortunately there is some evidence that radiation-induced genetic damage is not always passed on to unconceived generations (Kato, Schull, and Neel, 1966; Livingstone, 1967; Lerner, 1968). Nevertheless, radiation hazards, whether they be from nuclear weapons testing, industrial reactors, or X-rays, represent a potential source of genetic mutation and somatic damage to all living organisms.

Further answers about genetic abnormalities and behavior will have to come from careful population sampling studies and from basic research in cell physiology. In the meantime, moral and legal questions are already upon us. Richard Speck, the convicted murderer of eight Chicago nurses, was widely rumored to be an XYY type and this abnormality reportedly was going to be used in his defense. It turned out that in fact he was *not* an XYY type (Shah, 1970a; 1970b), but an XYY defense has been used in other trials. In Paris in 1968 Daniel Hugon was convicted of murder but given a reduced sentence, partly because of his XYY constitution (XYY chromosome defense, 1969). His lawyers argued that the extra Y chromosome rendered him not responsible for his crime. In Australia, Lawrence Hannell was acquitted for murder based on reasons of insanity (Bartholomew and Sutherland, 1969). Although his XYY constitution was pointed out at the trial, the verdict appears to have been influenced more by the likelihood of temporal lobe brain disease. Additional legal and ethical questions remain to be solved. For example, if a newborn baby is discovered to be an XYY type, should the parent or family physician be told? Or will this cause unusually protective rearing which may jeopardize the boy even more?

Domestication

It was previously pointed out that animals can be selectively bred for aggressiveness; as a result we have special breeds of hunting dogs as well as bulls guaranteed not to behave like Ferdinand in the bull ring. But animals can also be bred for their domestic qualities, and in many cases this has been the natural and gradual course of evolution. Paradise fish (*Macropodus opercularis*) belong to the same family as the Siamese fighting fish, and wild specimens found in the rice paddies of China are noted for their aggressiveness. But, unlike *Betta splendens,* Paradise fish have been bred for their docility rather than their fighting ability so that they can be kept together and sold commercially to fish hobbyists. Experiments have clearly shown that wild and domestic Paradise fish differ greatly in their aggressive behavior, with the wild fish being much more ferocious (Ward, 1967).

Dog owners may not realize it, but man's best friend evolved from wolves and has been greatly pacified after thousands of years of use as pets (Scott, 1968b). Even wild wolves can be tamed with a little patience, particularly if they are obtained when very young (Ginsburg, 1970). Not all dogs, of course, are gentle and harmless, for some have been bred for companionship while others are selected for their ability to frighten strangers. A considerable amount of research has been devoted to the social behavior of dogs (Scott and Fuller, 1965) which indicates that genetic factors, in addition to environmental factors, are of great importance in determining whether a particular breed is docile or savage.

The common laboratory rat is another example of a highly domesticated animal, and because it is so widely used for behavioral research it is worth tracing its checkered background. The brown Norway rat, *Rattus norvegicus,* is a native of eastern Asia and found its way to Europe with the returning crusaders. Here it began to thrive (Lockard, 1968; Walker, 1964). *Rattus norvegicus* appeared in the United States about the time of the American Revolution, and during the following centuries psychologists discovered the rat and began to concentrate on it more and more to the relative exclusion of other species (Beach, 1950; Bitterman, 1960). To keep pace with the demand, animal suppliers and breeders developed a number of similar strains (such as Long Evans, Sprague-Dawley, Wistar) which, after countless generations of inbreeding, are heavily domesticated and something of an evolutionary freak. This problem is frequently overlooked by researchers, who sometimes rely on rats for the solution of nearly every behavioral question, a strategy which is obviously inappropriate. In the case of aggressive behavior, domestication has clearly had an impact on the Norway rat. Karli (1956), for example, reported that in laboratory tests 70 per cent of wild rats will attack and kill mice while only about 12 per cent of domesticated rats will do the same.

Just how domestication comes about is not completely understood. It is often assumed that domestication is achieved after a long gradual process of gene substitution, and while this is probably true, it can also take place much more quickly. Keeler and King (1942) showed that the mutation of a single gene in wild Norway rats can lead to domestication. In the laboratory, domestication of wild rats has been achieved in as few as 10 generations (King and Donaldson, 1929), and it may be the ease of domestication which has contributed to their popularity.

The fact that an animal has been domesticated does not mean that its aggressiveness is lost. A peaceful pussy cat can be provoked into a screeching rage and so can a gentle laboratory rat. Human beings pride themselves on being "civilized" rather than "acting like animals," yet modern man is capable of destructive violence which makes cave men seem angelic by comparison. Thus, it is important to distinguish between the capacity to destroy and the tendency to destroy. Studies on the physiological basis of aggression clearly show that the normal mammalian brain is so constructed that it has the organization either to activate or to suppress aggressive behavior regardless of experience. Inappropriate activation (or a failure of suppression) may result from brain malfunction with disastrous effects, but an understanding of this process can help us to counteract such abnormalities. When the brain is functioning normally we must look to other "causes" of aggressive behavior, particularly developmental and social influences based on learning and previous experience.

SEX AND AGGRESSION

Aggressive behavior has long been linked to sexual motivation, perhaps due to the writings of Freud and other psychoanalysts. More recently, Moyer (1968) has included maternal and intermale aggression as major distinct forms of aggression in his physiological model. Tinbergen (1953) goes so far as to state that most fighting in animals can be considered reproductive fighting. This may be true if territorial fighting and battles for dominance are considered instrumental aggression in the pursuit of sexual privileges. Possessing an established territory or maintaining high social rank permits a better selection of mates and more favorable breeding grounds. Therefore it is not surprising that in many species fighting is intense only during the mating season. Chaffinches, for example, are relatively peaceful during the winter, but when spring arrives they are notoriously combative. Stag fighting in deer shows marked seasonal variation, with most fights occurring during the mating season. Male stickleback fish which have built nests are much more aggressive than those which have not (Wootton, 1970). Other animals, such as camels, will fight throughout the year, but their conflicts are much more intense during the rutting season. The same is true of the rhesus monkeys of Cayo Santiago Island, where aggressiveness fluctuates cyclically as a function of the colony's reproductive state (Wilson and Boelkins, 1970). More males die or are wounded during mating season than at any other time of year. Even humans have some cyclical variations in their aggressive behavior, as we shall see.

Sexual Monopolies and Harems

At mating time, social status becomes extremely important because males (and sometimes females) of nearly all species compete for the favors of the opposite sex. To take camels as an example, fighting becomes so intense in breeding season that nomads of the Sahara Desert typically separate their herds so that only one male is kept with about thirty females. During this December-to-April period the lone male will fight off any other male which attempts to approach his harem (Cloudsley-Thompson, 1965). Similar monopolies are found in the Pacific Coast elephant lions (Le Boeuf and Peterson, 1969). Close observation of their natural behavior reveals that 85 per cent of the females are inseminated by only 4 per cent of the males. This certainly gives the other 96 per cent something to fight about. During breeding season the American chameleon (*Anolis carobirensis*) may harbor a number of females in his territory and keep all other males away. One male may dominate as many as 15 other males which must constantly make submissive gestures by nodding their heads (Cloudsley-Thompson, 1965).

Monopolies are also common among wolves, where the dominant animal tries to prevent competitors from mating (Ginsburg, 1970). A male may fight off rivals showing an interest in his females, or he may abuse and injure a member of his harem when she comes into heat so that she cannot mate with others. By the time she has recovered she is no longer receptive and will fight off the males herself. Male deer engage in bitter stag fights over rights to a harem of females, but outside of the breeding season the males are quite peaceful (Etkin and Freedman, 1964).

Sexual monopolies are easy to observe in mixed groups of captive monkeys. The alpha male will invariably dominate all the others, and he will attack and intimidate any other males which attempt to mate with receptive females. But if a human enters the pen, the alpha male immediately becomes subordinate to the human, and this releases the inhibitions of lower ranking males who make a beeline to the nearest female and attempt to copulate.

Monogamy, Polygamy, and Promiscuity

A number of mating arrangements are common in nature, although none completely eliminates fighting. But jealously guarding a harem of females undoubtedly involves much more conflict than open promiscuity. In many fish and birds, one male may incubate the eggs of many females. Male rats attempt to mate with any receptive female but they make no attempt to monopolize the female or to keep other males from mating. Polygamy in the sense of repeated matings of males with different partners is actually quite common in nature and has been observed in horses, zebras, asses, pigs, hippos, camels, deer, buffaloes, cattle, sheep, goats, antelopes, sperm whales, and most wild primates (Wynne-Edwards, 1962). The reverse practice, polyandry, is rare, and exists only in a few species, including some quail and pheasants, where the female is dominant.

The invigorating influence of a novel sex partner has been known for some time, and in the laboratory it has come to be referred to as the "Coolidge Effect" in honor of the late President. Allegedly it refers to an incident in which the First Lady was admiring some barnyard activity, which led her to remark that the males seemed to have impressive sexual powers. The President agreed, but also noted that the males never stayed with the same partner. In the laboratory, Grunt and Young (1952) confirmed this effect by studying the mating behavior of guinea pigs. Males usually rest at least an hour after copulating, but if their partner is removed and replaced with a novel female, sexual activity is quickly renewed. If the original partner is removed and then reintroduced, no sexual invigoration takes place. In rats, the procedure can be repeated over and over again (Fowler and Whalen, 1961; Fisher, 1962; Wilson, Kuehn, and Beach, 1963). If males are allowed to copulate until they are satiated with one partner, they will begin again with the introduction of a new partner. The Coolidge Effect appears to be quite widespread and has been documented for rats, mice, guinea pigs, dairy bulls, water buffaloes, sheep, swine, boars, and cats.

Is such behavior characteristic of primates? Both caged monkeys and married people tend to have frequent intercourse with their partners, but as time passes the frequency diminishes. Married men sometimes worry about being impotent as they grow older, but often it turns out that they can be quickly aroused by women other than their wives. According to the Kinsey reports about three-quarters of the 6000 men interviewed expressed a desire for extramarital affairs and about half admitted to having sexual relations outside of marriage. Cross-cultural studies reveal that 84 per cent of 185 societies (Ford and Beach, 1951) or 75 per cent of 554 societies (Murdock, 1957) practice legalized polygamy. In the few like our own which do not, more subtle forms of multiple mating are common (i.e., premarital experimentation, extramarital affairs, and prostitution). The recognition of the stimulating properties of sexual novelty may be the reason why most societies overtly or covertly condone such behavior, particularly with regard to males (the so-called double standard). Sexual experimentation by females is less widely tolerated, and it has been suggested that being cuckolded by another male may be the most frequent cause of murder throughout the world (Etkin and Freedman, 1964).

It may be argued whether *homo sapiens* is monogamous or polygamous, but it is clear that humans are more monogamous than some animals and less monogamous (or more polygamous) than others. Chimpanzees and baboons may develop consort relationships between individual males and females, and simple family-type relationships are sometimes observed, usually centered around the mother. The tree shrew, a primitive primate, also shows strong indications of pair formation (Martin, 1968). Faithful monogamy has been reported in some birds, such as eagles, which remain paired to death (Cowden, 1969). Zebra finches show remarkably strong pair-formation: they mate for life and quarrels between partners are virtually nonexistent (Butterfield, 1970). Unlike married humans who have a roving eye, male finches prefer to remain with, and even look at, their own mate rather than novel females. Butterfield (1970) demonstrated this in an ingenious experiment in which he compared the reinforcing value of a mate with that of a novel female. He constructed a two-compartment apparatus in which the experimental subject (a male zebra finch) could look through a window and view his mate. But the male had to work to see his mate, for her compartment remained dark and was illuminated for 10 sec. only when the male landed on his perch and then departed (the release triggered a microswitch). This allowed the experimenter to measure the number of responses made by the male and the interval between responses. Using these measures it was possible to conclude that male zebra finches are more attracted to their mates than to novel females. Apparently zebra finches haven't heard of the Coolidge Effect.

One reason for dwelling so much on courtship and mating behavior is that they not only cause much agonistic behavior, but they also sometimes closely resemble it. The distinctive bird songs we hear in the spring have two functions: to attract passing females, and to mark a territory in which other males will be challenged and threatened. In Siamese fighting fish, the same colorful display which is used as a threat gesture against males is also effectively used to lure females to the male's bubble nest, where mating takes place. Barlow (1962) made detailed observations of the Asian teleost fish (*Badis badis*) and found that courtship patterns closely resembled true fights.

In many species, the mere presence of females increases the amount of fighting in males. Crook and Butterfield (1970) observed the agonistic behavior of the African quelea bird and compared the number of encounters between males when no females were present with periods in mixed company when females were introduced, and again in a control period when the females were removed. Their data indicate that agonistic encounters were roughly doubled when females were present. Similarities may be found in the behavior of adolescent boys and street gangs among whom rough-housing and showing off is stimulated by the presence of girls.

Neural Control of Sex and Aggression

Physiological studies also point to a close connection between sexual and aggressive behavior. Mapping experiments of the monkey brain (MacLean and Ploog, 1962) indicate that electrical stimulation of neural structures which elicit immediate penile erection are located in close proximity (within a millimeter) to sites which elicit a rage response. Clinical cases of brain damage in humans have been known to affect both sexual and aggressive behavior. In one case history (Mark and Ervin, 1970) a woman was examined after she had attacked others with razor blades and broken bottles and indicated a strong pattern of abusive assaults. Her sexual behavior was also relatively unusual since she masturbated 18 to 20 times each day and frequently participated in group orgies and lesbian activities. Psychiatric treatment failed to have any effect, and it was finally discovered that portions of her brain (the right frontal temporal region) were malfunctioning. She was given Dilantin, an antiseizure medication, to help control the abnormal neural activity, and it immediately reduced both her assaultive behavior and her desire for continuous sexual gratification. Certain drugs, such as PCPA (parachlorophenylalanine, a tryptophan hydroxylase inhibitor which lowers serotonin concentrations in the brain), have been reported to increase aggressiveness in cats and also act as an aphrodisiac (Ferguson, et al., 1970). The latest reports, however, fail to confirm these effects (Conner, et al., 1970; Zitrin, et al., 1970).

Sexual Dimorphism

No attempt is being made to argue that sex and aggression are the same, or that they are controlled by exactly the same mechanisms, but merely that they are interrelated. This raises the profound observation that males are different from females, at least in appearance, and this sexual dimorphism has important implications with respect to aggressive behavior. Males and females respond differently to the same stimuli, and there is evidence that males and females are neurologically different, at least in the case of rodents (Edwards, 1968). Aggressive behavior may be linked to sexual differences, and this may be shown by the fact that throughout the course of evolution the male of the species is usually larger and more aggressive (Scott, 1958a). The male crayfish has larger claws than the female and uses them to advantage in both fighting and mating when he has to pin the female down. In the hermit crab, size is correlated with aggressiveness (Hazlett, 1968). Female fighting fish are small and drab in appearance compared to the glamorous male, and while they do fight (Braddock and Braddock, 1955) they can be housed together and they are not nearly as vicious as the males. In mice there is a striking sex difference, with males being highly aggressive and females being comparatively peaceful. Other examples can be cited from the tales of hunters who know that it is nearly always the male which is larger and potentially more dangerous (at least to the hunter). This is true for a variety of game animals, including fish, pheasants, grizzly bears, and elephants. In some species of seals the male may be up to 10 times the size of the female (Bartholomew, 1952). Even nonhunters are acquainted with the legendary ferociousness of stallions and bulls.

The notion of universal male aggressiveness is not without important exceptions, and like most sweeping generalizations about aggression it is only partly true. In bees, it is the females, not the males, which possess stingers and defend against predators. Similarly, male wasps are generally dominated by the larger females, and the same is true in the praying mantis. Male spiders must carefully wave a distinctive appendage at the large females, who will quickly devour the males if they are not recognized. Male mice tend to be larger and more aggressive than females, but the opposite is true of another common rodent, the hamster. Males which attempt to mate with unreceptive females risk serious injury or even death (Hediger, 1965). Among the black eagles of South Africa, the females are larger and more aggressive than the males (Cowden, 1969). There are also reports of some deep-sea fish in which the female is large and fully developed while the male remains nothing but a tiny parasite (Etkin and Freedman, 1964).

In some species, sex is related to aggressiveness, but size is not. The brown booby (*Sula leucogaster*) is a large seabird with a wingspan of about three feet, and while the females are larger, heavier, and stronger, the males are more aggressive (Simmons, 1970). Among primates, males are usually more aggressive than females, but in some species, such as the gibbon, there is little sexual dimorphism. In highly social primates, particularly man, the factors which regulate sexual behavior may also influence aggressive behavior, but in general aggressive behavior is shaped more by social and developmental experience than by any specific biological factor. These factors will be discussed in more detail in Chapters 4 and 5.

It may be safe to conclude that males are usually more aggressive, but whether it is the male or the female which fights more depends on the type of sexual dimorphism and social organization of the species. For example, there is little sexual dimorphism in howler monkeys, and neither sex is highly aggressive (their agonistic behavior tends to be confined to screeching from the tops of trees.) Correlated with this is the fact that, unlike macaques, the male howler monkeys show cooperation with females in the care of the young (Etkin and Freedman, 1964). In some animals it is extremely difficult to tell males from females without examining the physiology of their reproductive organs. Usually, however, there are conspicuous secondary sexual characteristics such as body hair, horns, coloring, size, and so forth. If the male is larger and more flashy in appearance, chances are that the female will be less aggressive and more reliable in bringing up the young. An example is found in the comparison of male and female deer. As males grow up, they do not cooperate in the care of the young and eventually they ignore the entire herd and wander off by themselves. They may join a loosely-formed group of males, but during rutting season they break apart and search for a harem of females. The doe are not as large, do not grow decorative antlers, and they fight less among themselves. A few females usually become dominant, and female herds are generally well organized to permit better care of the young (Etkin and Freedman, 1964).

Sex Hormones and Aggression

For centuries it has been common knowledge that a castrated wild stallion becomes relatively tame, and for this reason only a few adult male horses kept for breeding purposes escape this treatment. Similarly, castration reduces a savage bull into a plodding ox, and many pet owners have their cats and dogs "fixed" to render them more docile.

Therapeutic castrations have also been carried out with humans. According to LeMaire (1956), such operations were first performed on prison convicts in Indiana, and the success in reducing criminality led to the passage of the first castration laws (later repealed). Germany, Switzerland, and the Scandanivian countries have legalized such treatment although the number of cases reported is relatively small. The most extensive use of this procedure has been in Denmark, where the treatment is usually (but not always) restricted to those who have committed sex crimes. The procedure is voluntary, but not agreeing to the operation reduces the chances of being released from prison. Based on the few hundred cases studied, castration leads to "general pacification" and a relatively low incidence of recidivism.

The importance of sex hormones in humans as well as other animals can also be seen in the dramatic increase in competitive behavior which usually accompanies sexual maturity and in the fact that aggressiveness often parallels sexual cycles. As previously pointed out, males of some species are most aggressive during the breeding season, and females may be relatively tame and "receptive" only when in estrus.

Does this apply to humans as well? Clinical observations confirm what most women already know: the premenstrual period is often accompanied by heightened tension, irritability, and feelings of hostility (Dalton, 1964; Hamburg, 1966). This syndrome appears to be correlated with a drop in the level of progesterone in the blood, and it has been reported that women taking contraceptive pills containing progestagenic agents are not bothered as much with premenstrual tension (Hamburg, Moos, and Yalom, 1968). As for antisocial behavior by women, a number of studies reveal that crimes are disproportionately committed during this premenstrual period (Dalton, 1964; Moyer, 1971).

The specific biological factors which influence sexual differentiation and later social behavior are the gonadal hormones, androgens and estrogens. Sexual determination is no longer thought to be genetically fixed at the time of fertilization, and the difference between males and females is probably more quantitative than qualitative (Goy, 1970). Both males and females produce both androgens and estrogens, and sexual determination can be reversed by changing the relative concentrations of these hormones very early in life. At critical states in an organism's development (generally before birth and just after birth) minute quantities of these chemicals are produced by the adrenal glands. They then influence the organism's nervous system and determine whether it will be male or female.

There are a number of different male and female sex hormones, but the most important with respect to aggression is testosterone, the male gonadal hormone that initiates puberty in males when it begins circulating in quantity. Rats do not fight much until puberty (Seward, 1945); however, they will begin fighting earlier if injected with testosterone (Levy and King, 1953). This hormone is normally present in both males and females, but it is produced in abundance by the male testes and in only minute concentrations in the female ovary. The fact that testosterone contributes to sexual dimorphism can be seen by injecting it into hens or castrated chickens (Fig. 24). These animals will then develop the secondary sex characteristics of a rooster, such as a larger comb and male plumage, but more importantly their aggressive behavior also intensifies. This was determined (Allee, Collias, and Lutherman, 1939) by injecting animals and then noting their rise or fall in the peck order (Fig. 25). It was found that hens injected with male hormones became more aggressive and fought their way up the peck order, sometimes going all the way from the bottom to the top. In addition, chickens which are castrated or treated with female sex hormones become more timid and lose status in the peck order. Testosterone

Figure 24. If the male hormone testosterone is injected into baby chicks it will cause premature accentuation of masculine characteristics. A normal eighteen-day-old chick is shown on the right and a testosterone-injected chick on the left. (After Selye, from Zuckerman. In Welty, J. C. The Life of Birds. Philadelphia, W. B. Saunders, 1962.)

also has an effect on territorial behavior, for if ring doves are injected with this male hormone they tend to enlarge their territories (Bennett, 1940).

The effects of hormone alterations are not always so simple and straightforward. In the chicken experiment described above, testosterone injections caused animals to fight their way up the peck order, but once the injections stopped they did not return to their old level but remained at the top. Gonadal hormones may have an important effect on aggressiveness, but the strength of

SOCIAL ORDER			
Hen Number	Before Injections		After Injections
	(Number of other hens pecked)		
RG	7		6
RW	7		6
YY	6		4
BR	6	**Dosage of**	4
GG	4	**Testosterone**	3
RR	3		1
BG	2	0.75 mg	1
RY	1	1.00 mg	7
BY	0	1.25 mg	7

Figure 25. Injecting testosterone into hens rapidly leads to a change in social rank. Before injections, hen BY was at rock bottom in the peck order and could peck at no one. After injections she rose to the top and pecked at everyone except RY, who also had hormone injections. The fact that BG did not elevate her status was attributed to the lower dosage used and the fact that she became sick during the experiment. (After Allee, Collias, and Lutherman, 1939.)

the effect may depend on when the injections are made. In general, treatments are most powerful if administered just after birth, at least in rodents. For example, if male rats are neonatally castrated they adopt female fighting patterns when they grow up (Conner and Levine, 1969). Castrating adult male rats that kill baby rats does not reduce this pup-killing behavior, but neonatal castration does (Denenberg, 1971). Female mice, normally much less aggressive than males, become much more aggressive as adults if they are given androgen (male hormone) treatments right after birth. Females treated in this way are difficult to breed when they grow up, for they do not respond to courtship gestures by males and instead attack and seriously cripple them (Bronson and Desjardins, 1968). But neonatal androgen treatments given to baby rats does not turn them into pup-killers when they grow up (Denenberg, 1971).

This illustrates another complication — namely, that hormone manipulations which affect aggressiveness in males may fail to do so in females. Castration of normally aggressive males by removing the testes reduces their aggressiveness, but castration of aggressive females by removing the ovaries may not. Female hamsters, which tend to be highly aggressive, are not made peaceful by removing their ovaries (Kislack and Beach, 1955). Aggressiveness is increased with estrogen injections but remains unchanged after progesterone treatments. Even more puzzling is the fact that if both estrogen and progesterone are administered, female hamsters become *less* aggressive. More recently, somewhat different results have been reported (Payne and Swanson, 1971). Payne and Swanson found that (a) spayed female hamsters become less aggressive; (b) administering progesterone increases aggressiveness; (c) injecting testosterone to spayed females does not decrease their submissiveness.

These results may be less puzzling if account is taken of recent evidence that there are structurally distinct neural systems which respond to androgens and to estrogens. More than a decade ago it was suggested (Phoenix, et al., 1959) that prenatally administered hormones may cause a permanent organizational change in the nervous system which affects adult sexual characteristics. Researchers found experimental support for this a few years later (Goy and Phoenix, 1963) when they demonstrated that hypothalamic lesions led to different kinds of sexual decrements in male and female guinea pigs. More recently, Singer (1968) found that preoptic lesions eliminated male sexual behavior while leaving female sexual behavior intact, and that anterior hypothalamic lesions which produced cessation of female sexual behavior only partly interfered with male sexual behavior. Similar results have been reported (Hitt, et al., 1970) which indicate that in both male and female rats the parafornical medial forebrain bundle is vital to the mediation of male sexual behavior but has no role in the execution of female sexual behavior. Similarly, the effect of septal lesions in rats depends in part on whether the subjects are male or female (Kondo and Lorens, 1971). It has also been shown that, given to female mice on the day of birth, both androgen and estrogen treatments have the same effect in that they facilitate the differentiation of androgen-sensitive mechanisms for the rest of the animal's life (Edwards and Herndon, 1970). This in turn has a marked effect on adult aggressive behavior, for when injected with testosterone, neonatally estrogenized or androgenized females fight like normal males, and all three fight more than females given a placebo at birth and injected with testosterone when adult. The design and results of this experiment are shown in Figure 26. Goy (1970) reports similar effects with rhesus mon-

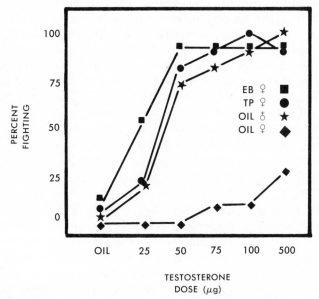

Figure 26. *On their day of birth, female mice were treated with a female hormone, estradiol benzoate (EB), a male hormone, testosterone propionate (TP), or a control injection of oil. Male mice were given only the control injection. As adults, all were castrated and then administered various dosages of testosterone as shown on the abscissa of the above graph. It can be seen that nearly all mice resumed fighting at higher dosages with the exception of females given oil at birth. It therefore appears that administering either male or female hormones shortly after birth makes mice permanently more sensitive to male hormones. (From Edwards and Herndon, 1970.)*

keys. If testosterone is injected into pregnant monkeys, the female offspring will show more masculine behavior patterns than normal females. In many cases masculine social behavior will not be evident until later stages of life. Such experiments lend support to the view that the brain is sexually dimorphous, with prenatal and neonatal hormones influencing neural differentiation that later affects sexual and other social behavior, including aggression.

Sexual Arousal and Aggressive Feelings

No review of sex and aggression would be complete without mentioning Freud. Freud believed that both sex and aggression are biological instincts and that human motivation fundamentally boils down to these primitive urges. These two forces were seen as being closely related, and such things as male dominance or female submissiveness were considered part of normal human sexuality. The supposed biological reason for this was that primitive man had to conquer and subdue a female before mating with her, and evolution tended to favor men who combined aggressiveness with sex (and also, presumably, women who were attracted by such tactics). In addition, Freud felt that inhibited sexual urges might find an outlet in the form of aggressive behavior, or that aggressive impulses might be sublimated into sexual perversions.

Most of Freud's ideas are based on conjecture rather than on scientific evidence, and for that reason they are difficult if not impossible to verify. Nevertheless, some laboratory studies have attempted to better understand the relation between sex and aggression. In one experiment (Barclay and Haber, 1965), manipulations were performed to generate hostile and aggressive feelings in male and female college students. This was done by having an instructor belittle his class for alleged poor performance on an exam, after which he made up a fictitious grading curve indicating that most of the class had flunked. He then instructed the students to participate in an experiment in which instructions were given in an arrogant and authorative manner. The experiment consisted of having everyone take a TAT (thematic apperception test) in which students made up short stories based on ambiguous pictures. In the control condition, a similar group of students took the TAT test without being insulted and ridiculed. The tests were then scored blindly (that is, the individuals doing the scoring did not know which tests were from the experimental group and which were from the control group). The results revealed statistically significant differences between the experimental and control groups, with the experimental group expressing more sexual and aggressive imagery in their stories. Thus, in this situation, increasing hostility tended to evoke sexual fantasies.

In a related study (Barclay, 1969), college students at the University of Minnesota were introduced to an experimenter supposedly from a prestigious Ivy League college. The experimenter quickly annoyed the subjects by stating that the task they were to perform had been simplified to accommodate the inferior type of student found at a place like Minnesota. In addition to fantasy measures of sexual arousal, subjects were persuaded to volunteer urine samples which were then analyzed for acid phosphatase, purportedly a physiological measure of sexual arousal. As in the previous study, it was found that sexual arousal also accompanied anger. Some experimenters have used different procedures and reported the same effect. Feshbach and Jaffee (1970) have experimentally reduced anger and aggression in the laboratory and found a parallel decline in the arousing qualities of erotic stimuli.

While manipulating aggression may influence sexual arousal, evidence for the reverse effect is mixed. Mosher and Katz (1970) showed either pornographic or neutral films to 120 male college students. Their level of verbal aggressiveness was assessed both before and after the films, and it was reported that exposure to sexually arousing stimuli did not heighten aggressiveness. Similar results were obtained by Clark and Sensibar (1955), who showed college males slides of nude females and then counted the number of aggression fantasies in a TAT test. They found that "aroused" subjects were significantly *less* likely to incorporate aggressive themes in their stories.

Different results were obtained by Clark (1952) who found that viewing sexually stimulating pictures increased aggressive fantasies in men. In a more recent study (cited in Berkowitz, 1970), subjects were first angered by the experimenter and then half of the group watched a sex film. Following this all subjects participated in an experiment in which their job was to administer punishment. Those who watched the sex film tended to dole out more punishment than those who had not seen the sex film. One possible explanation for this is that generalized activation rather than sexual arousal may increase aggressiveness. Geen and O'Neal (1969) found that exposure to nothing more than white noise tends to make subjects more aggressive.

Another approach has been to study the attitudes and previous experience of known sexual offenders. Lindner (1953) reported that sexual offenders had more fantasies of aggression in response to a projective test compared to offenders in nonsexual crimes.

Propper (1970) interviewed 476 male reformatory inmates 16 to 21 years old about their previous exposure to pornography. Eighty-two per cent of those with considerable previous exposure committed serious antisocial crimes while only 55 per cent of those with little pornographic experience committed such crimes. These data are tricky to interpret, for correlations of course do not prove causality. Many other experiments report just the opposite: that criminals and sexual offenders are similar to "normal" control groups with respect to what they judge to be sexually arousing (Cook and Fosen, 1970; Gebhard, et al., 1965; Goldstein, et al., 1970).

The entire question of the effect of sexual arousal on crime was considered by the Presidential Commission on Obscenity and Pornography (1970), and their conclusions are as follows:

> In sum, the empirical research has found no evidence to date that exposure to explicit sexual materials plays a significant role in the causation of delinquent or criminal behavior among youths or adults. The Commission cannot conclude that exposure to erotic materials is a factor in the causation of sex crimes or sex delinquency.

4 DEVELOPMENTAL DETERMINANTS OF AGGRESSION

Chapter 3 focused on the various physiological processes which underlie the expression of aggressive behavior. But physiological factors often interact with, and are modulated by, social and experiential factors. For example, it has been mentioned that there is a striking sex difference in the social behavior of the red deer, with the males being much more aggressive than the females. This can be attributed in part directly to hormonal factors, but sex differences are also partly influenced by rearing patterns (Etkin and Freedman, 1964). The red deer herd is a matriarchal organization controlled by the females, and at a very early age the males drift away and grow up in relative isolation with a minimum of social organization. The females, on the other hand, stick close to their mothers and continue to mature while becoming thoroughly socialized to the traditions of the herd. Thus, adult males and females have entirely different developmental histories.

Several experiments may help illustrate the importance of previous social experience on adult aggressive behavior. Southwick (1968) selected newborn mice from a genetic strain known to be passive in their social behavior, and placed them with mothers of a different strain, known to be aggressive. When these mice reached maturity, their chasing, attacking, and fighting behavior was compared with litter mates of the same strain which had not been raised with aggressive mothers. He found that aggressive behavior increased by about 85 per cent as a result of their upbringing. In another experiment, Beeman (1947) castrated mice, and as expected, this eliminated their social fighting. He then injected them with testosterone, and again as expected, they resumed fighting. The procedure was changed for other groups of mice which were first forced into fighting matches and then castrated.

These animals continued to fight even after castration, thus demonstrating that the learned fighting habit had a stronger influence than the reduction in hormone level. Other experiments (Bevan, Daves, and Levy, 1960) have also shown that prior fighting experience can outweigh the effects of hormone manipulations, although this may be true only when the experiment is done with adolescent or mature animals. The importance of factors other than genes or hormones is even better illustrated by studying the development of sex roles in humans.

SEX-TYPING AND GENDER ROLE DEVELOPMENT

Aggressiveness seems to be a well-entrenched masculine characteristic in humans. This is supported by the fact that the bulk of all violent crimes are committed by males. Homicide rates are five times as high for males compared to females, and for robbery the figure is twenty times as great (Violent Crime, 1969). Hormones clearly influence social and aggressive behavior, as we have seen, but "masculine" or "feminine" behavior is also strongly influenced by the long socialization process through which children learn society's values.

A newborn child is not only recognized, but *treated* as a boy or as a girl. This differential treatment continues for the rest of his life and appears to be an important factor in the development of gender roles (Sears, 1965). Western civilization has almost universally defined the gender roles as polar opposites, such as active versus passive, independent versus dependent, and aggressive versus submissive. Thus, it has been argued that humans are basically psychosexually neutral at birth, and that gender roles are learned through socialization (Hampson, 1965; Money, 1965; Mischel, 1970). Clinical cases of ambisexual incongruities (e.g., various types of human hermaphroditism) indicate that until language develops toward the end of the second year, reversal in sex rearing can be successfully imposed. Beyond this age it gradually becomes more difficult to reverse sex roles while maintaining a healthy psychological adjustment. With these sexual anomalies, the most successful sex-role reversals are accomplished if genital surgery is performed very early in life, and if the parents resolve their ambiguities and doubts and unfailingly treat their child according to the altered role. In addition, pubertal secondary sexual development should be timed and regulated hormonally (Money, 1965). We now know that psychosexual differentiation

can take place in opposition to
1. genetic sex (chromosome count);
2. hormonal sex (distribution of hormone concentrations);
3. gonadal sex: ovarian, testicular, or mixed;
4. morphology of the internal reproductive organs;
5. morphology of the external genitals.

Sexual incongruities are sometimes resolved even without extensive medical and psychiatric care. Money describes cases of females who have a penis-sized clitoris and masculine characteristics such as a muscular physique and a deep voice, yet maintain a feminine gender role and psychosexual identity.

Thus, there is considerable plasticity in the development of sex roles in humans, and definite patterns become apparent early in life. Sex roles, and aggressive behavior, are continuously influenced by child rearing practices, an issue to which we will return. At this point it might be appropriate only to summarize the results of extensive factor analysis studies relating child rearing practices with appropriate gender role development. Sears (1965) mentions four factors which contribute to feminizing children of both sexes:
1. the father's anxiety about sex;
2. the mother's punitiveness and nonpermissiveness with respect to aggression;
3. the use of physical punishment and ridicule;
4. severe training practices in realms such as table manners or toilet habits.

Significant correlations related to masculinization are less apparent although Sears reports that the "affectionate intrusion" of the father into a girl's rearing may have such an effect. One puzzling feature of these findings is that the use of physical punishment correlates with both feminization and increased aggressiveness, which does not agree with the presumption that aggression is more of a masculine characteristic.

The importance of gender-role development and its relation to aggressive behavior can be illustrated by an experiment involving binocular rivalry with a stereoscope (Moore, 1966). Males and females were shown two pictures simultaneously, a different picture for each eye. One picture showed a mailman and the other depicted a man with a dagger in his back. Since the pictures were flashed on and off very quickly, the situation created a "rivalry" over which elements would be more strongly perceived. It was discovered that males saw significantly more violence than did females, and that the tendency to perceive violence increased with age for both males and females. Thus, amount of previous experience (as reflected in age) and the type of experience (reflected by sex) affected perception. A similar situation was used by Toch and Schulte (1961) in comparing men who had just finished a program in police administration with others who were just entering. It was found that those just completing the program were more likely to see violence.

Thus, society exerts its influence through cultural definitions and social roles, and these factors are probably largely responsible for differences between men and women with regard to criminal violence. Further evidence of this comes from the fact that where cultural roles are more nearly equal for men and women, the rates of criminal offenses are also (Mulvihill and Tumin, 1969). This can also be seen in recent years where increased emancipation of women has been accompanied by a relative decrease in differences in delinquency and criminal rates for males and females.

SOCIAL ISOLATION

One of the traditional ways of studying the effects of developmental experience has been to separate individuals shortly after birth and raise them under different conditions. Obviously, this procedure lends itself to animal rather than human experimentation, and many such experiments have been carried out with the goal of determining how social experience during rearing, or the lack of it, influences adult aggressive behavior. One of the most radical procedures involves social isolation. Kuo (1967) summarized a number of his experiments in which various breeds of dogs, cats, birds, and fish were isolated from shortly after birth until maturity. He reported that, when tested as adults, most isolated animals show unusual aggressiveness toward members of their own species. This aggressiveness may also be directed at members of other species. Psychologists frequently raise laboratory rats in individual cages for easier identification and better control over their past learning experiences. But compared to animals housed in group cages, isolated rats are more prone to bite the experimenter (Hatch, et al., 1963). This necessitates the use of gloves and pre-experimental gentling sessions in which the rat gets used to the experimenter (and vice versa). Similarly, isolated rats are more apt to attack and kill some alien species, such as frogs (Johnson, DeSisto, and Koenig, 1972), although isolation is reported to have little effect on mouse-killing (Myer, 1969).

In monkeys, lack of peer experience during development leads to increased aggressiveness in adulthood, and this aggressiveness may be directed at other monkeys (Mason, 1960), alien species

(Mason and Green, 1962), or even themselves (Harlow and Harlow, 1962). The effects are not always predictable, for severely isolated monkeys may emerge unusually aggressive or unusually fearful, depending partly on the length of isolation (Harlow, Dodsworth, and Harlow, 1965). Monkeys isolated for the first six months of life may show suicidal tendencies in the presence of adults and may molest other infants, while 12 months of isolation tends to produce fearful animals who try to avoid any social contact. If monkeys are isolated early in life and then placed in a normal group setting for several years they are likely to continue avoiding contact with their peers (Sackett, 1967). But when isolated monkeys are first placed in a group setting, prolonged and destructive fighting usually takes place (Mason, 1963). Normally reared monkeys will also engage in destructive fighting if placed in a new group setting, but usually a dominance hierarchy is soon established after which there is relatively little overt quarreling.

Experimenters often do not make it clear what they mean by isolation, for it may refer to anything from lack of physical contact to total visual, auditory, and olfactory quarantine. But even partially isolated monkeys raised in bare wire cages show severe disturbances such as self-biting, agitated motor patterns, neglect and abuse of their babies, and inability to appropriately direct their aggressive behavior (Cross and Harlow, 1965; Sackett, 1968). (See Figure 27.) Sometimes the masochistic behavior becomes severe enough to lead to open bleeding and broken bones. Fearful withdrawal is also common in both males and females, with occasional violent outbursts being confined mostly to males. In general, social isolation during development produces severe behavioral pathology in all primates studied. Abnormal behavior at first includes rocking, finger-sucking, grimacing, and self-clutching, and if isolation is continued animals become threatening, aggressive and self-mutilating, develop stereotyped postures, and engage in pacing and masturbation (Mitchell, 1970). More severe and nearly total sensory isolation from conspecifics has been studied in chimpanzees; the result is that the chimps try to escape and avoid almost any stimulus (Davenport and Menzel, 1963). Severely isolated dogs show a startling inability to escape from punishment and it has been suggested that such isolation impairs the capacity to perceive pain (Melzack and Scott, 1957). More recent experimenters have attributed this effect in dogs to hyperemotionality caused by novel stimuli (Lore, 1969).

Another way to study the effects of social isolation is to compare "wild" animals with those reared in captivity. Zookeepers know that mere captivity may have a strong effect, for their animals often

Figure 27. Monkeys raised in social isolation develop abnormal behavior patterns including self-clutching (A) and self-biting (B). Such self-mutilation may result in open wounds and broken bones. (From Sackett, 1968, in Fox, M. W. Abnormal Behavior in Animals. Philadelphia, W. B. Saunders, 1968.)

prefer to fight rather than to mate. The difference between monkeys raised in captivity and those captured in the wild can be seen by comparing their sexual and aggressive behavior (Fig. 28) as measured by the number of threats, fights, acts of self-mutilation, and normal mountings (Sackett, 1968; Southwick, 1969). It is clear that the relative isolation of the laboratory makes monkeys more aggressive and withdrawn and more retarded in many of their social activities. Rearing in a restricted environment causes females to become indifferent and violently abusive mothers (Mitchell, 1970; Harlow, et al., 1963). Such abnormal behavior is not due to intellectual deficits and is caused more by lack of peers than by lack of mothering (Harlow and Harlow, 1962; Sackett, 1968). Aggressive behavior also may vary with ecologic as well as social

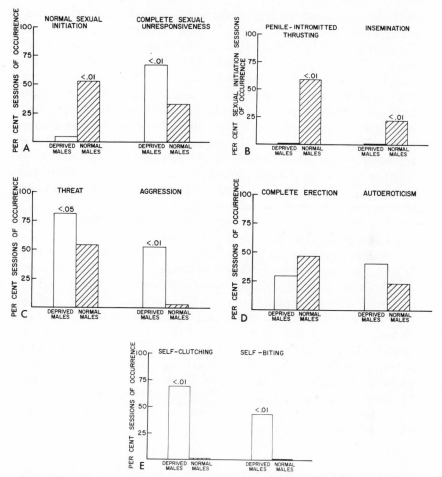

Figure 28. Monkeys raised in the laboratory display many forms of abnormal sexual and aggressive behavior as can be seen in comparisons with normal monkeys raised in the wild. Behaviors measured included (A) sexual responsiveness; (B) sexual success; (C) aggression; (D) autoeroticism; (E) self-mutilation. (From Sackett, 1968, in Fox, M. W. Abnormal Behavior in Animals. Philadelphia, W. B. Saunders, 1968.)

conditions. For example, monkeys inhabiting the rural villages of India are much more aggressive than others of the same species found in the forests (Southwick, 1969). Similarities may be noted in humans, for violent crime is disproportionately found in cities.

Of course, total social isolation is a condition which exists only in the laboratory, and where humans are concerned it does not exist at all. Unfortunately, there are a few scattered reports (Davis, 1940; 1947) of illegitimate children hidden in an attic during early childhood with no human contact other than that with an occasional feeder, sometimes deaf and mute. When such relative isolates are discovered, their cognitive capacities are severely retarded (although they may later recover to some extent). Such isolation may be accompanied by other debilitating circumstances such as malnutrition and disease, so it is difficult to draw any conclusions about the effects of isolation alone. Other attempts have been made to compare the health and physical development of institutionalized babies given little handling or stimulation with others given lots of TLC (tender loving care). Spitz (1945) reported severe detrimental effects ("hospitalism") from such relative isolation; however, his study has been widely criticized for methodological reasons, so the reported effect may have been due to factors other than isolation. It also contrasts with Harlow's monkey studies, in which isolation alone had little effect on health but had a disastrous effect on social adjustment.

Another indirect way of studying the effects of partial isolation in humans is to examine the effect of being an only child (Schacter, 1959), or growing up in a sheltered environment surrounded by maternal overprotection (Levy, 1943). Both experiences appear to increase the chances of deviant or maladjusted behavior although they may not directly contribute to aggressive behavior. We also know that for a child, being made to stand in a corner for a few minutes can be a very punishing experience. Isolating a child for as little as 10 minutes in a strange place quickly leads to emotional arousal and anxiety (Walters and Parke, 1964), although the exact effect may depend on other variables such as the social class of the child (Endo, 1968).

Theories of Social Deprivation

The studies of social isolation clearly reveal the importance of developmental variables in aggression, although it should be noted that the isolation procedure has also been used to argue just the opposite—namely, that aggression is innate and unaffected by developmental experience. For example, Eibl-Eibesfeldt (1961) raised wild rats in isolation and found that when put together as adults they would spontaneously begin fighting, thus suggesting that learning is not important because there was no opportunity for learning how to fight. But this mistakenly treats isolation as a neutral variable having no effect, and as we have already seen isolation is a powerful treatment which *increases* both intra- and interspecific aggression in rats. There is no such thing as "lack of experience," for isolated animals are marked both by what they learn and by what they fail to learn. Social isolation may teach an animal to fear anything novel and may also prevent an animal from learning the social rituals which inhibit aggression. Clearly, isolated animals have the capacity to fight, but where learning plays an important role is in the initiating factors, including the choice of opponents. Thus, an isolated animal may know how to fight, but he may not know how to recognize a threat or appeasement gesture and he may fight unnecessarily. The opposite may also happen: by failing to recognize provocations he may fight less. This is illustrated by the fact that if genetically aggressive mice (King and Gurney, 1954) or dogs (Fisher, 1955; Fuller and Clark, 1966; Scott and Fuller, 1965) are raised in isolation they will fight less rather than more. For example, fox terriers raised normally in a litter with their mother become extremely aggressive by the age of seven weeks, and after that it is difficult to keep more than three puppies together in safety. If the terriers are isolated, they are not exposed to this fighting and as adults they tend to ignore rather than to challenge other terriers. Broadly speaking, social isolation may be conceived of either as a neutral variable which alters behavior because it deprives an organism of learning what it normally would learn, or as an active variable which modifies behavior because of what is learned (not what is *not* learned). The traditional view is that isolation has a serious deleterious effect on behavior because it deprives an organism of sensory experience which is necessary for the normal development of the nervous system (Hebb, 1949).

More recently, Lessac and Solomon (1969) have proposed that isolation does more than merely retard behavior development, for it may actively distort development. For example, dogs placed in isolation may perform more poorly on tasks after the isolation period than before they were put in isolation. Thus, maladaptive behavior may be due to active interference on previously organized processes. Another interpretation (Fuller, 1967) is that isolated animals become used to low levels of general stimulation so that after isolation they are likely to be hyperreactive to even moderate levels of stimulation (e.g., the presence of another conspecific). In this way an isolated animal may react to normal stimulation the way a normal animal would react to violent stimulation.

In summary, it appears that social isolation has no unitary effect on behavior. It may either increase or decrease aggressiveness, and the exact effect depends on genetically determined species-typical behavior patterns as well as on the kind and amount of deprivation. As was pointed out in Chapter 3, all mammals have a built-in capacity to fight, but how often they do so and against whom appears to be strongly influenced by developmental experience. In addition, infantile experience can have an important effect on related processes such as fear and emotional arousal.

EARLY EXPERIENCE, EMOTIONALITY, AND AGGRESSIVENESS

Isolation and social deprivation are thus active rather than passive forms of early experience, and they clearly have an effect on the adult aggressive behavior, at least for animals reared in a controlled laboratory environment. Rather than isolating animals, the problem can be turned around by studying the effects of early stimulation rather than early deprivation. Treated in this manner the question becomes one of the kind and amount of early experience rather than simply the presence or absence of such experience.

In 1956, Levine, Chevalier, and Korchin discovered that merely picking up baby rats later made them superior to controls in their ability to learn a conditioned avoidance task. The procedure consisted of handling each rat pup for about three minutes a day from birth until weaning at 20 days. In a follow-up experiment (Levine, 1956) it was reported that the age at which the pups were handled was important because rats handled the same way later in life did not show the "emotional stability" of those handled right after birth.

The procedures for studying early handling and emotionality have been carefully worked out by Denenberg and his associates (1964; 1965; 1967; 1968; 1969; 1970). In the typical experiment, subjects (usually rats) are tested by placing them in an "open field," which is a boxlike apparatus marked off into 25 identical squares. The main dependent variables for assessing emotionality are: (a) the total number of squares entered in a three-minute period; (b) the number of interior as opposed to peripheral squares entered; (c) the latency of leaving the first square; (d) the number of fecal boluses. The open field test is based on the assumptions that a terrified rat will freeze, urinate and defecate, and be timid about exploring a novel environment. A rat with more emotional stability, on the other hand, will freely explore his new environment and is more likely to venture into the center of the apparatus. A number of experiments verified the fact that handling shortly after birth produced a relatively permanent effect in reducing emotionality. For example, Hunt and Otis (1963) showed that such infantile experience continues to have a measurable effect even in relatively old (544 days) rats.

It was soon discovered that the early experience effect could be produced without handling the animals simply by subjecting them to stress. Thus, baby rats could be electrically shocked (Baron, Brookshire, and Littman, 1957), jiggled in an oscillating shaker (Levine and Lewis, 1959), or placed in a refrigerator (Schaefer, Weingarten, and Towne, 1962), all with the same effect of reducing emotionality. Such manipulations produce physiological as well as behavioral effects which indicate that the adrenal glands of neonate rats are responsive either to stimulation or to stress (Zarrow, et al., 1966). If an assay is made of blood plasma, there will be a significant difference in plasma corticosterone between handled and nonhandled rats (Denenberg, et al., 1967).

The early handling effect seems well established, or at least well researched; however, it is not without controversy, for the variety of independent and dependent variables sometimes produce kaleidoscopic effects which are difficult to interpret. Some other laboratories (King, 1969; 1970) have failed to replicate the effect, which has resulted in speculation that the effect may operate only in certain strains or may be confounded by differences in litter sizes, treatment of the mother, and subtle differences in testing conditions (e.g., temperature, humidity, barometric pressure) on different days. The effect can be reliably found under certain specified conditions; however, if it is a powerful phenomenon it should be robust enough to emerge despite small differences in methodology. To give an example, the adult performance on open field scores may depend as much on how animals are treated after weaning as before weaning. The handling effect has been reported when subjects are housed in group cages following weaning, but stronger effects are generally obtained if they are housed in individual cages. Perhaps for this reason the latter procedure is more frequently employed. But social isolation is an abnormal condition with detrimental behavioral effects, particularly for rats, which are social animals. One therefore questions the generality of the effect which may occur in an artificial laboratory environment but be washed out when the conditions resemble those found in nature. For example, Ader (1965) compared handled and nonhandled rats which were housed either individually or in groups following weaning, and he reported that social interactions following weaning reduced or eliminated the differential effects of early handling.

It is interesting to observe that theorizing about the early handling effect has come full circle in the past several decades. At first it was thought that extra handling might have something to do with the mother by providing additional "mothering" or "contact comfort." But when it was discovered that the same effect could be produced by noxious stimuli such as electric shock, the effect was assumed to operate directly on the stimulated infant. Strong support for this view came from experiments which showed that brain chemistry was altered by many kinds of stimulation, ranging from caresses to near-torture. It was even suggested that the underlying variable in the entire effect is the slight drop in body temperature as a result of being moved (Schaefer, Weingarten, and Towne, 1962). But the most recent evidence (Thoman and Levine, 1969; 1970) once again suggests that the effect may be mediated through the mother, possibly because the experimental procedures cause slight hormonal changes in the mother which may affect the quality of her maternal behavior, which is in turn reflected in the behavior of the offspring. This is shown by the fact that if the mothers are molested by the experimenter (e.g., removed without disturbing the pups), then the offspring will be similar whether handled or not. Thus, manipulations which affect the mother also affect the development of the young. Such manipulations are effective not only when the mother is nursing, but when she is pregnant or even in her own childhood (Denenberg and Whimbey, 1963; Levine, 1967; Denenberg and Rosenberg, 1967). It appears that the experiences of a grandmother rat in her infancy may affect the behavior of her grandchildren (grandrats?) several generations away.

A final note on early handling is that it may not affect different strains and different species the same way. For example, early handling or stimulation of mice tends to make them *more* rather than *less* emotional (Hall and Whiteman, 1951; Lindzey, Winston, and Manosevitz, 1963; Imes and Etaugh, 1971). It thus appears that early stimulation, like social isolation, may either increase or decrease emotionality depending in part on species differences and genetic factors. Similarly, emotionality is not always related to aggressiveness in a simple way. For example, emotionality in a beagle is reflected by withdrawal while emotionality in a terrier leads to hyperactivity (Fuller, 1967). Rats judged to be emotionally stable fight much more with each other than rats considered hyper-emotional (Billingslea, 1941; Hall and Klein, 1942). But early handling, which increases emotional stability, appears to have no effect on pup-killing (Denenberg, 1971). Perhaps the best example of the complex interactions between genetics and developmental experience is reported by Ginsburg (1967). He found that early handling increased intraspecific fighting in one strain of mice, decreased it in a second strain, and had no effect at all in a third strain. Southwick and Clark (1968) have also reported similar strain differences in correlating emotionality with aggressiveness.

In humans, experiments on early stimulation generally involve sensory or perceptual stimulation and the effects on cognitive growth. A few experimenters (Casler, 1965; White and Castle, 1964) have attempted to carry out early handling manipulations by giving babies an extra 20 minutes of tactile stimulation for a number of weeks shortly after birth. The effects, as measured in general health, weight gain, and Gesell scores, have been small. Hopper and Pinneau (1957) persuaded 21 mothers to bounce and tickle their babies for an extra 10 minutes at each feeding, telling them that it might be related to speech development. They kept track of the amount of regurgitation over a two-week period but found that the extra stimulation had no effect when compared to controls. Freedman (1968, 1971) reported that premature babies which are handled and swaddled have a higher survival rate than those left undisturbed in an incubator. Similarly, babies placed in mechanically rocking incubators showed significantly faster weight gains compared to controls who were not rocked. Gerber (1958) has noted that African children from Uganda develop much faster than European children, and suggests that this may be due to the massive maternal attention and stimulation they receive very early in life. Quite naturally, more stressful types of early stimulation have not been studied with human infants, although again some cross-cultural data may be partially relevant. Landauer and Whiting (1964) compared societies which practiced body-piercing, shaping, and other painful practices on babies with other societies which did not. They reported that adults tended to be 2.5 inches taller in those societies which "stressed" their infants ($p < .01$). Kagan (1969) studied infants with mechanical trauma or mild anoxia (but no brain damage) at birth but later found no difference in I.Q. scores or learning ability when compared to infants who had had an easy delivery.

Attachments and Affectional Bonds

Due to some of Harlow's early work with monkeys (Harlow, 1959) it was thought that the lack of early stimulation and growing up without a mother contributed to later abnormal behavior. As it turned out, the kind of early experience is possibly more important than the amount, and Harlow (et al., 1963) defined five separate affectional systems: (1) the infant-mother system; (2) the infant-infant system; (3) the heterosexual or adult male-female system; (4) the maternal or mother-infant system; (5) the paternal or father-infant system. The mere presence of a mother does not guarantee normal development, for if the mother is unusually hostile during the first few months, her offspring may develop a hyperaggressiveness which may be observed as many as four years later (Sackett, 1967).

An important part of what takes place in early socialization and development is the formation of affectional bonds and emotional attachments. Sometimes the bond which develops is referred to as a dependency relationship; however, the term dependency has been criticized as being too global a concept to be of use beyond infancy, and instead the terms attachment or affectional system are preferred (Maccoby and Masters, 1970). For many years psychoanalysts stressed the view that events during the first three to five years determined adult behavior patterns (Bowlby, et al., 1956) so that deviant adult behavior might be "caused" by infantile experiences. The traditional psychoanalytic view has also argued that there is an "instinctive" mother-child bond and that the breaking of this innate attachment has permanent serious consequences (Bowlby, 1969). In spite of decades of research on such questions there seems to be little sound support for the psychoanalytic position (Orlansky, 1949; O'Connor, 1968; Thompson and Grusec, 1970). Adversity early in life appears to be reversible or at least modifiable, and permanent effects are probably due to continuing adversity rather than to some infantile trauma. The detrimental effects of institutionalization and other restricted environments are often only temporary and sometimes can be accounted for by general lack of stimulation and perceptual deprivation. The presence of social and perceptual stimulation appears to be necessary for normal behavior, but such stimulation can be provided in a variety of ways. Some reviewers (e.g., Casler, 1968) have concluded that social stimulation is not necessarily best administered by a loving mother, and that separation from the mother is not of crucial importance. Sackett (1970), for example, found that young monkeys were upset when separated from their mothers, but after associating with age-mates for as little as two weeks they preferred to be with peers rather than adult females. Others (Hinde and Spencer-Booth, 1970; Spencer-Booth and Hinde, 1972) have reported more profound and long-lasting disturbances from mother-infant separation in monkeys. Controlled experiments on human babies are of course difficult to carry out for ethical reasons; however, limited observations suggest that brief separations of very young children from their mother cause distress and an intensification of attachment behavior upon reunion (Maccoby and Masters, 1970).

Psychoanalytic views of separation and dependency are mainly based on unsystematic clinical impressions (Bowlby, 1958) and need not be confused with more accepted theories of attachment behavior. Attachments are found in nearly all social animals including man, but they are not necessarily permanent nor do they have to be with the mother. Attachments are facilitated by emotional arousal (Scott, 1962a) and can take place between a young organism and whatever is present in the environment regardless of whether the organism is rewarded, punished, or treated indifferently (Scott and Fuller, 1965). Although there exists an extensive literature on early experience, socialization, and attachment behavior, the present discussion is restricted to the direct effects of these developmental processes on aggressive behavior. For a more general review, the reader may wish to consult Thompson and Grusec (1970), Maccoby and Masters (1970), and Mischel (1970).

Cross-species Rearing and the Inhibition of Aggression

The fact that early social experience can dramatically affect aggressive and defensive behavior is easily illustrated by experiments in which cross-species bonds are formed. For example, sheep are traditionally supposed to have an "innate fear" of dogs, and farmers make good use of this behavior by employing only a few dogs to keep entire herds of sheep under control. But if a lamb is bottle-reared on a farm where puppies are also growing up, this "natural" fear never develops and in fact the lamb may become attached to dogs and consider them playmates (Scott, 1968a).

An even better example is the "natural" antagonism between cats and rats found in Hollywood cartoons. Kuo (1930) attempted to discover the origin of the cat's response to rats, and carried out an experiment in which he manipulated developmental conditions. One group of kittens was raised so that they never saw any rats. A second group was raised in an environment where they watched their mother chase and kill rats, and in a third group cats and rats were raised together from birth to maturity. Kuo found that about half (9 of 20) of the cats raised in isolation spontaneously killed rats when they grew up and that nearly all (18 of 21) of the cats reared in a rat-killing environment became killers. But if cats and rats were raised together, no killing took place during the rearing period and only a few cats (3 of 18) later killed rats.

Similar experiments have been carried out between rats and mice (Denenberg, Paschke, and Zarrow, 1969; Myer, 1969) which indicate that few if any rats will attack and kill mice if the two species are raised together. It has also been shown that if mice are reared with rat "aunts" they will later choose to be with rats rather than other mice (Hudgens, Denenberg, and Zarrow, 1968). Mice fostered by rat aunts tend to become, overall, more ratlike, in realms including their open field behavior, their plasma corticosterone response (Denenberg, et al., 1969), and their aggressiveness. In the case of aggressiveness, genetically aggressive mice show a sharp reduction in intraspecific fighting if they are raised with rats, probably because they become so thoroughly socialized to rats that they no longer treat mice as conspecifics.

Social attachments are commonly found in many species of mammals, birds, and even some insects (Scott, 1968b), and these attachments can be formed to an alien species or even to an inanimate object (Cairns, 1966a). Cross-species attachments have been demonstrated between cats and rats (McDougall and McDougall, 1927; Kuo, 1930), rats and monkeys (Mason and Green, 1962), cats and birds (Kuo, 1967), and lambs and dogs (Cairns, 1964). More impressive is the fact that emotional attachments can be formed to stationary and inanimate objects in monkeys (Harlow, 1958), dogs (Igel and Calvin, 1960), lambs (Cairns, 1966b), and chicks (Gray, 1960).

These attachments resemble the imprinting effect found in many birds and some mammals. In imprinting, the young animal will become attached to the most prominent moving object it sees during a "critical period" shortly after birth, and will attempt to follow it. In nature, the "following" response is an indication of a primary social bond, and it usually takes place with the mother. In the laboratory, a chick or duckling can be imprinted to a decoy, a rubber ball, or even the experimenter. The strength of this first attachment can be seen by the fact that the organism will continue to follow that to which it was imprinted, even if it means rejection of the mother and acceptance of an alien and inappropriate object. Although the strength and permanence of the imprinting effect is often overstated, it does represent a dramatic form of social behavior which is acquired at a very early age and continues to have lasting effects.

But it would be a mistake to leap to the conclusion that social behavior is infinitely modifiable through developmental experience. In Kuo's classic (1930) experiment, for example, half of the cats killed the first rat they saw as adults and the other half did not, even though all cats were raised in an identical environment. Also, a few of the cats raised with rats became rat-killers anyhow, and some of the cats "taught" to kill rats by their mothers never did acquire this response. And, while cross-species attachments

can be formed by cohabitation during development, such demonstrations are usually carried out between mammals in which
spontaneous interspecific aggressive behavior is not powerful
(e.g., rats and mice).

A more stringent test of the ability of early social experience
to inhibit aggression is to test more distantly related species in
which the killing response is strong. For example, nearly all rats
will quickly attack and kill a frog placed in the rat's home cage
(DeSisto and Huston, 1971). Can this killing response be modified
by early social experience with frogs? An attempt was made to
test this (Johnson, DeSisto, and Koenig, 1972) by raising both
species in either a frog-like environment (rats on a raft surrounded
by water containing frogs) or a rat-like environment (large community cages with shallow pans of water for the frogs). In both cases
the baby rats got along well with the frogs until 50 to 60 days of
age, when the rats began to trap and kill the frogs: interspecific
aggression took place in spite of early social experience. Another
attempt was made to raise rats and frogs together by protecting
the frogs within a wire mesh screen which allowed only visual and
olfactory exposure. When the rats reached maturity they were
individually tested with a frog, and more than three-quarters
quickly attacked and killed (the mean latency of attack was 25
seconds). It is possible that rats raised in a group situation form
attachments to each other rather than to an alien species, and so a
final attempt was made in which individual rats were housed
with individual (but protected) frogs so that the only social contact for the rats from weaning to maturity was with a frog. When
the rats were tested as adults, nearly all (94 per cent) quickly
attacked and killed the first unprotected frog they met. Similar
experiments were carried out between weanling rats and giant
cockroaches, and in this case as well no attachments were formed
and developmental experience failed to modify interspecific
aggressive behavior.

It is commonly noted that the more dissimilar two species are,
the less inclined they are to engage in social fighting (Fisher,
1964); however, dissimilarity may increase the chances of a preda-
tor-prey relationship. The rat-frog-cockroach data might be more
closely related to predation rather than social fighting, but the
rats were not hungry and few attempted to eat their victims. What
is important is the failure of developmental experience to modify
their killing behavior. Karli (1956) has reported that some rats,
either wild or domesticated, will always attack and kill mice, and
others will never kill, even if starving to death. Apparently there
are limits to which developmental experience can modify aggres-

sive behavior. Thus, any generalizations based on total rigidity or total plasticity are bound to be only partly correct. But as we get closer to the primates, and particularly among humans, we find that social and environmental conditions during rearing are of great significance.

AGGRESSION AND CHILD REARING PRACTICES

Sometimes it is assumed that aggressive parents produce aggressive children ("like father, like son"), but unfortunately parental influences are not quite so simple (McCord, McCord, and Howard, 1961). Few parents knowingly train their children to be aggressive, and most parents firmly believe they are doing what is "right." For example, some parents make a virtue out of being strict disciplinarians and live by the saying, "Spare the rod and spoil the child." All their efforts may backfire, for no other variable is as strongly related to the development of aggressive behavior as the use of physical punishment (Feshbach, 1970). This is true even if the punishment is doled out in an effort to eliminate aggressive behavior. In the laboratory, punishment in the form of verbal abuse may elicit a stronger aggressive response than frustrating a subject by interfering with an ongoing task (Buss, 1961). In the home, the angry display of the parent may be more important than the severity of the punishment, and the inhibition, if any, may be only temporary. Discipline may achieve its immediate goal of producing a "well-behaved" child at home; however, the same child may continue to be a problem elsewhere. The child may simply learn that aggression is acceptable as long as the father doesn't find out and that the use of physical force is an effective way of achieving goals.

A number of correlational studies have attempted to test the effects of parental punitiveness and children's aggression. Hoffman (1960) rated mothers according to the severity of discipline they employed and the extent to which they asserted unqualified power over their children. He found that the use of such unqualified power was significantly correlated with the child's hostility toward other children and his resistance to social influence. Bandura and Walters (1963) studied punitive and nonpunitive fathers, and found that the sons of the former revealed more antisocial values when they made up stories. The correlation between parental punitiveness and children's aggressive behavior has also been reported in other studies (Glueck and Glueck, 1950; Bandura and Walters, 1959); however, it should be cautioned that such correlations do not necessarily imply a causal relationship. Rather than punishment causing aggression, it is also possible for the reverse to happen. For example, children who are aggressive for some other reason (e.g., brain dysfunction) are likely to be punished more often.

One of the difficulties in evaluating different child rearing practices is the problem of identifying "aggressive" and "non-aggressive" children. Sometimes delinquency records are used, although, strictly speaking, delinquency cannot be equated with aggression. Other times the parents are interviewed, as in an extensive study carried out by Sears, Maccoby, and Levin (1957). They interviewed 379 middle class mothers from New England in an effort to discover familial correlates of aggressive behavior. The factors which they singled out as being correlated with the development of aggressiveness are: (a) the use of physical punishment; (b) parental permissiveness in the expression of aggression; (c) frequent disagreements between the parents; (d) the mother's general dissatisfaction with her role in life and particularly her low esteem of her husband. There were no independent behavioral measures of aggressiveness, and aggressiveness was assessed by what the mothers said about their children. In another study (Sears, et al., 1953), aggressiveness was measured in a nursery school setting, and once again physical punishment in the home emerged as an important factor correlated with aggressive behavior.

Other studies have come to similar conclusions by studying adolescent delinquents (Bandura and Walters, 1959) and non-delinquents (McCord, McCord, and Howard, 1961). In the Bandura and Walters study, 26 white boys with a history of delinquency were studied in interviews with both the boys and their parents. All of the boys were of average or above average intelligence, and all came from intact families which did not reside in a high-delinquency neighborhood. Rating scales similar to those used by Sears and his associates were employed to compare the delinquent boys with a control group of nondelinquents. The major findings were that the two groups did not differ in their affection for their mothers; however, delinquent boys exhibited considerable hostility for their fathers. The mothers of delinquent boys often displayed lack of warmth for their husbands, and this feeling was usually reciprocated. The delinquent boys showed less guilt for wrong-doings and their behavior was maintained by fear rather than by any moral standards. In general, the socialization of delinquent boys seemed to be characterized by a lack of modeling after the father and the failure to develop a personal conscience.

In the McCord study, 174 nondelinquent boys and their parents were studied over a five-year period, and it was concluded that "aggressive," "assertive," and "nonaggressive" boys came from radically different backgrounds. Aggressive boys were usually raised by parents who were (a) rejecting, punitive, and inconsistent in their guidance, and (b) constantly fighting themselves and undermining each other's values. Nonaggressive boys came from environments which emphasized: (a) warmth, consistency, and lack of punitive controls, and (b) social conformity and mutual respect. Assertive boys often came from families which were (a) affectionate and non-threatening, but (b) where parents exerted inconsistent controls with lack of conformity and some open conflict.

AGGRESSION AS A PERSONALITY TRAIT

It is difficult to relate aggression to personality because there seems to be no single cluster of traits which describes the aggressive child (Feshbach, 1970). A profile of behavior may be judged aggressive or nonaggressive depending on the age, sex, and other circumstances. Aggressiveness cannot simply be equated with delinquency or possession of a police record, and if people are asked to judge aggressiveness in others they are likely to use widely varying standards. In some contexts, aggressiveness may be an admired quality, and be equated with achievement and accomplishment. For example, in the Moore and Gilliland (1921) study described in Chapter 1, the Dartmouth students rated most aggressive were popular and respected while those judged unaggressive were considered without prominence. Butcher (1965) tested eighth-graders on the M.M.P.I. and found that the most disturbed boys were those judged *either* very high or very low in aggressiveness by schoolmates and teachers.

One way to apply personality to aggressive behavior is to label different character types. For example, Hartmann, et al., (1949) categorize the following types of aggressive personality:
1. reputation defenders;
2. norm enforcers;
3. self-image compensators;
4. self-defenders;
5. pressure removers;
6. bullies;
7. exploiters;
8. self-indulgers;
9. catharters.

Another descriptive procedure is to classify individual personality types as chronically overcontrolled, undercontrolled, or under appropriate control (Megargee and Mendelsohn, 1962; Megargee, 1966). A chronically *overcontrolled* person normally operates under rigid inhibitions which prevent him from responding to provocations or displacing his aggressive tendencies. An *under-controlled* individual is just the opposite in that he lacks social controls to inhibit his antisocial behavior. *Appropriate control* refers to a balance between assertiveness and inhibition so that an individual usually restrains himself except when aggression might be considered justified. Megargee's work is interesting in that it suggests that violent aggression (e.g., a brutal murder) may be more than an extension of milder forms of aggression (e.g., a fist fight) and may have entirely different personality dynamics. The undercontrolled individual may be responsible for numerous acts that are antisocial, but the chronically overcontrolled person is much more dangerous in the long run. Many brutal and senseless crimes are committed by persons who were thought to be mild-mannered, unemotional, and in firm control. But on rare occasions when this control breaks down their aggression bursts forth and is likely to be much more violent.

Others have related the aggressive personality to an active-independent behavior pattern. Millon (1969) describes the aggressive personality as being brusque, argumentative, and sometimes abusive. Accordingly, such individuals are often dogmatic in their views and insist on being "right." When matters are to their liking they can be very gracious and cheerful; however, generally their behavior is guarded, and expressions of softer emotions are rare. Millon considers aggressive personality types to have a low frustration tolerance and be quick to be provoked into retaliation. Others may consider them insensitive and coarse, but often they are keenly aware of the feelings of others and merely dislike displays of weakness, either in others or in themselves. The active-independent personality regards himself as being assertive, energetic, self-reliant, strong, honest, and realistic.

However one chooses to describe the aggressive personality, characteristic traits tend to appear early and remain relatively stable throughout childhood into adulthood. In young children, aggressiveness may be displayed through a variety of inflexible and almost stereotyped behavior patterns (Dittman and Goodrich, 1961). Nursery school teachers who rate the expression of aggression in children find that it remains remarkably stable between the ages of three to five, and that aggressive behavior in nursery school is a good predictor of what happens in kindergarten (Jersild and Markey, 1935; Emmerich, 1966).

Kagan and Moss (1962) carried out a longitudinal study of the continuity of aggressive behavior in 36 men and 35 women from birth through adolescence and reported that behavioral instability before three years of age was not an indication of later instability. After three years, however, aggressive tendencies tend to stabilize, particularly in boys. This trend continues into adulthood, with the boys showing frequent tantrums in school becoming short-tempered adults. As girls grow older they tend to express less aggression, probably because of the difference in sex roles ingrained by society. Boys are expected to be more assertive and they are encouraged to fight when necessary to "prove their manhood." But overt expression of aggression in girls is frowned upon and punished as they grow older. This leads to an inhibition of aggressive tendencies or at least a restriction to more subtle forms of hostility (Sears, Maccoby, and Levin, 1957; Maccoby, 1966).

An example of how aggressiveness continues from childhood into adulthood is seen in the following example (Kagan and Moss, 1962):

At seven years:
An impetuous, irresponsible child with lack of judgment and often purposely mean and malicious. He likes to bust up constructive activities of others with destructive and violent acts. He was noisy most of the time and, in any group, would disrupt its organization. He was rather infantile in these destructive activities. He cried easily, was easily frustrated, and would kick up a crying tantrum when he didn't get his way.

At eleven years:
S's [subject's] play was of a blustering, aggressive sort with little quiet persistence in it. He liked active games, easy activities with quick success, lots of noise and action. He appeared to like "baiting" the adults; he liked daring authorities by a slim balance more than the actual end product. He liked to run wild in the yard and did this most of the time with an abandoned sort of violent physical effort. S had a loud voice, grunted and groaned and sang at the top of his voice. He had no real group cooperative play. He showed off, clowned a lot, and initiated a lot of aggressive play with other boys.

Excerpts from an interview at age 27:
E: "Can you remember the last time you were mildly irritated at anyone?"
S: "I get irritated at drivers every day. I'm driving in traffic — there's usually some idiot that wants to pull out in front of you or something like that. I'm inclined to get too upset about things like that and be criticized for blowing-up like that."
E: "What do you tend to do if you come home at night and your wife is irritated with you?"
S: "Well — that depends on the mood I'm in. Sometimes I'll blow up. Generally, I get too obnoxious and get to feeling guilty and try to smooth things over."

E: "What do you tend to do when someone insults you?"
S: "If somebody gets to insulting me, I insult them right back."

Kagan and Moss found that the continuity of aggressive behavior from childhood to adulthood was particularly evident in males. Another case illustrates this point:

> Subject 1650 was examined at 3½ yrs. of age and had a spell of uncontrolled rage. When the doctor tried to get near him he screamed and held his breath. In his early years in school S was unusually destructive and violent. He gradually gave up holding his breath when he got irritated, but he was easily angered and provoked. When he was 8 he was observed to take some baby birds from a nest and torture them. In his preadolescent years his outbursts of temper continued and he was highly resistant to being interviewed by adults. At 12 he was a rough-house when playing with other boys but was rebellious and openly resentful toward adults. In his twenties he remained easily angered and frustrated, and often verbally attacked his wife, child, and strangers. He felt that being tough and aggressive was the only way to get anywhere in the world and that hate and power strivings were basic qualities of human nature.

CULTURE AND THE FAMILY

In a broader sense, the developmental process becomes the socialization process through which children grow up internalizing and finally practicing approved cultural norms. The importance of this socialization process is evident from the variety of attitudes about aggressive behavior found in different cultures. Many subtle (and not-so-subtle) distinctions in social norms relate to situations when aggressive behavior is or is not appropriate, against whom it may be directed, by whom, and with what intensity. Benedict (1934) points out that the Aztecs fought wars only to obtain captives for religious sacrifices. They were therefore ill-prepared to fight the Spaniards who fought in order to kill and to conquer. Benedict tried to discuss warfare with the Mission Indians of California but was unsuccessful because the entire concept was so alien to their culture that they couldn't understand what she meant. Similarly, in many societies the killing of a baby is a serious offense, but in others the first two children are killed by custom. Sometimes children are expected to kill their parents when they get old, but in other cultures this would be regarded as a capital crime. Killing one's wife or causing accidental death may be treated very lightly or very punitively. In some cultures, children are killed for being born on Wednesday, cutting their upper teeth first, or stealing a fowl.

Many primitive tribes are quite peaceful, even if they are skilled hunters and weapon-makers, and bravery and aggressiveness are not always admired traits. In tribes which do sanction killing, it is usually only that outsiders can be killed without the act being considered murder. Even head-hunters may have very strict norms about in-group fighting, but when head-hunting there are no inhibitions and the victim may be a woman or child, just as long as she is from another tribe (Mead, 1963). Violence against outsiders may be sanctioned in a number of cultures whether it be in New Guinea, Pakistan, or Mississippi. Sometimes "outsiders" means anyone other than the immediate family, as in the case of a tribe referred to by Gorer (1966). In this New Guinea tribe, power and prestige were gained by killing, but the victim had to be outside the family.

In our own society, intrafamilial violence is not sanctioned, but it is surprisingly common (Bard, 1971; Shah and Weber, 1968). The Uniform Crime Reports (1969) assembled by the Federal Bureau of Investigation reveal that most aggravated assaults occur among family members, about half of these being spouse-killings. Husbands killed their wives (uxoricide) slightly more often than vice versa (54 per cent versus 46 per cent), and for men who were killed by a woman the murderess was likely to be their wife. It turns out that wives are most likely to attack in the kitchen while husbands generally prefer to kill in the bedroom (Wolfgang, 1958). About 3.7 per cent of all reported murders involve child-killing (filicide) and infant murder (infanticide); the murderer is nearly always the mother (Shah and Weber, 1968). Matricide and patricide are relatively rare, with the former being somewhat more common, the son most often being the killer. Such murders frequently involve men with powerful attachments to their mothers, and often the killing is precipitated by a trivial cause. Each year about 700 children kill someone, with about one-third of the victims being other family members. Much more frequent than intrafamilial murder is child abuse and neglect (the battered child syndrome). Such abuse is statistically more common in lower socioeconomic families; however, this may be partly due to the fact that wealthier families can more easily conceal intrafamilial quarrels than those more closely connected with public agencies (e.g., welfare).

It is clear that violence within the family is all too common, and this may be both the result and the cause of weakened family structure. The family is the cornerstone of human society, and patterns of behavior established in childhood and adolescence make an important contribution to adult social behavior. Nearly all children have the potential to engage in violent and destructive behavior and at one time or another nearly all children make a reality out of this capacity. The degree to which such behavior is augmented, redirected, or diminished depends to a great extent on how it is dealt with by the parents. To some, the problem of violence in contemporary society is a reflection of a loss in solidarity of the family structure (Campbell and Shoham, 1970). Marital conflicts and divorce are more common than ever, both parents now spend more time outside the home, and television fills the void. Young people find it easier to become attached to peer groups and various subcultures, thus widening the gap between the generations. Parents sometimes react by becoming more rigid and impatient and by attempting to control behavior with punishment and "discipline." Adults preach traditional virtues but fail to practice them, thereby providing inadequate and dysfunctional role models. All things considered, the stability of family life is an important factor in the normal development of the child, and the strengthening of family life may go a long way toward reducing delinquent and antisocial behavior in children (Monahan, 1957).

But no one really knows the best model to follow for child rearing practices, and it is likely that no single pattern would be best for everyone. Different rearing habits may have the same result, and similar rearing practices may have entirely different results, depending on a host of other interacting factors. Parents may unwittingly reward aggressive behavior, overpunish aggressive behavior, fail to punish aggressive behavior, inconsistently punish aggressive behavior, unwittingly provoke aggressive behavior, respond aggressively to provocations, become aggressive models, and become threatening and rejecting. Certainly developmental experience influences adult aggressive behavior, for, as Wordsworth put it, "The Child is father of the Man." But infantile experiences do not completely determine adult behavior patterns. Children quickly reach the point where they are no longer easily "trained," but this training, combined with examples set by the parents, continues to modify behavior well into maturity (Berkowitz, 1964). The following chapter will take up the question of learning, particularly social learning, and how it relates to aggression.

5 LEARNING THEORY AND AGGRESSION

Learning has always played a central role in scientific psychology, and it is not surprising that most theoretical analyses of human aggression place special emphasis on learning. Experimental and social psychologists have found this a fruitful approach; however, Feshbach (1971) points out that the contributions may be more an illumination of ways to conceptualize aggressive phenomena than to account for them. Chapter 1 described many of the conceptual problems in dealing with aggressive behavior and stressed that difficulties with adequate definitions stem from that fact that aggression is not a unitary concept. Thus, we find that learning theory can be applied to some types of aggressive behavior but not to others. For those which do lend themselves to a learning analysis, different types of conditioning and learning principles best fit different types of aggressive behavior. When aggression is viewed as a learned habit, it is possible to subject it to a behavioral analysis just like any other habit. Buss (1961), for example, describes the habit strength of aggression in terms of: (a) the antecedents of aggression, such as the number of previous fights or provocations; (b) the history of reinforcement for aggression, that is, the frequency and intensity of reward or punishment which followed aggressive acts; (c) social facilitation, including cultural norms about the expression of hostility and aggression; (d) temperament or personality characteristics such as permissiveness, impulsiveness, independence, frustration-tolerance, and so on. Contemporary formulations borrow concepts from classical and instrumental conditioning, reinforcement theory, and social learning theory — ideas which were first put to use by learning theorists in the frustration-aggression hypothesis.

THE FRUSTRATION-AGGRESSION HYPOTHESIS

From a theoretical point of view, the social psychological analysis of aggression began in earnest with the publication of the classic monograph, *Frustration and Aggression* (Dollard, et al., 1939). The authors borrowed some of their ideas from Freud but attempted to formulate them in a testable manner. They rejected the idea of a death wish or aggressive instinct and instead linked aggressive behavior to motivational antecedents — namely, incidences of frustration. For several decades the frustration-aggression hypothesis was the focal point of psychological studies on aggression, but while much research was generated, it was constantly plagued by circularity and by definitional problems. The presence of frustration was taken to mean that subsequent behavior was likely to be aggressive, and the presence of aggression was used as evidence that the preceding experience had been frustrating.

In attempting to gain independent measures of each term, it was soon discovered that defining frustration was even more difficult than defining aggression, and perhaps as a result most theorists concentrated on the problem of frustration at the expense of aggression. As time passed, psychologists gradually realized that both frustration and aggression are far too complex to be "explained" by any single theory. Today, the frustration-aggression hypothesis is more of an interesting historical document than a definitive statement about aggression. Nevertheless, considerable contemporary theorizing on the subject finds its roots in this classical hypothesis.

Originally, it was stated that "the frustration-aggression hypothesis assumes a universal causal relation between frustration and aggression" and that "aggression is always a consequence of frustration." This rather strong position was soon liberalized (Miller, 1941) to mean that aggression is the *dominant* response to frustration and that it is really an *instigation* rather than aggression itself which is aroused. For some, these concessions were taken to mean that aggression had other causes, and that frustration might have other effects. The "instigation" clause could mean that frustration elicited an instigation to aggression which sometimes failed to get translated into overt aggression. Another important qualification (Miller, 1941) was that the relation between frustration and aggression was not necessarily innate and could be learned. The idea that aggression could be a learned response had some novelty at the time, although now, of course, it is routinely accepted. As originally formulated, aggression was a function of: (a) the strength of instigation to the frustrated response; (b) the amount of interference with the response; and (c) the number of frustrated responses. As Berkowitz (1958) pointed out, most research has concentrated on inhibition, displacement, and catharsis rather than on how aggressive responses are learned and maintained.

A few examples may help illustrate the flavor of the theory. In an early experiment (Barker, Dembo, and Lewin, 1941), children were led to a playroom containing many attractive and desirable toys. But they were not allowed into the room and instead could only look at the toys through a window (i.e., frustration). A nonfrustration control group was allowed immediate access to the toys, and finally both groups could play in the room. Observers recorded the constructiveness of play of the two groups, and noted that the frustrated group frequently smashed toys and was much more destructive. By comparison, the nonfrustrated control group was much more quiet and constructive in their play.

Another study (Haner and Brown, 1955) manipulated frustration by promising children a prize for successfully pushing marbles through holes in a board. If the subjects failed to do so within a certain time period, they had to depress a plunger and start all over again. The strength of the plunger response could be measured easily, and this response served as the dependent variable for assessing aggression. It was found that the closer they were to finishing and getting the prize when they failed, the harder they pushed on the plunger. In a similar experiment, Olds (1953) trained children to crank a machine to get poker chips which could be exchanged for toys. When the number of turns needed to get a chip was increased, the force on the crank increased; when the number of required turns was decreased, the force was also decreased. Thus, making the task more difficult and frustrating energized their cranking behavior.

Studies from "real life" have also been used to support the frustration-aggression hypothesis. Hovland and Sears (1940) correlated the lynching of Negroes in the South with measures of economic prosperity during the years 1882 to 1930. They found that the number of lynchings was inversely related to the price of cotton: during prosperity, the price of cotton was high and lynchings were few. But in hard times (i.e., frustration), lynchings were more common. This widely quoted finding illustrates the application of frustration-aggression theory, but it should not be taken too literally (some have claimed the effect is a statistical artifact). A somewhat similar experiment (Feierabend and Feierabend, 1966) was carried out to explore the relationship between political stability and public frustrations. Political stability in different countries was independently rated on a seven-point scale, and frustration was estimated by examining the literacy rate, the number of calories in the average diet, the gross national product, the per cent of urbanization, and the number of radios, telephones, newspapers, and physicians. It was found that political instability tended to accompany high degrees of "frustration."

Prejudice may also be a form of aggression produced by frustration. Miller and Bugelski (1948) played a trick on a number of young men working at a camp. The subjects were led to look forward to a big night in town, but when the time arrived they had to take a tedious and difficult test instead. A scale was devised to measure their attitudes towards Mexicans and Japanese both before they were frustrated and after they were frustrated. It was found that subjects reported more undesirable traits and fewer desirable traits following the test, thus indicating that in this situation frustration increased hostility toward foreigners who had nothing to do with the problem.

While these and many other examples show that frustration can lead to aggression, they do not prove the theory, for proof rests on an adequate definition of each term. For example, a failure to elicit aggression in the testing situation might be attributed to inadequate frustration; or, more commonly, whenever aggression appeared it could be claimed that components of frustration could be found in the preceding events. Frustration was originally conceived as a blocking or thwarting of a goal response; however, later theories emphasized such things as internal arousal (Brown and Farber, 1951), the arbitrariness of rewards (Pastore, 1952), and the absence of reward following a history of reward (Amsel, 1958). In Amsel's frustration effect, animals were trained to run down a double runway with a goal box at the end of each runway. When running times had stabilized, Amsel systematically withheld reward from the first goal box (in order to "frustrate" the animal) and then measured running speed to the second goal box. It was found that frustrating lack of reward had an energizing effect in that the animals ran faster after they "expected" reward but did not get it. This energizing effect of frustration has been found with many species, including fish (Gonzalez, 1970), and with many types of rewards, including brain stimulation (Johnson, Lobdell, and Levy, 1969).

It may be fair to conclude that frustration can be manipulated in the laboratory, and that increased frustration may produce faster or more vigorous responding. But does this shed any light on the problem of aggression? In some experiments aggression has been a dependent variable. For example, Azrin, Hutchinson, and Hake (1966) demonstrated that aggression could be produced in pigeons as a result of experimental extinction. In this procedure pigeons learned to peck a key for food reward, but when the experimenter disconnected the feeding mechanism, pigeons would turn and attack another pigeon. Such attacks would not take place if the trained pigeon was no longer hungry, or if the food could be seen but not eaten. In order to obtain this extinction-induced aggression it appears that the subject has to be actively responding for food and consuming it when food delivery is terminated.

The endless and seemingly fruitless search for a valid conception of frustration (Lawson, 1965) sidetracked many from the original problem of aggression, and frequently it was argued that frustration leads to displacement, fixation, regression, and so on. In the Barker, Dembo, and Lewin (1941) experiment cited above, the frustrated children were both more destructive (aggressive) and less constructive (regressive in the sense of reverting to a more primitive form of play). Regression rather than aggression has also been argued from experiments with rats (Mowrer, 1940). But whatever frustration leads to, it is neither the only nor the fastest path to aggression. Buss (1961) has pointed out that threats and attack can elicit stronger aggressive responses than frustration. In the long run, the frustration-aggression hypothesis contains considerable truth, but it is too simple and too sweeping (Berkowtiz, 1969b), and its contribution to the understanding of aggression is at best limited.

CLASSICAL CONDITIONING AND AGGRESSION

The frustration-aggression model involves a stimulus-response analysis in which aggression is considered a response to a stimulus situation (frustration). Other stimulus-response models have been offered, most notably the pain-aggression model (Ulrich and Azrin, 1962), more fully described in Chapter 1. This model treats aggression as a response to painful stimuli; in behavioral conditioning terms, pain is an unconditional stimulus (UCS) and aggression is an unconditional response (UCR). In Pavlov's classic experiments with dogs, the UCS is the meat powder and the UCR is the salivation. The UCR is considered to be a reflexive response to the UCS. We know that associating a neutral stimulus (CS) with the UCS-UCR reflex results in a learned or conditioned response (CR) which eventually will be evoked by the conditioned stimulus alone. Vernon and Ulrich (1966) applied this classical conditioning paradigm to pain-elicited aggression (Table 1). If fighting (UCR) is considered a reflexive response to a UCS (painful foot-shock),

TABLE 1. THE CLASSICAL CONDITIONING OF AGGRESSION

(1)	CS (tone) ——— · O (neutral)	
	UCS (shock) ——— · UCR (fighting)	
(2)	CS ———UCS——— · UCR	
(3)	CS ———· CR (fighting)	

a neutral tone (CS) should elicit fighting (CR) after many pairings with shock, and this is what eventually happens. Using the same classical conditioning paradigm, Siamese fighting fish can be conditioned to emit a threat display to an arbitrary neutral stimulus (Adler and Hogan, 1963).

These experiments demonstrate that in principle certain kinds of aggression can be classically conditioned. But when it comes to humans, there are no unlearned, reflexive aggressive responses, and the classical conditioning model, if appropriate at all, becomes more subtle. For example, Berkowitz (1970) argues that aggressive behavior sometimes functions like a conditioned response to situational stimuli, particularly when environmental cues may combine with states of internal excitation to produce impulsive aggressive reactions. When this happens, aggression may come to resemble a conditioned response to situational stimuli, and the behavior more closely fits a classical conditioning model than other learning paradigms. To illustrate this effect, Berkowitz and LePage (1967) arranged a situation in which subjects were instructed to play the role of an experimenter trying to teach others to learn a task. When their subjects made mistakes, the experimenter (i.e., the subject) administered punishment in the form of electric shock. In the experimental condition, a gun or rifle was placed on a nearby table, and in the control condition these weapons were absent. The gun thus served as situational cue, and it was discovered that the experimenters (i.e., the subjects) punished their subjects more severely (by applying more intense electric shock) when guns were present compared to when they were absent.

In the Berkowitz and LePage experiment, guns facilitated aggressive behavior, presumably because of their well-ingrained association with violence and bloodshed. But aggression-eliciting stimuli need not have well-established previous associations, for such associations can be rapidly acquired. Berkowitz and Geen (1966) demonstrated this by linking the name of a stranger to an unsavory film character. In the first stage of this experiment, a stooge acted as experimenter and evaluated the performance of his subjects by administering electric shock to them for poor work. Following this, some subjects saw film clips of the movie *Champion* in which Kirk Douglas takes a beating in a boxing match. Control subjects saw a neutral film of a foot race. When the movies were over the subjects returned to take their turns playing the experimenter who doled out electric shocks. Each group was again subdivided so that for half of the subjects the stooge was referred to as "Bob," while for the remaining subjects his name was "Kirk." The main dependent variable was the number of shocks the subjects (playing experimenter) administered to the stooges. The results showed that subjects who had been angered by being shocked in the first stage of the experiment and who had seen the boxing film, were significantly more punitive toward stooges named "Kirk" than to stooges named "Bob." Thus, aggressive behavior was heightened by (a) prior anger, (b) observing aggression, and (c) associating the stooge with the person in the film.

In another similar experiment (Berkowitz, 1965) the following variables were manipulated: (a) anger was manipulated either by insulting subjects or by treating them in a neutral fashion; (b) observation of aggression was manipulated by showing either the Kirk Douglas flick or a boring travelog about Marco Polo; (c) association with the movie was manipulated by labeling the stooges as either physical education majors or as speech majors. The results showed that subjects were more hostile if they had been insulted, regardless of which film they viewed, but most aggression spilled out if subjects thought the stooges were physical education majors. Berkowitz and Knurek (1969) further demonstrated that a person's name elicited stronger aggressive behavior if his name had been previously paired with unpleasant words.

Classical conditioning experiments seem clearly to implicate the role of stimulus associations in some types of human aggression. Although the experimental evidence is gathered in the laboratory under highly contrived conditions, the value of the work is that the variables operating can be carefully controlled and specified and the changes in aggressive behavior measured objectively. If significant changes take place in such sterile laboratory surroundings, what can we reasonably expect from the real threats and provocations of everyday life? The principle of association through contiguity which is the basis of classical conditioning is commonly seen in situations involving persuasion and attitude change. Politicians stumble over each other in their eagerness to be associated with motherhood, apple pie, and the flag. They are equally enthusiastic about being linked with sure causes, such as opposing child beating, pornography, atheism, and people who don't take baths. The charge of being "soft on Communism" still evokes a knee-jerk reflex from much of the population, and in

Communist countries the thought of capitalism is still strongly associated with decadence and war-mongering.

A consideration of the classical conditioning of aggression does not necessarily mean that aggressive behavior is a rigidly controlled response to a particular cue, for stimulus and response generalization are assumed to take place. Thus, a class of stimuli may become associated with a class of responses, and the strength of the associations will vary systematically along generalization gradients as a function of the conditions under which the learning took place. For example, semantic generalization of hostile meaning takes place as measured by GSR (galvanic skin response), an indication of autonomic arousal (Lang, Geer, and Hnatiow, 1963). Associations can also be developed for eliciting nonaggressive behavior as well as aggressive behavior. Scott (1958, 1958a) reports that picking dogs up from an early age teaches them to associate helplessness with being lifted. With such training, even aggressive terriers stop fighting as soon as they are picked up. Berkowitz (1970) has reviewed much of the research on the learning of aggressive behavior and he concludes that the classical conditioning model best fits many (but not all) types of human aggression, particularly those impulsive kinds of violence which are influenced by situational cues. The principle of association is also important in social learning and modeling behavior, as we shall see in a later section. But before turning to social learning, it is appropriate to examine another important learning model, that of instrumental conditioning.

AGGRESSION AND INSTRUMENTAL BEHAVIOR

In the animal kingdom, purposeless fighting is rare, and much social conflict is an elaboration of defensive behavior (Scott, 1966). Animals will fight to defend their territory, their mates, or their status, but fighting ceases when appeasements are offered or threats are withdrawn. Even predatory killing ceases if animals are not hungry and food is abundant. In this case potential meals may be tolerated by "natural enemies." Thus, nearly all animal aggression is instrumental in character. It is goal-directed, but the goal is absence of competition rather than injury to an opponent.

If certain types of aggression are instrumental in character, then they should be under the control of positive and negative reinforcement (reward and punishment). This is easy to demonstrate in the laboratory by shocking rats and then turning off the electric current when they begin to fight (Miller, 1948). Fighting now becomes instrumental to pain avoidance, and the termination of shock acts as a reward. As a result, fighting tends to increase. Similarly, mice can be trained to fight by matching them with a restrained mouse which has difficulty fighting back. The "free" mouse soon becomes encouraged and rewarded by his "success" and develops the habit of attacking all mice, including females and young mice with which he ordinarily would not fight (Scott, 1958a).

Humans may respond in a similar fashion. In 1969 there were over six and one-half times as many crimes against property as there were crimes against persons (Uniform Crime Reports, 1969). Many of the property crimes involved no violence, but when violence did take place it was generally a means rather than a goal. In everyday life we often find that mildly aggressive behavior is instrumental in making a sale, defeating an opponent, and so on. A football coach usually tries to schedule a few easy opponents to build up confidence and to reward competitiveness. In times of war, governments reward citizens for fighting and dying by giving out medals, extolling bravery, and praising sacrifice. In the laboratory, studies have shown that humans may become more aggressive if aggressive behavior is rewarded. Geen and Pigg (1970) carried out an experiment in which college students played the role of teacher by operating an "aggression machine" (Buss, 1961). The procedure used involves elaborate deceptions in which the subject is led to believe that he is the experimenter, while the subject he is supposed to be experimenting upon is really nonexistent. The subject, as experimenter, is supposed to teach a task to another by electrically shocking him for mistakes. But the fake subject is the real experimenter who makes sure that no one ever gets shocked and that the fake subject appears to make mistakes and to absorb punishment. In any case, one group of subjects (experimenters) in Geen and Pigg's experiment was verbally praised for administering punishment while another group was not. It was discovered that (a) reinforced subjects delivered more frequent shocks at higher intensities, and (b) subjects praised for being aggressive later emitted more aggressive words on a word association test. In a somewhat similar experiment, Loew (1967) rewarded college students for making hostile remarks, and later found that rewarded subjects were more punitive toward others compared to a control group which was reinforced for verbalizing nonaggressive words. It has also been found that if children are rewarded for making hostile remarks they are more likely to select toys which have aggressive functions (Lovaas, 1961).

Another aspect of instrumental aggressive behavior in humans involves self-esteem. Often manliness is equated with pride and self-esteem, as in the traditional warrior definition of masculinity. By putting down others one demonstrates status and power, but being put down represents a significant blow to one's self-esteem. Feshbach (1970; 1971) has argued that humiliation and threats to self-esteem may be among the most powerful elicitors of aggressive behavior in humans. No one likes to be humiliated, and most people feel that retaliation is instrumental in patching an injured pride. It should be noted that if aggression is instrumental and is maintained by reward, it should be possible to modify this behavior by removing the reward and substituting punishment. This kind of behavior modification treatment for aggressive behavior will be discussed in Chapter 7.

Is Aggression Reinforcing?

Rather than a means to an end, it is sometimes argued that aggression is an end in itself and serves as its own reinforcement. A number of experiments have been carried out with animals to see if killing can be considered a goal in itself rather than instrumental behavior for some other goal. This is generally done by observing whether a response will be learned which provides an opportunity to attack and kill. Myer (1964) found that some rats, if given the opportunity, will continue to attack and kill mice even though they are given no conventional reinforcement for doing so. If placed in a T-maze with mice in one goal box and baby rats in the other, mouse-killing rats will choose the arm of he maze where they can attack a mouse, while non-mouse-killers prefer the company of baby rats (Myer and White, 1965). The opportunity to attack a mouse can also be used to teach rats a spatial discrimination and a reversal (Tellegen, Horn, and LeGrand, 1969). If monkeys are given a painful tail shock, they will learn to perform a response which gives them access to a canvas ball they can attack (Azrin, Hutchinson, and McLaughlin, 1965). Rats given inescapable electric shock will choose the arm of a T-maze containing another rat with which they can fight (Dreyer and Church, 1970), and cats under the influence of hypothalamic stimulation will seek out a rat to attack (Roberts and Kiess, 1964). Fighting fish (Thompson, 1963) and fighting cocks (Thompson, 1964) will perform an operant response in order to be rewarded with visual exposure to a conspecific. (A more complete discussion of the behavior of fighting fish, including alternative explanations, is given in Chapter 1.)

It is also possible to shape lever- and key-pressing responses in a Skinner box using a live mouse as reinforcement (Van Hemel, 1970). Rats will perform operant responses for the reward of killing mice (Van Hemel and Myer, 1970) or frogs (Huston, DeSisto, and Meyer, 1969) with little apparent satiation, although some experimenters have reported evidence of satiation (Kulkarni, 1968). In an operant situation, killing latencies decrease with practice, just as with conventional reinforcers, and prior killing experience makes such behavior more resistant to the suppressive effects of punishment (Myer, 1967).

Whether aggression is rewarding for its own sake is a more difficult question to answer than might be supposed, for it is necessary to show that killing is not instrumental. It is possible that some animals kill because they "enjoy" killing, but it is also possible that they are defending a quasi-territory, killing defensively because they feel cornered or threatened, or responding to the possibility of a tastier meal than Purina lab chow. The reinforcement may come, not from killing, but from the cessation of distracting stimuli or from the removal of a potential competitor. Killing might also be the result of being trapped in a foreign environment such as a Skinner box where nearly everything is irrelevant to the natural behavior of the animal. It might also be a neurotic reaction resulting from abnormal rearing conditions (e.g., isolated cages).

While some experimenters have tried to show that aggression is rewarding in animals, others have tried to show that "altruism" is rewarding. Rice and Gainer (1962) suspended rats in the air, and found that other rats would learn to press a bar which would lower the distressed rat. Lavery and Foley (1963) argued that the effect might be due to arousal rather than altruism, for rats will learn to make a response which will terminate either distress calls or white noise. Greene (1969) found that rats would rescue a conspecific in distress only if the rescuer himself had previously experienced the distress (e.g., electric shock).

On the other side of the coin, animals will sometimes not only fail to rescue, but may actively torment a conspecific in distress. Mice, termites, and piranha fish are known to attack and kill conspecifics which are injured. In the laboratory, Sidowski (1970) strapped a monkey to a cross to see if other monkeys would aid the helpless victim. At first the other monkeys withdrew, but later they ignored the obvious distress of the "crucified" monkey and began to pull his hair, gouge his eyes, and lick his genitals. It should be noted that the animals in this experiment were partially isolated or totally isolated from birth and, unfortunately, no control group of normal monkeys was tested. Distress experiments may not be critical tests of altruism, for they are usually carried out in an artificial social situation. A restrained animal is prevented from communicating with gestures so that other animals might feel threatened by the victim's apparent refusal to participate in rituals. Certainly an upright position on a cross easily could be mistaken for a posture of threat.

In the long run, it is doubtful that it will ever be established that animals in general are either altruistic or aggressive. Individual aggressive and helping behavior is likely to vary with social, developmental, situational, and species differences. There is some evidence that consummatory behaviors such as eating, drinking, or copulating are reinforcing in their own right, or in terms of Glickman and Schiff's (1967) model, the neural activity underlying such consummatory behavior may be reinforcing. Predatory or defensive killing may be a form of such consummatory behavior, but offensive killing for its own sake appears to be the exception, at least in nonhuman animals. Aside from a few clever laboratory demonstrations, the natural aggressive behavior of animals appears to be confined to instrumental aggression. This was stated many years ago by Craig (1928), when he said, "... Fighting is not sought nor valued for its own sake ... when an animal does fight, he aims not to destroy the enemy, but only to get rid of his presence and interference."

Do Humans Enjoy Violence?

Amateur analysts are forever speculating that people have a morbid fascination with violence. People flock to war movies, spy thrillers, and action-packed Westerns, and Hollywood considers violence as one of the keys to box office success. It is sometimes claimed that people enjoy professional football for its roughness, car races for the collisions, hockey games for the fist fights, and bull fights for the blood. Indeed, fans are not always content merely to watch the action. In Peru in 1964 a referee disallowed a goal in an Olympic soccer match and the crowd rioted. Before it was over there were 300 killed, 500 injured, and numerous buildings were destroyed. Hunters and gun enthusiasts often speak of the joy and thrill of shooting and killing. In 1968, the *American Rifleman* featured articles under the title "Happiness Is a Warm Gun."

More commonly, people do not participate in violence, but sometimes feel gratification at the injury or suffering of others.

A case in point is the public reaction to the assassination of President Kennedy and the subsequent slaying of the alleged assassin, Lee Harvey Oswald, by Jack Ruby. A surprising number of people openly admitted that they were pleased when Oswald was killed (Feshbach and Feshbach, 1965). One study found that 11 per cent of those interviewed expressed wishes that the assassin be lynched or shot (Sheatsley and Feldman, 1964). Although nearly all of the Presidential assassination attempts have involved individuals with mental disorders, these well-publicized and dramatic events tend to have a marked impact on both normal people and those who are mentally ill (Taylor and Weisz, 1970).

People do not automatically rejoice at the spilling of blood, of course, and their reaction usually depends on their moral preconceptions about the justifiability of an act. When police attack and beat peace marchers, some elements of the population are delighted and others are furious. The killing of policemen is considered an act of cowardice by most people, but some militants regard it as an act of bravery. In the Kent State shootings, a surprising number of adults expressed satisfaction at the killing of college students, and some felt that even more should have been shot. On the other hand, those who sympathized with the students regarded the National Guard as criminals. Another incident of this sort which polarized the population was the My Lai massacre. American soldiers admitted executing unarmed prisoners, including women and children, yet many people somehow viewed the executions as entirely legitimate. A surprising number of people came to regard Lieutenant Calley as a folk hero, even though he was convicted of murder (Hero Calley, 1971). At the Nuremberg trials following World War II many of those executed as criminals had previously enjoyed roles as heroes.

Attribution theorists have pointed out that in many kinds of social conflict the attribution of violence or aggression depends more on the personal values of the beholder than on objective facts. For example, if protesting college students are portrayed as spoiled rich kids, effete snobs, or bums, their cause may be considered unworthy. At the Democratic convention riots in Chicago in 1968, many felt the police went berserk and rioted. Mayor Daley, on the other hand, claimed the police were merely restoring order. Sometimes justifications can be completely twisted so that opposite forms of behavior are legitimized. Feshbach (1970) has pointed out that many individuals defended the role of the military both at Kent State and at My Lai. It was argued that the soldiers at My Lai were not to blame because they just happened to be there when the incidents occurred. But at Kent State the students deserved to be shot *because* they happened to be present. Thus, the same reason was given to justify both innocence and guilt.

In the laboratory, only a few experiments have attempted to test whether witnessing or participating in aggression can act as a reward. In one (Feshbach, Stiles and Bitter, 1967), college coeds were first either insulted (experimental group) or treated in a friendly fashion (control group). They were then given a verbal learning task which was arranged so that, for each group, half of the subjects would be reinforced with a flash of light for a correct response while the other half was reinforced by watching someone receive electric shock. (The someone, naturally, was a stooge of the experimenter and the shock and pain were faked.) It was found that if subjects had been insulted, watching someone else get shocked served as a reinforcer in that more correct responses were made compared to when the light was the reinforcer. If subjects had not been insulted, witnessing punishment had the opposite effect and decreased performance, thus acting as a negative reinforcer. Hokanson (1970) has noted that the performance of an aggressive response sometimes reduces physiological tension. But it does not always have such a cathartic effect, and nonaggressive responses may have the same effect.

Anger, Hostility, and Drive-Mediated Aggression

The question of whether aggression in general is rewarding can be answered in the negative, but this is partly because the question is too simply formulated for a more meaningful answer. A more appropriate question is whether certain types of aggression may be rewarding in certain situations. Sometimes aggression is a goal rather than a means to a goal, and in this case it more closely resembles what Feshbach (1970; 1971) calls drive-mediated aggression. A desire to injure when injury alone is the goal might be an example of aggressive drive. It was noted earlier that Freud conceived of all aggression as reflecting this kind of destructive motivation, but as we have seen, much aggression is only instrumental to some other nonaggressive goal and is not a goal in itself. This distinction between drive-mediated aggression and instrumental aggression is important because the two types are entirely different, both functionally and dynamically. In instrumental aggression, attack and injury are not carried out for their own sake but rather in the pursuit of another goal. Drive-mediated aggression, on the other hand, usually involves expressive or affective behavior in which injury itself is an end rather than a means. Drive-mediated aggression is sometimes equated with the emotional response of anger, which is easily measured in terms of physio-logical arousal (heart rate, sweating, pupil dilation, and so forth).

Emotional factors are clearly important in aggressive behavior, for most violent crime is impulsive rather than premeditated. Berkowitz (1970) argues that in certain situations, environmental stimuli associated with aggressive reactions can be reinforcing in the sense that they may be sought out. But this may occur only if a person is already angry, and it may be difficult to tell if the re-inforcing stimuli actually elicit aggressive behavior or whether they function mainly to reduce inhibitions against expressing it. Certainly situational stimuli and emotional factors are important, for studies show that many violent attacks are provoked by the victim (Wolfgang, 1957), and conflicts with the law are often precipitated by the behavior of the police (Toch, 1969). But as Kauf-mann (1970) points out, an individual may be boiling with anger and yet show no antisocial behavior; conversely, atrocities have been committed with little or no emotional involvement. The importance of anger is that it may have drive properties which intensify aggressive behavior; however, it should not be assumed that anger is *the* drive motivating aggressive behavior (Buss, 1961). Hostility is another term frequently used, but unlike anger, it develops gradually and dissipates slowly. Hostility usually refers to a negative attitude which is learned, and some theorists (Fesh-bach, 1964) make a distinction between hostile aggression (the desire to injure) and expressive aggression (the desire to hit). In this terminology, the latter emphasizes the act and the former the result.

Unfortunately, drive and habit components are not neatly separated. Most aggressive responses are a combination of expres-sive, hostile, and instrumental components, and these functions are further obscured by inhibitory factors. Hostile drives may be learned from childhood as cultural norms, or as Sears (1958) suggests, they may be acquired through secondary reinforcement. For example, if injuring others becomes associated with removing frustrations, then feedback of pain alone may come to maintain behavior. Sometimes it is difficult to distinguish between drive-mediated aggression and instrumental aggression. For example, a person who has been insulted may lash out with verbal or physical abuse. But it is difficult to tell if this aggressive behavior is instru-mental, that is, intended to restore self-esteem, or drive-mediated, that is, intended to injure an opponent. Often the individual him-self may not understand his own motives or intentions.

The issue of intentionality has troubled theorists for many years, for resting an explanation on inscrutable mental events may weaken rather than strengthen a theory. Both Buss (1961, 1971) and Kaufmann (1965, 1970) have emphasized that human aggression is an interpersonal attack *intended* to produce injury or harm, but neither theorist is comfortable with the concept of intention. Kaufmann says that the attacker must have a subjective probability greater than zero of imparting a noxious stimulus toward some object. Buss operationally defines intent as the process of examining the stimuli antecedent to the response and its consequences.

It was noted in Chapter 1 that the psychology of aggression cannot avoid coming to grips with the problem of intention, for much injury is unintentional and therefore involves no aggression. Similarly, many aggressive attacks are intended to produce injury, and are still considered aggression even after they fail for one reason or another. It appears that traditional learning concepts involving stimulus, response, and reinforcement contingencies are not fully sufficient to account for all of human aggression. It is necessary to supplement conditioning constructs with additional factors which take into consideration cognitive, mediational, and intentional processes. The most successful integration of cognitive factors with learning constructs has come from social learning theory.

SOCIAL LEARNING THEORY
AND MODELING BEHAVIOR

Social learning and modeling theory appears to be especially relevant to human behavior, and in recent years it has emerged as one of the most fruitful approaches to the social psychology of aggression. Such behavior is also referred to as observational learning, imitation, identification, copying, role-taking, and a variety of other terms, all with subtle distinctions (Bandura, 1970). In general, modeling is a broader term since it implies more than simple response mimicry, and modeling influences can have at least three distinct effects: (a) the acquisition of new behavior, such as solving a puzzle after watching someone else learn its solution; (b) inhibitory effects, such as a reduced tendency to engage in a behavior for which others have been punished, or disinhibitory effects, such as losing a fear of elevators by watching other people successfully use them; (c) facilitation of responses already in the organism's repertoire. An easy demonstration of this is to point to the sky in a public place and watch everyone look up.

Bandura (1970) has reviewed how different theories have attempted to explain modeling behavior. For example, instinct theories going back to the turn of the century declared that there is an "innate propensity" (i.e., instinct) to imitate others. The tendency to use instincts as explanations enjoyed a short popularity; however, this approach fell into disrepute under the criticism of behavioristic psychologists who emphasized the role of learning. Some behaviorists argued that imitation is a result of associative processes while others emphasized the role of reinforcement. The later view was given impetus with the publication of Miller and Dollard's *Social Learning and Imitation* in 1941, which led to much research on the instrumental function of imitative responses. More recently, popularity has switched to social learning theory (Rotter, 1954; Bandura, 1969), which stresses cognitive functions as well as stimulus-response associations. Important to Bandura's theory is the informational function of observational learning which is controlled by attentional and retentional processes, motoric reproduction, and motivation.

Social modeling in a natural setting is difficult to study except by correlating the behavior of children with that of influential peers or elders. While this is a valuable procedure, it is plagued by uncontrolled variables which unfortunately limit the conclusions which can be reached. For this reason, most experiments have been performed under more controlled conditions in the laboratory. Sometimes these experiments resemble contrived parlor games, but nevertheless they illustrate that social modeling can take place among strangers in a single sitting, and this offers some clue as to what might be expected after decades of exposure to friends, family, or TV. As a result of extensive research, we now know that both children and adults can acquire complex behavioral patterns, emotional reactions, and a variety of attitudes through exposure to models (Bandura, 1969; Flanders, 1968).

Many experiments have been specifically directed to the question of whether aggressive behavior can be socially learned, and if so, just what factors influence modeling behavior. An example is the following experiment. Bandura and Huston (1961) arranged a game in which children watched an adult solve a problem. The adult model made many irrelevant responses including aggressive responses which were directed at a nearby doll. When the children were tested in the same game, they imitated the aggressive behavior even though it was unrelated to the solution of the problem.

In another series of experiments (Bandura, Ross, and Ross, 1961; 1963a) nursery school children were led into a room containing various playthings, including a large inflated doll looking something like a clown. The children were independently rated for their interpersonal aggressiveness before the experiment began so that they could be assigned to matched experimental groups of about equal aggressiveness. One group of children observed adult models punch and kick the doll, with half of the children watching models of the same sex and the other half watching the opposite sex. A second group observed the same events, but through a TV monitor rather than in person. A third group watched an aggressive model which was costumed as a cat. Several control groups were also employed, including one in which the adult model played nonaggressively with various playthings such as tinker toys, and another in which subjects had no previous exposure to models at all (to rule out the possibility that the playthings alone instigated aggressive behavior without any help from the model).

All children were subjected to mild frustration and then led into the playroom where observers recorded their behavior. The major findings were that exposure to aggressive models increased aggressive behavior, both verbal and physical. The extent to which children copied the behavior of the models can be seen in Figure 29, which shows how closely particular aggressive responses are learned and imitated. Further analyses revealed that watching the models on television was just as effective in increasing aggressiveness as watching them in person. When the aggressive model was dressed like a cat, it had less influence on the children.

Figure 29. *In the top row of pictures, an adult model performs various aggressive acts against a large inflated doll. Children who observe this tend to imitate such behavior (bottom two rows). (Courtesy of A. Bandura.)*

It is worth noting that the children did not always directly imitate the behavior of the model, but sometimes displayed novel aggressive behavior of their own. This indicates that the function of the model may be simply to release inhibitions. It has also been shown (Kuhn, Madsen, and Becker, 1967) that it is not necessary to frustrate the children before they are allowed to play, and that frustration may even partially disrupt rather than facilitate the influence of an aggressive model. Punishment may have unusual effects, for it can eliminate aggressive behavior toward dolls in a playing situation, but the observer may learn to apply punishment against others, or to be more discriminating and confine aggression to situations where punishment is less probable (Hollenberg and Sperry, 1950).

In other studies it has been shown that verbalizing the model's behavior increases the influence of the model (Bandura, Grusec, and Menlove, 1966) and that the presence of another person can affect the amount of imitative aggression displayed by children. In addition, the effect of the model depends to some extent on the model's perceived social power and whether the model is rewarded or punished for his aggression (Bandura, Ross, and Ross, 1963b; Bandura, 1965a). Punishment may only delay the influence of the model so that imitative behavior may show up in a safer time and place.

Stimulus characteristics also affect the strength of modeling behavior (Bandura, 1969; 1970). For example, modeling can take place to cartoon characters, although the influence is weaker than if the model is a peer. It is interesting to note that the identity of the model is also important in animal modeling behavior, for it has been shown that kittens will show faster observational learning if the model is their mother rather than a strange cat (Chester, 1969).

An important point both in experimental studies and in "real life" situations is that just where and when the effect of modeling shows up in the behavior of the observer is difficult to predict. Because of this, it is necessary to make a distinction between learning and performance in modeling behavior (Bandura, 1962; 1965). The fact that watching aggression does not immediately instigate aggression does not necessarily indicate that nothing was learned. The observer may retain what he has learned from the model and perform it at some future time, perhaps the next time he is angry. This problem often makes it difficult to evaluate social learning, for research has shown that modeling influences can be retained for many months before being performed (Hicks, 1965).

Models may also function to instill moral values and cultural stereotypes rather than to instigate a specific imitative motor response. This is illustrated by a study (Siegel, 1958) in which second-graders were exposed to a series of radio dramas about taxi cab drivers with an experimental group of children hearing episodes in which the cab drivers got into fights. A control group heard similar stories but without any violence. The children were later quizzed on their beliefs about taxi drivers in their home town, and about half of the experimental group attributed highly aggressive behavior toward all taxi drivers. Two-thirds of the control group attributed no aggressive qualities to taxi drivers and the remaining third only moderately aggressive behavior.

The choice of taxi drivers in this study was appropriate because there is no universal stereotype about them, at least among second-graders. It leads us to wonder to what extent known cultural and racial stereotypes may have been created or perpetuated

Figure 30. *Modeling behavior may be seen in "real life" situations as well as in the laboratory. (Photo by G. Cole, in Wallace, J. Psychology: A Social Science. Philadelphia, W. B. Saunders, 1971.)*

through modeling processes by the mass media. Decade after decade Hollywood movies and television shows portrayed the American Negro as being lazy and incompetent, shuffling along "Amos and Andy"-style with few redeeming qualities other than good rhythm. Stereotyped roles such as maids, chauffeurs, waiters, and shoeshine boys were generally reserved for Negroes. Roles of status and sophistication were always played by whites, even in the commercials. In the last several years this situation has improved somewhat, but this raises the more general question of the effect of the mass media in influencing behavior and attitudes.

Violence and the Mass Media

In the Presidential elections of 1968, a reporter interviewed farmers in rural Iowa and, much to his surprise, found that farmers were preoccupied with life on college campuses and crime in large cities (Kneeland, 1968). It is unlikely that such concerns stemmed from any personal experience but rather reflected the extent to which the farmers had been influenced by campaign rhetoric on TV.

A number of other stories provide more dramatic examples of media influence. On December 13, 1966 the National Broadcasting Company presented a television drama entitled "The Doomsday Flight" which concerned a hoax to blow up an airliner. Before the program was over a bomb threat had been telephoned to one airline, and within 24 hours there were four more, a highly unusual number of hoaxes, not easily dismissed as mere coincidence (Gould, 1966). A rerun of the show appeared on Montreal television on July 26, 1971, and a few days later a BOAC 747 with 379 persons aboard was threatened shortly after leaving Montreal. The bomb scare closely followed the movie script, with an anonymous caller insisting that the bomb would go off at 5000 feet. (The airliner was diverted to Denver, which has an altitude of 5339 feet.) Subsequently the Federal Aviation Administration wrote to 500 television stations and asked them to refrain from showing the film (FAA, 1971).

Following the mass murders by Richard Speck in Chicago and Charles Whitman at the University of Texas there was a rash of shootings which may have been instigated by these events. In one multiple shooting, a high school boy claimed that he got the idea from Speck and Whitman (Berkowitz, 1970). In fact, analyses of violent crime rates indicate that there is often a significant rise following some widely publicized tragedy. In the bloody Sharon Tate murders, Susan Atkins testified that the reason for the murders was to remove suspicion from Robert Beausoleil, who had been arrested in connection with a previous murder actually committed by Miss Atkins. By committing more murders she thought the police would decide they were holding the wrong man and release Robert Beausoleil. The idea apparently was inspired by a movie on television: "I saw a movie on television like that once. They arrested a man and then there were eight more killings before police realized they had the wrong man." (Neumeyer, 1971).

For many years society has condoned gangster comics, war toys, and horror movies, perhaps because no one could prove any direct ill effects. But in the past few years television and the press have mushroomed into a highly competitive and effective industry which now saturates the public as never before. Crimes and even wars are graphically portrayed every day in nearly everyone's living room. Television has dramatically altered political campaigns, conventions, and even voting patterns, and it may be affecting personal values just as much. Because of its influence on the lives of nearly everyone, television has become enormously wealthy and powerful. The Presidential commission which studied violence and the mass media specifically pointed out that commercial television is one of the most profitable industries in the world (Baker and Ball, 1969); its lobbyists, therefore, wield vast influence.

Media spokesmen argue that they are only doing their job and giving the public what it wants. Violence (referred to as "action") is dwelled upon, they claim, because people are attracted to violence. This may be true, but is it partly a *result* of watching television? Television executives deny that television has such an influence, but such denials have a distinctly hollow ring, because the television industry is supported and maintained by two and a half billion dollars a year from an enthusiastic advertising industry. The paradox, of course, is that billions are poured into advertising by private business because of the firm conviction that values and behavior can be influenced by television. If commercials can change behavior, why can't the programs? Why do politicians and movie stars struggle so hard for television exposure? If the sales of X deodorant or Y toothpaste go up as a result of viewing habits, what are people "buying" with constant exposure to violence? Are our media an unwitting "school for delinquency?" (Berkowitz, 1962).

Needless to say, the social impact of the mass media is a heated issue, and all too many critics are eager to leap to conclusions without adequate evidence and to blame the media for nearly every category of evil. We know for sure that the effects of observing violence are complex, and anyone seeking a simple answer is likely to be disappointed. It is almost impossible to prove that any particular crime was "caused" by watching a movie or television show. It is even more difficult to prove that it was not. Still more difficult to assess is the effect on personality and character, for television may have detrimental social effects not directly related to causing crime. Even if watching violence does not cause normal people to become criminals, how does it affect their attitude toward tolerance of violence by others? Are they more likely to approve of violence as an acceptable way of solving problems, whether it be by the police, by the Pentagon, or by political radicals? Does repeated exposure to violence brutalize people and make them insensitive to genuine suffering? Does society pay a price when the media fails to emphasize the finer aspects of civilization?

Feshbach and Singer (1971) discuss such questions in a recent book on television aggression. They point out that logically, television violence could (a) have no discernible effect; (b) reduce aggressive tendencies through catharsis; (c) increase aggressive-

Figure 31. Watching violence may neither reduce feelings of hostility nor turn people into hardened criminals. But it may have a brutalizing effect, so that individuals become insensitive to suffering while also accepting violence carried out by others. Above, Chicago police hassle student demonstrators. (Courtesy of United Press International.)

ness. If aggression is affected, it could be due to (a) specific or general learning; (b) a generalized arousal of passions; (c) reduction of inhibitions. The variables which could influence the effect of watching violent acts seem endless: the amount of violence observed, the quality of violence observed, the dramatic context, the personal qualities of the aggressor, the justifiability of the aggression, whether the act of aggression is "successful," whether it is rewarded or punished, the relation to previously witnessed aggression, the emotional state of the beholder, the personality of the beholder, the age, sex, and intelligence of the beholder, the beholder's opportunities and expectancies about the consequences, and many more. It seems safe to say that the question has genuine complexities, complexities which are not likely to be disposed of in a few "crucial" experiments.

The Content of Television Programs

A good way to start examining this issue is by documenting the kinds of violence depicted by the media and their frequency. Television has received special attention because it is potentially the most influential of the media, and numerous attempts have been made to catalog the contents of television programs. The most recent study was carried out for a report entitled *Violence and the Media* (Baker and Ball, 1969) in conjunction with the National Commission on the Causes and Prevention of Violence. During prime viewing hours in the first week of October in 1967 and again in 1968, detailed accounts were taken of all programs on the three major networks. Some of the findings were the following:

(a) Violence occurred in eight out of ten programs;

(b) Violence occurred in 93.5 per cent of all cartoons directed at children;

(c) More than half of the major characters were violent;

(d) The "good guys" committed as much violence as the "bad guys;"

(e) The pain and suffering accompanying violence is rarely shown;

(f) For every bystander who attempted to prevent violence there was another who assisted or encouraged it;

(g) Nearly half of the killers suffered no consequences from their acts;

(h) The majority of Americans interviewed believe that there is too much violence on television.

The report was relatively critical of the television industry, and went on to speculate about norms which might be drawn from watching TV:

(a) Violence is more likely to be committed by minority groups and foreigners;

(b) Strangers shouldn't be trusted, for they are responsible for most violence;

(c) White people do not get killed as often as nonwhite people;

(d) Law enforcement officials are frequently violent;

(e) Violence and killing are usually clean and painless;

(f) Apathy is the usual reaction to violence;

(g) Violence often goes unpunished;

(h) Good people as well as bad people often resort to violence;

(i) Violence is usually a successful means to an end.

The Catharsis Hypothesis

There can be little question about whether television contains excessive violence, although in the past year or two it has been toned down a little. The real question is what effect, if any, this has on the viewer. Sometimes it is argued that observing violence actually reduces rather than increases aggressive tendencies. For example, hostile fantasies may be aroused, but they in turn evoke fear of retaliation and feelings of guilt which may lead to the inhibition of aggression. A more standard argument is that of the catharsis hypothesis, which suggests that vicarious participation in aggression provides the viewer with a harmless outlet with which to dissipate aggressive impulses.

The idea of catharsis can be traced to the early days of the classic Greek theater in which the purpose of great drama was not just to tell a good story, but to get the audience emotionally involved in a moral dilemma. According to Aristotle's *Poetics* there were certain key ingredients to great tragedy, including the underlying nobility of character which contributes to an almost inevitable tragic downfall. The audience grasps the philosophical and moral struggle and suffers along with characters like Oedipus. Death becomes the embodiment of some great principle, and by the end the audience has gone through a catharsis which leaves their emotions drained.

Few people dispute the cathartic effect of great tragedy, but when was the last time anyone saw great tragedy on television? Instead we are swamped with shallow pseudo-dramas which Newton Minow (former chairman of the Federal Communications Commission) politely called a "vast wasteland." Others call it pure garbage. What the public sees on television bears no resemblance to the dramatic principles of tragedy and catharsis.

We see callous heroes who live by violence, suffer very little, represent no principles, and get rewarded in the end.

The question remains whether a more corrupted concept of catharsis may still operate, one which simply refers to the reduction of hostile tendencies after participating in real or fantasied aggression. Freud believed that emotional expression provides an outlet for stored up aggressive "instincts," and many later psychoanalysts thought that a regular "draining" of the emotions was beneficial and even therapeutic. Some advocate that children be encouraged to engage in hostile play in order to provide an outlet for the natural "need" to express aggression.

There is little scientific evidence which supports the value of such cathartic therapy, and there is some which suggests that in the long run it may have the opposite effect. Participating in destructive play may exhaust a child and temporarily render him less aggressive, but what has the child learned? If he is encouraged and rewarded for being aggressive, he is more likely to be aggressive in the future. If he sees adult models participating in or condoning aggression, the modeling influences may teach him to have fewer inhibitions against fighting. If carried to an extreme, the catharsis hypothesis becomes ludicrous. Kaufmann (1970) points out that if it really worked we should require all children to be maximally exposed to violence and bloodshed in an effort to *reduce* crime and delinquency. In the same vein, we should be able to *reduce* sexual desire by exposure to erotic stimuli; perhaps a starving man would feel less hungry if he were teased with pictures of filet mignon and caviar.

The great faith in the catharsis hypothesis is somewhat surprising in view of the paucity of experimental evidence which supports it. In one experiment (Rosenbaum and DeCharms, 1960) it was shown that if subject B attacks subject A, and the attacker (B) is then punished by subject C, the original victim (A) will then be less aggressive compared to the situation in which the attacker (B) goes unpunished. The problem with this kind of experiment is that a reduction in hostility toward someone who has been punished might be a result of guilt feelings rather than catharsis.

A more complex experiment offering limited support for the catharsis hypothesis was one in which a mild reduction in hostility took place when victimized subjects were able to experience vicariously some suffering of their attacker that was unrelated to the provocation (Bramel, Taub, and Blum, 1968). In this experiment, college students began in the usual manner by being abused and insulted by an obnoxious experimenter. Through a series of elaborate deceptions, the first experimenter departed and was replaced by another, who then played tapes of people experiencing hallucinogenic drugs. By a contrived coincidence, the person in the recording was none other than—guess who?—the obnoxious experimenter. In one condition, subjects heard their tormenter in states of agony and suffering. Other subjects heard him responding neutrally or in apparent euphoria. Subjects then rated their own mood, their attitude toward the first experimenter, and their overall interest in the experiment. The results indicated that hostility toward the obnoxious experimenter decreased if the subjects had heard him suffering from drugs, and slightly increased if he was having a pleasurable experience with the drugs. According to the authors, the differences were statistically acceptable, but not dramatic.

Another qualified version of the catharsis hypothesis is that it takes place mainly when the observer is already angry (Buss, 1961; Feshbach, 1964), however even this limited view is not supported by some evidence (Mallick and McCandless, 1966; Hartmann, 1969). It should be observed that feedback about suffering and initial anger are both uncommon when watching television, so if these factors are critical to the catharsis effect there can be little catharsis from watching television violence.

As far as laboratory studies go, more convincing evidence indicates that watching violence may amplify or instigate aggressive tendencies rather than reduce them. Such studies are similar to those testing social learning and modeling behavior and generally indicate that both children and adults may have heightened aggressive behavior following episodes of watching filmed violence. In one experiment (Walters, Thomas, and Acker, 1962) normal adult males were shown either (a) a film depicting a knife fight, or (b) a neutral film. They were then persuaded to take part in an experiment testing the effects of punishment on learning (the aggression machine again). The intensity of shock they thought they were administering was the dependent measure of aggression. It was found that subjects who had previously witnessed the aggressive film administered more severe punishment than those who had witnessed a neutral film. Thus, watching violence tended to make normal people somewhat more aggressive, even though their punishment was directed toward a stranger and administered in a different manner from what they had witnessed.

Berkowitz and his associates have extensively studied film-mediated aggression and generally found that aggressive tendencies are heightened by watching aggression (some of these experiments were reviewed earlier in this chapter). Precisely how these tendencies are directed may depend in part on characteristics of the available targets, situational cues, and how the observer perceives the situation. In addition, aggressive tendencies can be heightened by a variety of arousing stimuli, not just those which are mediated by film or TV. For example, effective stimuli may include visual material from comic books, scenes from an athletic contest, routines by a hostile comedian such as Don Rickles, and even white noise (Berkowitz, 1970). Sometimes the effects have unusual twists. Berkowitz and LePage (1967) showed that the presence of a gun in the experimental setting tends to make subjects more aggressive on the aggression machine. But Fischer, Kelm, and Rose (1969) reported than an ordinary table knife was a more effective aggression-eliciting cue than a switchblade knife. In addition, these experimenters found a significant effect for males but not for females, and this adds a sex dimension to the social learning of aggressive behavior. Eron (1963) also reported a sex difference, in this case the effects of television viewing habits on aggressive behavior (see below).

The overall pattern of laboratory investigations seems to indicate that normal adults and children can become more aggressive after exposure to aggressive stimuli. But an important and relatively neglected problem remains: can results obtained in the laboratory be generalized to the real world? Kniveton and Stephenson (1970) found that children will be influenced by aggressive models if they are observed in a laboratory setting, but significantly less aggressive modeling takes place in a more familiar environment. Furthermore, the experimental effect attributed to an aggressive film is transient and disappears within a week. It may be that a formal experiment in a psychology laboratory adds prestige and credibility to stimuli which would be less effective if they were observed at home. The problem of naturalistic research is a perennial one (Willems and Raush, 1969), for the outcome and interpretations may depend more on the methodology than anything else. Just as the Skinner box is worthless for investigating many problems (e.g., social behavior) in animals, the perfectly-controlled human laboratory with its aggression machines and contrived deceptions may also have inherent limitations. Much pseudo-knowledge has been accumulated by rat psychologists and social psychologists alike, for often the research is not relevant to the problem being studied (Lockard, 1968; 1971; Silverman, 1971). In the case of TV violence, Singer (1971) has pointed out that many of the studies measure play or simulated aggression rather than overt aggression and that much of the filmed material used is unrepresentative of television programs or movies. Furthermore, most studies have used only middle class subjects.

Feshbach and Singer (1971) have pointed out that the content of aggressive material may be less important than both the context in which it is perceived and the extent to which the observer distinguishes between fantasy and reality. An observer who recognizes that Buggs Bunny, Batman, and James Bond are not for real may be difficult to influence. What is really needed is more extensive longitudinal research in naturalistic settings, for such studies may contain relevant variables not present in single-session laboratory experiments. Eron (1963) tried to do this by correlating viewing preferences with reported aggressive behavior. Children were rated for their aggressive tendencies by interviewing their playmates, and parents were independently consulted about the viewing habits of the children. No significant relationships were found between viewing habits and aggressive behavior in girls. Among boys, those who preferred more programs of violence tended to be more aggressive in school. These boys did not necessarily watch more television in terms of hours per day, and it turned out that those who watched TV the most were actually the least aggressive. It should be pointed out that the correlations do not establish the direction of the causality. It could be that watching violent television makes boys aggressive, or that boys who are aggressive tend to like violent TV. Other correlational studies have been attempted (Himmelweit, Oppenheim and Vince, 1958; Klapper, 1960), but no unambiguous results have been obtained.

In one short longitudinal study, 665 boys from 10 to 17 years of age in three private schools and four boys' camps were studied over a period of six weeks. Half of the boys in each institution were required to watch a minimum of six hours per week of programs containing violence, including such shows as "Combat," "Gunsmoke," "FBI," and "Route 66." The other half watched non-aggressive programs for an equivalent time (e.g., "Lawrence Welk," "Walt Disney," "Beverly Hillbillies," and "Dick Van Dyke"). Aside from the six-hour limit, great latitude was permitted in viewing habits. At the end of six weeks the boys were given questionnaires, TAT's (thematic apperception tests), and peer ratings to assess differences in aggressive behavior. It was found that in the boys' homes, but not in the private schools, those who watched violent television showed significantly less verbal and physical aggression compared to those who watched nonviolent television. Not all measures showed this effect, but at least no evidence was obtained to suggest that watching violent television increased aggressiveness. Further details of this study and other related findings are discussed at length in the recent book, *Television and Aggression* (Feshbach and Singer, 1971).

Additional studies are now being carried out and it is probably premature to attempt any firm conclusions. Exposure to violence does not guarantee catharsis, and in fact the catharsis hypothesis enjoys little support. But children do not imitate everything they see, and there is no reason to believe that an otherwise normal child will turn into a criminal from television exposure. Whether the same is true of disturbed children is more difficult to assess. Perhaps more distressing is the possibility that television is helping to mold shallow and callous individuals and ultimately a brutalized society with warped values. We know that much of positive value can be learned from television, as has been the case with programs like "Sesame Street." It would be naive to assume that television teaches only good things and not bad things (or vice versa). No one advocates censoring all violence, for sometimes it plays a crucial role in artistic expression or in the reporting of world news events. Any such regulation would be fundamentally incompatible with a free society. As yet, we have no firm evidence for a causal link between viewing violence and heightened aggression. This will no doubt relieve those who worried about the fact that President Nixon enjoyed a war movie (*Patton*) so much that he asked to see it a second time.

But failure to prove a causal link should not be interpreted as a license to pollute the airways with more trash. The bulk of scientific studies clearly warn about the detrimental effects of media violence (Berkowitz, 1962; Bryan and Schwartz, 1971; Goransen, 1969; 1970; Baker and Ball, 1969; Kaufmann, 1970; Siegel, 1970). Only a few (Feshbach, 1970; Feshbach and Singer, 1971) have taken a different view. For what it is worth, the Commission Report on Violence and the Media offered the following general conclusions (Baker and Ball, 1969):

1. The weight of social science stands in opposition to the conclusion that mass media portrayals of violence have no effect upon individuals, groups, and society.

2. To the extent that mass media portrayals of violence have effects upon individuals, groups, and society, it is a variety that most persons would deem costly and harmful to individuals and society.

3. The direction of effects of mass media portrayals of violence is to extend the behavioral and attitudinal boundaries of acceptable violence beyond legal and social norms currently espoused by a majority of Americans.

A more recent review by Singer (1971) offers somewhat different conclusions:

1. Scientific evidence does not yet conclusively link increased violence in the United States to material presented in the media.

2. Some children and adults may imitate witnessed aggression under certain conditions, but other conditions may lead to a reduction in tension and overt aggression.

3. The behavioral sciences have developed sophisticated procedures for studying the effects of mass media, but relatively little research has been done under conditions which simulate actual viewing experiences.

4. Pending the outcome of present and future investigations, some voluntary restraint on the part of the media would seem to be wise.

More recently, the Surgeon General of the United States released a preliminary report which concluded that television violence does not have a uniformly adverse effect on the majority of children. It also noted that under certain circumstances it may increase aggressiveness in some children already predisposed toward aggressive behavior. Unfortunately, the Surgeon General gave the television industry veto power over the selection of individuals who helped write the report. Television executives blackballed some of the best experts on the subject, including Leonard Berkowitz, Albert Bandura, Ralph Garry, Otto Larsen, Percy Tannenbaum, Leo Bogart, and Leon Eisenberg (Gould, 1972). Some of the work of Bandura and Berkowitz is now almost classic, and in general it tends to show the possible harmful effects of observing violence, as we have seen on previous pages. Because of the biased manner in which Surgeon General William Stewart selected his committee, his report will be of questionable value.

6 VIOLENCE AND SOCIETY

It is often said that war begins in the minds of men. This view probably owes its popularity to its simplicity, for simplicity is often confused with truth. It suggests that social conflict can be understood in terms of individual motivation. Unfortunately, war and other forms of institutional violence cannot be understood by generalizing from individual behavior, nor can they be understood directly on the basis of animal or preverbal human behavior (Scott, 1962). This book has concentrated on animal behavior and simple forms of human behavior because these problems are scientifically significant, and because they are researchable. The direct benefits to society may seem limited, but in all fairness they should be compared to the nonscientific contributions. What lasting wisdom has come from centuries of effort by politicians, diplomats, police, or even poets and philosophers? Social conflict is probably worse today than ever before, so the modest contributions of science in recent years may provide reason for cautious optimism.

Hopefully, basic facts about aggressive phenomena will provide a cumulative base of support for an analysis of some of the broader problems of society. Unfortunately, it seems that as problems become more relevant they also become more complex. This complexity often defies scientific analysis and leaves us with a mélange of facts, myths, and opinions which must be sorted out in a painstaking fashion. A good example is the problem of the effect of television violence, a problem considered in the last chapter but one which is equally pertinent to sociological issues. A direct approach to the problem of violence and society forces us into a gray area containing more speculation and controversy. An awareness of such problems should not cause social scientists to avoid the area, but only to admit the inherent limitations and tentative conclusions. There are no ultimate facts in this area, and there are not likely to be any for some time. We have only educated insights, which are admittedly based on opinion as well as on fact.

The reader who insists on facts without opinions should skip the present chapter, which begins with guesses about the extent of violent crime and the conditions under which it occurs.

VIOLENT CRIME IN THE U.S.A.

In the decade of the 1960's, the crime rate in the United States grew about 10 times as fast as the population. According to the Uniform Crime Reports of the FBI (1969) crimes of violence increased in number by 130 per cent and in rate (i.e., taking population increases into account) by 104 per cent. Between 1960 and 1970 the rate of murder increased by 44 per cent, forcible rape by 93 per cent, aggravated assault by 79 per cent, and robbery by 146 per cent. Although some major cities have seen higher crime rates during earlier periods in the 20th century, crimes of violence in general appear to be increasing at an unprecedented rate (Fig. 32). Such statements, however, must be tempered by the fact that the FBI crime statistics are neither entirely objective nor accurate. The Uniform Crime Reports assembles at face value the voluntary disclosures of local police, and such reports are often unreliable and self-serving. Local law enforcement agencies sometimes inflate crime statistics to scare taxpayers into spending more money for the police, or they may juggle figures to make it look as though local politicians have done a good job in reducing crime. There is a trend toward improving the accuracy of crime statistics in recent years; however, the United States lags considerably behind many European countries in this respect. Some of the apparent increase in crime rate over the past 10 years no doubt stems from more complete reporting by the police.

A profile of violent crime in the United States has been summarized in a report to the National Commission on the Causes and Prevention of Violence (Violent Crime, 1969):

1. Violent crime is concentrated in large cities. The 26 largest cities in the United States contain only 17 per cent of the total population, but contribute 45 per cent of the major crimes of violence. Baltimore leads all major cities, with one resident out of 49 being victimized each year.

2. Violent crime is overwhelmingly committed by males. The ratio of males to females arrested in connection with murder is five to one.

3. Most crime in the cities is concentrated among youths between 15 and 24 years of age. Crime rates for those from 10 to 14 have risen dramatically in the past few years.

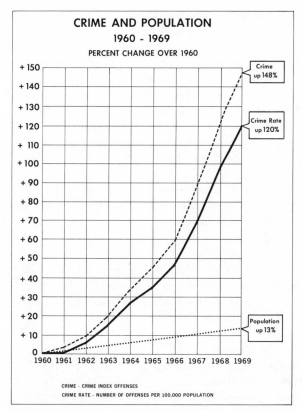

CRIME AND POPULATION
1960 - 1969
PERCENT CHANGE OVER 1960

Crime up 148%

Crime Rate up 120%

Population up 13%

CRIME · CRIME INDEX OFFENSES
CRIME RATE · NUMBER OF OFFENSES PER 100,000 POPULATION

Figure 32. *According to the FBI, the overall rate of crime in the United States increased by 120 per cent between 1960 and 1969. But the Uniform Crime Reports are based on voluntary disclosures by local police, and such reports are often notoriously unreliable and self-serving. In addition, most crimes are never even reported, so it is difficult to get a true picture of crime in America. (FBI Uniform Crime Reports, 1969.)*

4. Violent crime is committed primarily by those in the lower occupational brackets. In Philadelphia, for example, over 90 per cent of homicides were committed by persons who ranged from the unemployed to skilled laborers.

5. Violent crime in cities is disproportionately more frequent in slums and ghettos.

6. Victims and offenders usually share similar characteristics. With the exception of robbery, most violent crime is not inter-racial. The victims of most black offenders are other blacks, while whites attack whites. Most robbery carried out against poor people is initiated by other poor people.

7. Most homicides and assaults take place between relatives, friends, or acquaintances. In 1969, one-quarter of all murders

took place within the family. Rapes and robberies, on the other hand, usually involve strangers.

8. Crimes of violence are frequently provoked by the victims, and the motives are usually trivial: petty arguments, family squabbles, and jealousy. Either the victim or the offender or both are likely to have been drinking when a violent crime is committed.

9. Most crimes are committed by repeaters. Among individuals convicted of crimes of assault, 76 per cent committed another crime within six years after being released. In a study of 10,000 Philadelphia boys, six per cent of the boys accounted for 53 per cent of all personal attacks.

Another report (Challenge of Crime, 1967) by the President's Commission on Law Enforcement and the Administration of Justice summarized the following sociological correlates of violent crime in urban areas:

1. low income;
2. physical deterioration of a community;
3. racial and ethnic concentrations;
4. overcrowding in substandard housing;
5. high population density;
6. mixed land use;
7. broken homes;
8. weak family structures;
9. poor education;
10. high unemployment;
11. poor health and medical care.

In general, violent crime feeds and perpetuates itself on social and environmental adversity, including poor housing and schools, lack of jobs, social disorganization, and racial prejudice. Many of these same factors lie at the root of urban riots, as we shall see later in this chapter.

GUNS AND VIOLENCE

Most murders are not premeditated, but rather are impulsive crimes of passion, often committed under the influence of alcohol when guns happen to be handy (Clark, 1970). Guns also tend to make suicides much easier for many people who would not have the courage to try another method. In the laboratory, Berkowitz and LePage (1967) showed that the mere presence of guns can significantly amplify aggressive actions. Whether or not the widespread ownership of guns and easy access to them contributes to violence is difficult to tell, but certainly there is enough evidence to indicate that the absence of strong gun control laws in the United States may be a major cause for concern. No one can forget the story of Lee Harvey Oswald: In 1963, Oswald read the February issue of the *American Rifleman* and clipped out a coupon which he sent to a Chicago mail order house along with $21.45. He quickly received the 6.5 millimeter Manchester-Carcano rifle that later killed President Kennedy.

The following are some revealing facts about guns, assembled by Clark (1970), Gillin and Ochberg (1970), and the Uniform Crime Reports of 1969:

1. Since 1900, guns have killed over 800,000 Americans. The total casualties from civilian gunfire in the 20th century exceed the military casualties in all wars from the Revolutionary War through the Vietnamese War.

2. About 20,000 Americans are killed and 200,000 injured by guns each year. Someone is shot on the average of once every 25 minutes. In one recent year guns were used in 126,000 robberies and assaults. About two-thirds of all homicides are committed with guns and more than half with hand guns.

3. There are over 100 million and perhaps as many as 200 million privately owned guns in the United States. More than half of the homes in the country have at least one gun, and a significant proportion are intended for purposes other than hunting or hobbies. Between 1963 and 1967 there has been a 132-per-cent increase in firearms sales. In 1967 alone there were 4,585,000 guns legally sold in the United States.

4. Many more people have used guns to kill themselves than to kill other people.

5. By a very wide margin, the United States leads all other advanced countries in homicides, suicides, and accidents with firearms. The rate of gun homicide is 35 times higher in the United States than in such countries as England, Germany, and Denmark. Only Canada comes close to the United States, and its rate is 30 times lower.

6. Compared to other countries, the United States is extremely lax in gun control laws. In Japan, for example, it was an old tradition that only a few people, such as samurai warriors, had the right to carry arms. In modern Japan, only the police and armed forces are permitted to own arms and there is little public pressure for the "right" to bear arms. Many Americans, on the other hand, seem to feel that almost anyone should be able to carry deadly weapons. Americans pay dearly for this "right." Taking population into account, the rate of gun homicide in the United States is 214 times higher than it is in Japan. In Tokyo, the world's largest city,

only three people were murdered by hand guns in 1970. During the same period in New York City over 500 persons were similarly murdered, even though New York has about three and a half million *fewer* citizens than Tokyo (Halloran, 1971). In addition, New Yorkers suffered from 74,102 robberies while Tokyo had only 474.

Such facts understandably lead many to conclude that the United States is gun crazy, and that we are paying for it dearly in the number of people killed and wounded each year. In the era of the 1920's and 1930's the rate of gun homicide was higher than it is today, but if the trend of the past decade continues we may soon be in another homicide wave. We may be in it already, for better emergency medical care may convert a higher shooting rate to a lower death rate (Block and Geis, 1962). Most opinion polls show that the majority of gun owners and about three-quarters of the general public favor more stringent gun control legislation (Daniels, et al., 1970). In fact, more than half of those interviewed back in 1959 favored outlawing all hand guns except for those carried by the police (Public . . . , 1959).

Following the assassinations of President Kennedy, Sen. Robert Kennedy, and Rev. Martin Luther King, there was a brief movement for stricter gun control laws. But because of the opposition of gun manufacturers, sporting groups, and radical political organizations such as the Black Panthers and the Minutemen, only a watered-down bill was finally passed. The most powerful opposition came from the National Rifle Association (NRA), with well over a million members and a multimillion dollar budget. Through their official publication, the *American Rifleman,* they rallied their membership in a letter-writing campaign to oppose gun laws. The campaign was successful, partly because the gun lobby distorted the issues (Harris, 1968). No attempt was being made to remove the constitutional freedom to bear arms, but only to register gun owners. We register automobiles, spouses, and dogs, so why not guns? In Washington, D. C., 25 per cent of those receiving guns through the mail had criminal records (Clark 1970). Even guns, let alone gun owners, are often unregistered. Following the Detroit riots of June, 1967, it was found that 90 per cent of the guns confiscated were not registered as required under Michigan law.

It is unfortunate that we have so many statistics on gun deaths, but so little scientific information on the psychological effects of gun possession. The indirect effects may be worse than is realized, for guns are a symbol of force and brutality and a glorification of violence. The psychological impact of gun possession is probably a much easier question to investigate than the effect of television violence. But it requires the cooperation of gun enthusiasts, and until such cooperation is forthcoming it is likely that we will be forced to continue speculation based on the counting of dead bodies.

VIOLENCE AND MENTAL ILLNESS

It is sometimes said that anyone who commits murder is by definition mentally unstable, and it is not surprising that those charged with vicious crimes often plead temporary insanity. But are the mentally ill really more dangerous and more prone to commit acts of violence? It is unfortunate that ignorance still surrounds the care and treatment of the mentally ill and that along with this ignorance goes distorted fear. In point of fact, individuals with a history of mental illness are probably no more prone to violence than anyone else.

Gulevich and Bourne (1970) reviewed a number of studies involving tens of thousands of discharged mental patients. In general, the studies tend to indicate that former mental patients have problems with the law at about the same or lower frequency after discharge. This does not answer the question of how people who are *currently* mentally ill behave, but these researchers do indicate that there is no need to have unusual fears of individuals who have been mentally ill at one time or another. The most recent and detailed studies (Rappeport, Lassen and Hay, 1967) support these general conclusions. For most crimes, with the possible exception of rape, rates for former mental patients are about the same as those in the general population. Those who frequently get into trouble with the law, either in the general population or among former patients, tend to be alcoholics and schizophrenics. But getting into trouble with the law may not be a good indicator, for released female mental patients are unlikely to commit robbery or murder, but they may be more abusive in their personal conduct.

Diagnoses of known criminal offenders are more difficult to evaluate because of widespread differences in classifications applied to the mentally ill, particularly with regard to aggressiveness (Buss, 1961). In a recent review (Gulevich and Bourne, 1970) it is pointed out that some psychiatrists find very few criminals whom they consider psychotic or even abnormal, while other psychiatrists report psychoses in nearly all of the criminals they examine. All things considered, there seems to be no justification for blaming an unusual amount of violence or crime on the mentally ill or insane.

More research could be done and should be done on this problem. In general there have been two major approaches to studying the relation between mental illness and crime. The first has been to examine the criminal tendencies of patients released from mental institutions, and the second has been to gauge the proportion of known criminals who are mentally ill. Both procedures are fraught with difficulties; for example, only the best-behaved patients are released from mental hospitals, while the more difficult cases, which remain behind, cannot be tested in society. In addition, crime rates tend to decrease with age, and patients naturally age while they are institutionalized. The problem of screening known criminals is that there is very little competent psychiatric care or evaluation of prisoners, and anyone examining them finds it difficult to be objective because they know that their "patients" are convicted criminals. A more objective test would be to obtain psychiatric evaluations of a mixed group of individuals, some of whom are criminals, with the person performing the evaluations not knowing which individuals are criminals and which are "normal." Another problem is that convicted criminals may be psychologically "together" when they enter prison, but may become "spaced out" as a result of the prison experience. Indeed, there is good reason to believe that prison life has many deleterious effects on behavior, as we shall see in the following section.

PRISONS: FACTORIES FOR CRIME

Vengeance is a strictly human invention, something not found in any other species. Somewhere along the line, human beings got the idea that punishment is a cure for aggression. In his book, *The Crime of Punishment* (1966), Karl Menninger writes, "I suspect that all the crimes committed by all the jailed criminals do not equal in total social damage that of the crimes committed against them." For most of ancient and modern history, individuals guilty of antisocial behavior have been executed, banished, beaten, maimed, or publicly ridiculed. Detention was used not as a form of punishment but only to hold prisoners until sentences could be carried out (Goldfarb, 1970). About the end of the 18th century the Pennsylvania Quakers, among others, reacted to the cruelties of corporal and capital punishment by locking up criminals so that they could contemplate their sins, wrestle with their consciences, and build up a desire to reform. Penitentiaries were places for penitence.

This American invention may have been an effective and humane treatment among Puritans in Colonial days, but it has since degenerated into an ugly nightmare, frequently involving regular physical and psychological torture. Society foots a bill of about one and a half billion dollars annually to keep over 400,000 Americans locked up in places where their criminal tendencies increase rather than decrease. A few jails now in use were built before the inauguration of George Washington, and a recent survey by the Census Bureau for the Law Enforcement Assistance Administration revealed that more than half (52 per cent) of the inmates of city and county jails throughout the country have not been convicted of any crime (Rosenthal, 1971). Those incarcerated while awaiting justice (*sic*) are mainly those too poor to afford bail or a competent lawyer who would speed their case. Whereas jails are supposed to hold individuals for only a short period of time, some have been known to keep people for five years, often in conditions not fit for any primate. Parish Prison in New Orleans, for example, was built in 1929 for 400 prisoners. It now cages 850: 75 per cent of them are as yet unsentenced (Shame of Prisons, 1971).

Former United States Attorney General Ramsey Clark (1970) paints a grim picture of American prisons, which he calls "factories of crime." Society tends to regard prisons as warehouses in which to store people as cheaply as possible to keep them from the public eye while also gaining vengeance. Money is saved at the expense of the prisoners, and the public rarely hears about it or shows any concern if it does. As recently as 1965 the only all-female federal prison lacked toilets in many of the units and women were compelled to use jars instead. The current system of "justice" tends to discriminate against the poor and minority groups. Minor offenders and the accused are lumped with hard-core criminals so that most prisons contain mixtures of dope addicts, sex deviates, alcoholics, tax evaders, the mentally ill, political activists, check forgers, those with brain damage, and so forth. Think of the possibilities for social learning!

Accordingly, the interior of most prisons is a jungle of violence in which the worst criminals determine the common denominator for everyone else. In addition to frequent beatings and homosexual rapings, the prison subculture often fosters and maintains extensive gambling and narcotics rackets. Prisons are generally located in remote areas, and workers have low salary scales, so it is difficult to obtain qualified personnel, even for guard duty. Many guards can be bribed with money or sexual favors, and extortion can be used against prisoners (and guards) who fail to participate. Because of these problems, prison officials usually make little attempt to control what goes on inside the walls and instead concentrate on just keeping the prisoners locked up. Sometimes prisoners themselves are used as armed guards, partly because guns in the hands of the most vicious inmates easily intimidate other prisoners. A recent scandal in several Arkansas prisons revealed that beatings were common and that those who were murdered or died from abuse were secretly buried in a hidden graveyard. Torture devices, such as "Tucker's telephone," which was an induction coil used to apply electric shock to prisoners' genitals until they were unconscious, were discovered.

In response to such practices, observers sometimes ask why anyone should feel sorry for prisoners and why any effort should be expended to correct their deplorable living conditions. After all, they are being punished for their crimes, which are their own fault. There are two replies to these questions, one based on humanitarian concerns for prisoners as human beings, and the other based on the selfish interests of the rest of society. The latter, of course, has the strongest appeal to the mass of the population: most prisoners are eventually released, and it would seem that society should take a strong interest in what prisoners learn in prison and what they are likely to do when they get out. What they learn is crime and more crime, piled on top of intense hatred and contempt of society at large. This is illustrated by the fact that fully 80 per cent of all felonies are committed by repeat offenders (Clark, 1970). Those who were dangerous criminals are likely to go on being dangerous criminals; those who were petty criminals are likely to become more dangerous criminals.

It would seem that an excellent way to reduce crime in the streets would be to shift the emphasis of prisons from vengeance to rehabilitation. Previous crimes cannot be undone, but future crimes can be prevented. In order to do this, major reforms will have to take place in the penal system and more money devoted to it. Today, 95 per cent of all "corrections" money goes to custody and security while only 5 per cent is spent on health, education, and rehabilitation (Clark, 1970). Eighty per cent of the manpower in penal systems is used for guard duty. Of the remaining 20 per cent only a few are devoted to rehabilitation. For example, there are only 20 full-time prison psychiatrists in the entire Federal system and probably only about 50 in the entire United States. When one realizes that a quarter of the prisoners in some states are mentally retarded, this seems like deliberate negligence. Year after year the budgets for prisons are among the most severely cut, for few people care about prisoners (70 per cent of all prisoners never have a single visitor).

Some people favor spending less money on the prison system, presumably to be "tough on crimes"; however, such policies are really soft on crime because they have the effect of spreading rather than stamping out crime. In the hearings on the Omnibus Crime Control Act of 1968, so-called "law and order" politicians such as Sen. John McClelland of Arkansas and Sen. Strom Thurmond of South Carolina wanted to impose 95 per cent cuts on the funds for corrections. In California, Governor Reagan showed his concern for crime by beefing up the police force and cutting back on allocations for prisons. No doubt politicians can win many votes by coming out strongly against convicted criminals, particularly if prisoners are usually poor people from minority groups with little voting power. The sad result is that our prisons continue to turn out hard-core criminals who will continue to molest the rest of the population. It would seem that money spent on prisons could be one of the cheapest and most effective ways of reducing crime.

The problem is unfortunately much deeper, for legal-judicial-law enforcement systems are proving increasingly clumsy at dealing with crime and social problems. Police are underpaid, district attorneys are under political pressure, and the enormous backlog of cases makes it difficult to get a speedy, fair trial. There are vast differences from city to city and from state to state in how strictly laws will be enforced and offenders punished. At the root of the problem is the election of politicians who thrive on the problems of social unrest by championing simple solutions. How often have politicians called for more police, stricter judges, harsher laws, all for the purpose of achieving law and order by putting more people in jail? Politicians rarely do anything to speed the rehabilitation of prisoners and, partly as a result, corrections programs receive the lowest priorities in virtually every state (Rugaber, 1971). Many judges are deliberately lenient on moderate criminals, knowing that imprisonment is a sure formula for producing hard-core criminals.

Many years ago Dostoyevsky remarked that a society can be judged by the humanity it shows toward its outcasts. No one seeks to pardon criminals for vicious crimes against society, but there is no excuse for barbaric treatment of prisoners. The attitude of contemporary society was blatantly exposed in the 1971 uprisings at Attica State Prison in New York. Nearly all of the prisoners were black and nearly all of the guards were white. The prisoners had legitimate grievances that the state had ignored, and finally, to publicize their plight, the prisoners took over part of the prison and captured hostages. Hundreds of guards were mobilized to storm the prison, and tensions mounted as rumors spread that the hostages were being mistreated and possibly tortured. From the news media's accounts it appeared as if the prisoners were violent and unreasonable while the state was being peaceful and rational. Not surprisingly, the public cried for "action" (i.e., force) and the mobilized guards spoiled for a fight. Nearly every observer agreed that there would be a massacre if the state decided to attack (Wicker, 1971), but the attack was nevertheless ordered. The police shot their way into the prison and dozens of people were indiscriminately gunned down, including a number of the hostages who were being "saved." It turned out that the hostages had not been tortured by the prisoners, but beating and torture *was* carried out by the police. As punishment for their actions, prisoners were deprived of legal rights and corrections officials tried to conceal and distort what actually happened. In the meantime, Governor Rockefeller (who had refused to go to the scene) and President Nixon supported and applauded the attack and ensuing bloodshed.

How often have the politicians, the supposed leaders of our society, come out strongly in favor of the rehabilitation of prisoners? Very rarely. Politicians will probably continue to exploit this situation to the detriment of society until the public realizes that punishment is *not* a cure for crime.

DRUGS AND VIOLENCE

Nearly everyone has heard the saying, "Speed Kills." This slogan was popularized a few years ago by the street subculture of San Francisco's Haight-Ashbury district after much unfortunate experimentation with methamphetamine, or "speed," a powerful central nervous system stimulant. In the minds of many, drugs are often linked with violence as a social menace. Do drugs "cause" violence?

This topic is an explosive issue of great social relevance, but unfortunately, facts are often confounded with myths. Some authorities argue that all drugs are dangerous and have undesirable, antisocial effects. Others see drugs as a means to beautiful, mind-expanding experiences which improve the quality of life. Neither of these extreme positions has much to offer. In general, it is necessary to distinguish between (a) the pharmacological and physiological effects, (b) the behavioral effects, and (c) the social effects of various drugs. For example, amphetamines are central nervous system stimulants, while barbiturates are physiological depressants, sometimes called sedative-hypnotics because awareness may be lessened. Powerful mind-altering drugs include psychotomimetics (drugs that produce manifestations resembling those of a psychosis) such as LSD (lysergic acid diethylamide), DMT (dimethyltryptamine), mescaline, and psilocybin. Marihuana may have the effect of a hallucinogen, a mild stimulant, or even a tranquilizer.

Legally, marihuana is classified as a narcotic along with opiate drugs like heroin, morphine, and opium, which are known for their analgesic properties. But marihuana differs from the opiates both pharmacologically and in the fact that it is not physically addicting. Alcohol, a central nervous system depressant, *can* be addicting; however, legally it is *not* a narcotic. The differences between the legal and the physiological classifications are further illustrated by the fact that a totally outlawed drug such as heroin may produce no permanent body damage even after decades of use (Fort, 1969), whereas freely available alcohol and tobacco may cause permanent physiological destruction or contribute to processes of cell degeneration (alcoholic brain damage, cirrhosis of the liver, lung cancer, heart disease, and so forth). Overdoses of heroin, as with many drugs, can cause death, but tolerable dosages of alcohol and tobacco over a long period of time contribute to hundreds of thousands of deaths each year.

This raises the provoking question of what parameters to adopt in evaluating the personal and social dangers of drugs. If drugs were measured quantitatively by their tendency to cause or contribute to deaths in the population, then alcohol would be by far the most dangerous drug. After alcohol would come tobacco as a major cause of drug-related deaths, and following tobacco would come barbiturates such as sleeping pills, which are among the leading methods of suicide. In combination with alcohol they are a common cause of accidental death.

If one looks at crime statistics instead of death rates, a different picture emerges, but not necessarily a more accurate one, because crime statistics may be very misleading. For example, possession of marihuana is illegal; therefore by definition a "crime" is committed by a possessor, even though no antisocial behavior may be involved. By carefully manipulating such statistics, it is possible to present "objective" data linking marihuana with crime. It is unfortunate that many narcotics officials and politicians have distorted drug information in the hopes of frightening young people away from all drugs. The net result is often a loss of credibility so that even legitimate drug information is ignored. Fort (1969) documents a number of cases of such distortions, sometimes well-intentioned and sometimes deliberate. Many drug laws are based on their political popularity rather than on medical or behavioral facts. Alcohol is known to be linked with violent aggression, yet legislation against it has been unpopular, as was shown by the successful campaign against prohibition. There appears to be little evidence linking marihuana to violence, yet smoking pot may land someone in jail for years. Deaths are common from alcohol but not from marihuana, yet the former is legal and the latter is illegal.

Sometimes drugs are difficult to classify, for they defy simple-minded categories such as hard and soft or safe and dangerous. Nearly any drug can be harmful at excessive dosage, and at normal dosage its effect may depend on the method of administration and subtle individual biological and psychological differences which still remain poorly understood. The possibilities of dangerous effects have led some authorities to urge a blanket rejection of all drugs, emphasizing such possible risks as blindness, insanity, brain damage, criminal behavior, birth defects, altered personality, and so on. Some of these dangers are real, particularly when the user has no sure way of knowing the type and concentration of a drug. Unfortunately, some users reject all information and trust only personal experience, thus making themselves guinea pigs.

Another common reason for assuming all drugs to be dangerous until proved safe is that a harmless drug may lead to the use of dangerous drugs. This domino theory is quoted over and over; it is based on the retrospective views of addicts. Statistics can be enumerated which show that many heroin addicts previously smoked pot; if we got people to give up pot, so the reasoning goes, they would not turn to heroin. But sequential events have never proved causal relationships. The same reasoning should lead us to ban milk because most heroin users drank milk before they turned to heroin. There are countries where marihuana smoking is rampant while the use of heroin is practically unknown (Fort, 1969). On the other hand, the enjoyment of a relatively harmless drug like marihuana may encourage experimentation with other drugs which are in fact deadly. Potentially deadly drugs may also produce some enjoyment, but the added risks greatly outweigh any temporary pleasure. If there is such a thing as a progression from one drug to another, probably the best example is from caffeine (in soft drinks, coffee, and some brands of aspirin) to tobacco and alcohol.

Just what medical evidence is there linking drugs to aggression that results in violence? Marihuana generally produces a pleasant, euphoric effect rarely associated with violence. In fact this drug may reduce aggressive behavior: Santos (1966) has reported that it causes fighting mice to stop fighting. In a recent report from the National Institutes of Mental Health (Marihuana and Health, 1971) it was concluded that present evidence fails to link marihuana with violent behavior or the subsequent use of other drugs such as heroin. In addition, marihuana has few detrimental physiological effects, almost never leads to death, and has little effect on fetal development.

The relation between many other drugs and violence has been recently reviewed by Tinklenberg and Stillman (1970). Potent psychotomimetics like LSD are often characterized by weakness, lethargy, and sometimes fear, which preclude assaultive behavior. Similarly, opiates are rarely associated with violence. Opium addiction today is a relatively minor problem compared to what it was at the turn of the century, and the most frequently addicted are physicians. Barbiturates tend to sedate and put people to sleep; however, they may produce paradoxical reactions, particularly in combination with other drugs. Barbiturates are commonly used to tranquilize individuals agitated by the conflicts of urban or suburban life and to sedate potentially dangerous institutionalized patients, but widespread misuse may create more problems than are solved. Some of these drugs may have legitimate medical uses, such as morphine or codeine for killing pain; as for psychotomimetics, anecdotes that they have beneficial value in increasing awareness, sensitivity, and creativity are without foundation.

Compared with other drugs, amphetamines and alcohol appear to be far more dangerous with respect to aggressive behavior. Amphetamines are stimulants which heighten excitability and muscular tension and may lead to more irritability and impulsive behavior. Paradoxically, some forms, such as methamphetamine (speed), appear to be conclusively linked to assaultive behavior whereas other amphetamines in low dosages can have the opposite effect, reducing violent outbursts. Methamphetamine administered to rats accentuates affective attack elicited by hypothalamic stimulation (Panksepp, 1971b).

From the point of view of society, alcohol is definitely the most dangerous drug, and according to the President's Commission on Law Enforcement and Administration of Justice (1967), alcohol is the only drug causally related to violence. Because of its easy availability and widespread usage it is not surprising to find alcohol as an integral part of many violent crimes. Mark and Ervin (1970) have pointed out that a drugged brain is like a diseased brain in that in both cases it and its owner may be out of control. We know that most homicides are impulsive actions between people who know each other, with the victim often provoking the killing. The impulsive violence of the attacker is likely to be heightened by alcohol, and drinking often precedes assaultive behavior. The close connection between alcohol and violence is no secret: liquor stores, bars, and taverns are often quickly closed at the first sign of a possible riot. Many states have "Blue Laws" restricting the sale of liquor to the six weekdays to help assure that Sunday will be a day of peace. Similar practices are found in other cultures. Horton (1943) describes primitive tribes in which the women routinely hide any weapons during tribal drinking bouts.

There is another important side to the drug story which deals not with direct effects but the more complicated psychological and social context within which drugs are obtained and used. Whether a drug increases or decreases aggressive behavior may depend on the user's personality, his mood at the time he takes it, where he takes it and with whom, how much he has had in the past, and what he expects to happen. It may be one thing to take a drug in a secure and comfortable setting among close friends and quite another thing to take it when feeling isolated, insecure, and desperate. In addition, the direct effect of the drug may cause no violent behavior, but the psychological reaction following "coming down" may do so.

Just as important is the fact that an illegal drug habit can be very expensive, forcing the user into crime and constant exposure to criminal elements. Addicts who need 75 to 100 dollars a day to buy drugs are willing to take great risks, whether they have to mug people on the streets or break into homes. They usually commit crimes against property and try to avoid interpersonal violence, but of course eventually someone gets hurt. Fort (1969) reports that 10 to 12 per cent of all property crimes in New York City are committed by admitted drug users. It is likely that the stereotyped association between drugs and violence (with the exception of alcohol) is due more to instrumental behavior in obtaining drugs than to any direct effects from the drugs themselves.

LA COSA NOSTRA

Organized crime is one of the topics covered by a task force for the National Commission on the Causes and Prevention of Violence (Violence and Organized Crime, 1969). Since the Kefauver hearings in the early 1950's, it has become known that the Mafia, or what is now called La Cosa Nostra ("this thing of ours"), is a growing nationwide crime syndicate which specializes in narcotics, gambling, loan sharking, extortion, labor racketeering, and the infiltration of legitimate businesses. No one knows exactly how large organized crime is, but it has been estimated that it accounts for 7.7 billion dollars a year in illegal goods and services, a price tag which is absorbed by the public in everyday price structures and the cost of living.

Today, the crime syndicate consists of 24 families of Italian descent which are highly organized on regional and national levels. A boss with absolute authority heads each family, and directly under him is a liaison officer and administrative assistant, along with a *consigliere* or counselor who is often a family elder. Below the consigliere are the *caporegine* or lieutenants, and finally come the *soldate* or buttonmen. While La Cosa Nostra does not have violence as its goal, its effectiveness is based on threats and fear, and occasionally there are brutal beatings and murders to set an example. The beatings may be performed with lead pipes, knives, and baseball bats, and sometimes those who are to be executed are tortured and then dismembered.

In gambling operations there is relatively little violence since credit is rarely accepted, but in the loan shark rackets credit payments must be forced illegally. The victims are usually members of the general public; the commission report describes the following typical case. A man borrowed 300 dollars to pay some medical bills but could not meet the 10 per cent per week (520 per cent per year) interest payments. He was beaten, his son was nearly kidnapped, and the syndicate tried to force his wife into prostitution. After having paid back 1000 dollars without reducing the original principal of 300 dollars he despaired and committed suicide.

In recent years, gangland murders have been fewer than in the past, but at the same time the crime syndicate has broadened and strengthened its influence. It has done this by using more sophisticated illegal business techniques and by winning the support of community residents who rely on the syndicate for protection. In addition, the wealth of the organization and its skill at blackmail and extortion makes bribery and corruption other powerful tools of La Cosa Nostra. In general, such organized crime flourishes only where it is supported by corrupt officials. For example, one underworld source maintains that half of the police department in one New England city is on the syndicate payroll. The police forewarn the syndicate of any raids or crackdowns which might disrupt the illegal activity of La Cosa Nostra.

In many ways, crimes against society are the worst crimes of all, for there are few defenses when the law is circumvented. The seriousness can be disguised by the fact that everyone is hurt a little but few are hurt very much. Organized crime claims that it is simply doing the same thing that businessmen and politicians do—namely, grabbing as much as they can get while also trying to stay out of trouble with the law. When people do this "above ground" as opposed to "under ground" it is usually referred to as white collar crime.

WHITE COLLAR AND CORPORATE CRIME

Late in 1970 an Illinois state politician named Paul Powell died after 36 years of service on the state payroll (Kifner, 1971). While he lay in state on the same catafalque that had once borne President Lincoln, thousands of admirers paid tribute. Mayor Richard Daley of Chicago called him a "natural leader" and Governor Richard Ogilvie quoted Shakespeare: "He was above all a man who demanded of himself a sense of honor. . . . " The Veterans of World War II bestowed upon him their coveted Americanism Award.

It is little wonder that Mr. Powell had so many friends. Shortly after his death it was discovered that in his apartment he had over 800,000 dollars in cash stuffed in shoe boxes, along with 49 cases of whiskey. His estate was valued at over three million dollars, an unbelievable sum, considering his salary. The complete story of Mr. Powell's career will probably never be known, but after his death much came to light concerning his wheelings and dealings with lobbyists, favor-seekers, patronage workers, campaign contributors, and businessmen. Mr. Powell used the muscle of his office to aid Chicago's lucrative horse racing tracks. He helped keep taxes low and profits high, and shared in the returns with kickbacks. He is reported to have received additional kickbacks from the trucking industry by allowing them to falsify information so they could make more money. Mr. Powell made a steady habit of soliciting "flower funds," a practice widespread among Midwestern politicians. This custom requires that those obligated should send money rather than flowers in appreciation. Another method of raising money was to get the state to help sponsor testimonial dinners for himself. Lobbyists and interest-seekers flocked to these affairs, some of which netted Mr. Powell over 100,000 dollars. Mr. Powell also administered the sales of low-numbered license plates, for which he received up to 1000 dollars. When the Roman Catholic Archdiocese of Chicago gave up license plate number "1," Mr. Powell used it for himself.

No deals were too small for Mr. Powell. He personally received all the coins out of the 18 Coca-Cola vending machines in the Illinois state capitol. He was reported to have taken funds earmarked for handicapped children and used the money to purchase glossy color photographs of himself. He harbored grudges against liberal politicians who attacked him, and in one case got the Springfield police to blanket an opponent with traffic tickets. He despised "hippies and other long haired animals," and at election time he openly bragged about fat contracts and plunder which awaited those who supported him. At Christmas he would tip his doorman two dollars, and when he died he left the bulk of his estate to preserve his home as a shrine.

Perhaps what is most interesting about this case is that decades of illegal activities and influence peddling gained rather than lost supporters. In a just and democratic political system that was efficiently operating, Mr. Powell could not possibly have succeeded; he represents a kind of corruption which the average citizen finances without knowing it. Many of Powell's friends continued to protect him after his death, saying that his wealth was obtained by saving money when he was young. Others, including some taxpayers, laughed off the whole affair, amused by how one man had managed to bilk the public of so much money.

Sociologists sometimes refer to "folk crimes"—those which are clearly illegal but nevertheless openly tolerated by the public. Sometimes they are tolerated because the average person never hears of them; this is because white collar crimes often lead to no court convictions (Sutherland, 1949). When business and professional people evince antisocial aggressions by evading taxes, advertising dishonestly, fixing prices, infringing on copyrights, or bribing decision makers, few people consider it as threatening as simple burglary. When businessmen are caught and convicted, which is rare, their corporations may pay any criminal fines and continue to employ the offender. Perhaps some of the hypocrisy is partly due to the fact that many businessmen hire lawyers who are skilled in the art of using (and changing) the law so that their activities are either technically legal or supported by loopholes. Sometimes the inequities are due simply to the status of the offender, for wealthy people can often find ways to stay out of jail while those of low status have no recourse to these methods. Take, for example, the recent case of a 23-year-old Negro who robbed a white girl of 30 dollars and a wrist watch (Robber . . . , 1970). An all-white Alabama jury found him guilty and sentenced him to death. Obviously this case eventually will be reversed, but the injustice done is almost a crime in itself.

Consider another recent case. The brokerage firm of Coggeshall and Hicks, members of the New York Stock Exchange, pleaded guilty to illegal trading over a five-year-period and using secret Swiss bank accounts to hide their 225,000 dollars in illegal commissions. Robert S. Keefer, Jr., senior partner in the firm, was fined 30,000 dollars. The presiding judge, Irving B. Cooper, suspended the jail sentence for Mr. Keefer, who was represented by a former New York district judge. The following week Judge Cooper tried an unemployed Negro for stealing a television set worth less than 100 dollars and sentenced him to a year in jail (Mintz and Cohen, 1971).

Just how flagrantly and frequently corporations violate the law has been illustrated in a classic study by Sutherland (1949). He carefully examined the 70 largest industrial and commercial corporations in the United States (excepting public utilities and oil companies). It was discovered that about half of these corporations were illegal in their origins or else began illegal activities shortly after they were founded. All 70 had been prosecuted and convicted of at least one crime. There were a total of 980 adverse decisions against these corporations, with the average company being convicted 14 times. This high rate of recidivism among these corporations is such that 90 per cent of them could be legally considered as habitual criminals.

Such blue chip corporate recidivism, as Ralph Nader calls it, is partly due to the fact that a substantial proportion of illegal activity carried out by corporation executives is deliberate and is highly organized. Nevertheless, such executives do not think of themselves as criminals. Like the Mafia, they have contempt for government and the law, both of which interfere with their illegal activities. Organized crime, whether corporate or underworld, usually adopts the old conservative philosophy that the best government is the one which governs least, a philosophy which would leave tycoons to their own methods.

> Businessmen differ from professional thieves principally in their greater interest in status and respectability. They think of themselves as honest men, not as criminals, whereas professional thieves, when they speak honestly, admit they are thieves. The businessman does regard himself as a lawbreaker, but he thinks the laws are wrong or at least that they should not restrict him, although they may well restrict others. He does not think of himself as a criminal, because he does not conform to the popular stereotype of the criminal. This popular stereotype is always taken from the lower socioeconomic class. (Sutherland, 1968)

An example might be taken from the well-known electrical equipment antitrust case of 1961. In this case a number of executives of General Electric, Westinghouse, and other companies met regularly with their competitors so that their prices would be fixed at a uniformly high level to the detriment of all buyers. One of the defendants was a vice president with a salary of 135,000 dollars a year. He was the father of three children and a Navy veteran who had risen to the rank of lieutenant commander. He had a degree in engineering from Georgia Tech and had been awarded an honorary doctorate from Siena College in 1958. He was a director of a boy's club, a trustee of a private girl's school, and a member of Governor Rockefeller's Temporary State Committee on Economic Expansion. Following his sentencing, he told the press that his conviction was "for conduct which has been interpreted as being in conflict with the complex antitrust laws" (Geis, G., 1968). Shortly after he was released from jail he was appointed president of a large product research corporation near Philadelphia.

Businessmen usually argue that fraud and deception are characteristic of only a few fly-by-night organizations. Others, however, argue that such practices are actually quite widespread among supposedly respectable blue-chip firms (Millones, 1970). How ethical are businessmen in general? This question was asked by Baumhart (1968), who polled 1700 businessmen, mostly top and middle management executives. Most respondents agreed that corporation executives cannot act in the interest of shareholders alone, but must also consider the interests of employees and consumers. But many businessmen tend to be cynical, and often they believe that while they themselves are ethical, others are not. When an executive acts ethically, he credits his own character. When he acts unethically, he tends to blame his superiors and the climate of the industry at large. About half of the respondents agreed with the statement, "The American business executive tends to ignore the great ethical laws as they apply immediately to his work. He is preoccupied chiefly with gain." Four out of seven executives believed that businessmen would violate ethics if they thought they could get away with it. About 80 per cent admitted that their own industry commonly engaged in practices which they personally considered unethical.

It is difficult to estimate to what extent business is engaged in illegal activity, for as Robert Morgenthau, nine years United States Attorney for New York City, points out, white collar crime is easy to conceal and evidence is difficult to obtain, even with great investigatory effort. Morgenthau recalls (as quoted in Mintz and Cohen, 1971) that he has convicted numerous lawyers (including law school professors), prominent doctors and surgeons, vice presidents of banks and publishing houses, executives in accounting and stock exchange firms, and high ranking politicians. Usually it is such people who are the first to complain about petty robberies and crime in the streets, and unfortunately the police spend the bulk of their time on the relatively easy to solve and generally more justifiable crimes — namely, the petty crimes committed by the poor. It was Morgenthau who pioneered attempts to crack down on secret numbered foreign bank accounts for illegal purposes, and not long thereafter he was fired by Attorney General John Mitchell, partly under pressure from the banking community.

It may be asked what white collar and corporation crime has to do with violence and aggression. The answer is that it is difficult to justify a double standard for crimes which cause death, injury and destruction. As Morgenthau pointed out, the legal-judicial system concentrates on relatively straightforward crimes, such as crimes of passion. But we tend to ignore more indirect and invisible behavior, sometimes deliberate, which eventually results in injury to someone else. Food processers, for example, sometimes extract vital nutrients from basic foods such as wheat and cereals, even though millions of Americans are suffering from hunger and malnutrition. They then pour money into expensive advertising campaigns to make the consumer believe he is getting a nutritious product. Deception is carefully employed not only in advertising but in packaging. This assures that the consumer will have a difficult time knowing what he is actually getting while also making it nearly impossible to compare products. Most processed foods are now adulterated with chemicals to change the color or flavor or to preserve it longer. Some foods, such as hot dogs, are now almost a third pure fat. When processing techniques become sloppy and government inspectors somehow remain "unaware" of conditions, people may actually die from food poisoning, as in a recent case with Bon Vivant vichyssoise soup.

Drug manufacturers have been notorious for flooding the public with worthless drugs on which they make great profits. Many potentially dangerous drugs are marketed without adequate scientific testing, and promotion campaigns place heavy pressure on doctors to use pills for everything. Advertising stresses unsubstantiated, magical wonders, while ill side-effects are played down. When drugs are proved harmful, many drug companies have been known to resort to extended litigation to keep the product on the market as long as possible before it must be withdrawn. With drugs which are essential, such as certain antibiotics, drug companies have been convicted of selling products at 30 times their manufacturing cost and conspiring with other companies to fix prices in order to maintain such profits. Once again the most vulnerable, the poor and the elderly, suffer the most.

Sometimes manufacturing and design defects are known but this information is suppressed, as Mintz and Cohen (1971) have documented in a number of specific cases. For many years automobile manufacturers resisted improvements in safety features, going back to the days when General Motors refused to put safety glass in their cars. Alfred Sloan, Jr., then GM president, said, "Accidents or no accidents, my concern in this is a matter of profit and loss.... You may say, perhaps, that I am selfish, but business is selfish. We are not a charitable institution—we are trying to make a profit for our stockholders." Before safety laws were passed in the 1960's, few manufacturers admitted to any defects. But when forced to by Federal law, over 12 million vehicles were recalled in the first three years.

In 1967 a Convair 580 crashed in Ohio killing 38 persons. An investigation revealed that a defect caused the propeller to come loose; it then penetrated the fuselage and made the plane crash. The manufacturer of the propeller, the Allison Division of General Motors, already knew about the defect, but had not advised any airlines about the dangers. The company was convicted and fined 8000 dollars.

Just how business interests win out over public interest is often an involved process of back-scratching in which many individuals are rewarded and no one is ultimately responsible. The oil industry is a prime example of how the consumer and the taxpayer indirectly support gigantic corporations which use their power to gain political favoritism and freedom from responsibility (e.g., the pollution issue). It seemed strange to many that for years the government policy on oil was almost indistinguishable from that of the industry itself. In 1959 President Eisenhower restricted the importation of foreign oil, supposedly for national security, although administration officials later admitted it was mainly for economic reasons. Forced to buy expensive American petroleum products, consumers paid an additional 40 to 70 billion dollars during the decade of the 1960s, a figure which by conservative calculations ended up costing the average family an extra 100 dollars a year. It is interesting to note that most industries pay about 40 per cent of their income in taxes, but the oil industry pays only 8 per cent. Between 1964 and 1967, Atlantic Richfield earned profits of 465 million dollars, yet made no federal tax payments whatsoever. It also turns out that oil men accounted for almost half of the large political contributions, nearly all of it going to the Republican Party. In the 1968 Presidential campaign, a number of Texas oil men visited Sen. Hubert Humphrey, the Democratic candidate. They offered several million dollars to aid his campaign if Humphrey would guarantee that he would continue to support the oil depletion allowance. Humphrey refused, and the oil men gave him nothing. Richard Nixon, on the other hand, was a partner in a Wall Street firm which often represented the oil interests before the 1968 elections. In 1967 Mr. Nixon successfully negotiated a tax-exempt status for an oil refinery run by a New York City financier, John Shaheen. In 1968, Mr. Shaheen made generous contributions to the Nixon-Agnew campaign. After being elected, President Nixon continued to make decisions favorable to the oil industry, and the oil industry continued to support the Republican Party. There is nothing illegal, of course, about supporting the oil industry at the expense of the taxpayer, but it does raise questions about whether politicians use their offices to serve themselves rather than the public. Many Congressmen have personal investments in the oil industry, and their re-election campaigns are often heavily financed by those favoring government subsidies, direct or indirect, for the oil industry. Further details can be found in Mintz and Cohen (1971).

It is encouraging to note that many businessmen, politicians, lawyers, and public offcials have advocated internal reforms, although much of the pressure has come from the consumer movement and an aroused public. When business and government combine to act against the public interest, it creates much unnecessary suffering and injustice and provides a foundation for social unrest. The United States has been fortunate to be wealthy enough so that wealth is spread, even if a handful of greedy individuals manipulate power and fortunes in their own interest. But in recent years the wealth that reaches the lower financial strata has been spread thinner and thinner until we have genuine suffering in the form of poverty, malnutrition, poor health, unemployment, and lack of education. The resulting inequality of wealth and opportunity is probably the most fundamental cause of social unrest and this is nowhere more evident than in America's troubled racial history.

INTERRACIAL VIOLENCE
IN AMERICAN HISTORY

During the decade of the 1960's, Americans witnessed an unusual number of ghetto revolts and civil riots in areas ranging from slums to college campuses. Many of the disorders were racial in character, and the National Commission on the Causes and Prevention of Violence reported that between 1964 and 1968 there were 239 violent riots with racial overtones. These involved over 200,000 people, resulting in 8000 casualties, including 191 dead, mostly blacks. More than 30,000 white Americans also participated in riots during this period, and there were about 200 major incidents involving white terrorism against blacks and civil rights workers.

To many, such civil disorders were something new. But not to all. As H. Rap Brown put it in 1967, "Violence is as American as cherry pie." There is considerable truth to this, and much of it is documented in the Kerner Report of the National Advisory Commission on Civil Disorders (Kerner, et al., 1968). The Kerner Commission shocked the nation when it concluded that the riots of 1967 were the direct result of 300 years of systematic racial discrimination in the United States. Perhaps it had not occurred to many that racial prejudice is a form of violence, for inevitably it leads to more violence.

Only 20 years after Columbus discovered America, Spanish, Dutch, and Portuguese slave traders brought African Negroes in chains to the New World. By the time of the American Revolution of 1776, one out of every six persons here was black; most of them were slaves. Often they were bought and sold like cattle and deprived of most human rights. In the Revolutionary War, orders were given to keep "Negroes or vagabonds" out of the Army, yet one of the very first Americans to die fighting the British was Crispus Attucks, a Boston Negro.

Many of the leaders in the American Revolution might be characterized as rabble-rousers dedicated to violent disruption. They successfully staged a number of violent incidents such as the Boston Tea Party and the so-called Boston Massacre in order to provoke the British and inflame public opinion. As occupying forces, the British were generally disliked, but there is considerable evidence that they treated most colonial settlers with respect. Today, of course, the American revolutionaries are remembered as patriots because they destroyed the established British colonial government.

In spite of the fact that the Declaration of Independence claimed that "all men are created equal," it was agreed at the Constitutional Convention that a black slave was actually only three-fifths of a person when it came to counting the population. It was not until the early part of the 19th century that Congress began trying to regulate slave trade, and while many Northern states abolished slavery, the institution became even more entrenched in the South. Most Negroes lived in the South, and it was there that repressive laws were passed so that blacks could not own property, get married, assemble in public, or have any rights in court.

The exploitation of Negroes was immensely profitable and therefore popular among white Southerners; however, "free" blacks in the North also fared poorly but for different reasons. Theoretically, Northern blacks could own property, but most knew only poverty and could not afford it. Those who could afford it were not permitted to live in white neighborhoods. In 1829, the white citizens of Cincinnati rioted and drove out half of the Negro population by invading their homes and burning their property. By the middle of the century, most Northern Negroes were "free" and living in poverty while Southern Negroes were slaves living in poverty. The Dred Scott decision of 1857 was an indication that the public was not yet ready to give Negroes the constitutional safeguards enjoyed by white Americans. But an abolitionist movement began to grow in popularity, partly because of the cruelty of slavery depicted in the book and play, *Uncle Tom's Cabin*. The trend toward emancipation was one of the principal causes of the Civil War, but blacks still were not allowed to join the Army until later when there were serious troop shortages. When blacks finally joined the Union armies, they were segregated in units of "colored troops," and not until the war was nearly over were they given equal pay.

Over one-half million Americans were killed in the Civil War, which made it one of the most costly and bloody episodes in American history. The ending of the war was the beginning of a whole new set of social conflicts, including those initiated by the assassination of President Lincoln by an embittered Southerner. Even before the war was over there were race riots in Cincinnati, Newark, Buffalo, and Troy, partly due to fears of cheaper black labor. Probably the worst riot in American history took place in New York City in 1863. The four-day melee (Figs. 33 and 34) was partly to protest the draft, and it is usually referred to as a draft riot. But racism due to fear of Negro competition in the labor market was the underlying explosive factor. The Irish-American workers, themselves much discriminated against, rioted throughout the city, and before it was over 2000 were killed and 8000 injured.

The ending of the Civil War had little immediate effect on white attitudes in the South. In New Orleans, 34 blacks were killed and 200 injured when they gathered at the city hall to discuss their new right to vote. The police attacked the Negroes and order was not restored until Federal troops were called in. General Sheridan later commented on the incident (Kerner, et al., 1968):

> At least nine-tenths of the casualties were perpetrated by the police and citizens by stabbing and smashing in the heads many who had already been wounded or killed by policemen. . . . it was not just a riot but an absolute massacre by the police . . . a murder which the mayor and police . . . perpetrated without the shadow of necessity.

Figure 33. *The New York City Draft Riot, which took place from July 13 to 16, 1863, was probably the worst riot in American history. Over two thousand were killed and eight thousand injured. (Courtesy of the Kean Archives.)*

The Reconstruction era saw the continuation of racial prejudice and the growth of other social and political conflicts. The Ku Klux Klan and other white supremacy movements became popular in the South. One Ku Klux Klan group in Mississippi boasted of killing 116 Negroes and throwing their bodies in the Tallahatchie River. Aided by the Supreme Court's *Plessy v. Ferguson* decision, separate but equal facilities gave legal sanction to segregation. Many other laws were rewritten: for example, the State of Louisiana had 130,344 registered black voters in 1896, but the law was rewritten so that only 5320 black voters remained. Not all civil violence was racial, for in the latter part of the 19th century there were a number of serious riots among railroad workers, miners, and other labor groups in which hundreds were killed.

This pattern of violence continued without abatement into the 20th century. In East St. Louis in 1917 a race riot erupted out of fear of social and economic competition from Negroes. Events were triggered in an aluminum plant in which Negro workers were hired to replace striking whites. The whites demanded that the mayor stop the influx of Negroes into St. Louis, and while tensions

Figure 34. *Racism was one of the underlying factors in the New York Draft Riots. This drawing depicts the lynching of a Negro on Clarkson Street. (Courtesy of the Kean Archives.)*

were running high a rumor spread that a Negro had shot a white person. Thousands of people congregated in angry mobs in search of vengeance, beating and killing any Negroes they found. The National Guard finally restored order, but the press continued to play up the Negro "crimes." Shortly thereafter, whites drove through black neighborhoods shooting at houses; Negroes then armed themselves and shot a police car. The following day the main street became a "bloody half-mile:" streetcars were stopped and searched for blacks, and those discovered, including women and children, were beaten and killed in front of cheering crowds of whites. White rioters later set fire to the Negro section of the city, resulting in 48 more deaths and 300 buildings destroyed.

In 1919 in Chicago, a Negro boy swam from a segregated black bathing area into a white swimming area and was stoned when he climbed onto the "white" raft. The boy drowned, and the in-flamed blacks demanded the arrest of the stone-throwers. Instead, the police arrested a Negro, and the Negroes then attacked the police. Racial unrest spread throughout the city and in the following week 38 were killed and hundreds were injured.

During World War I, Negroes were still heavily discriminated against in the armed forces, and a number were beaten and lynched, some still in uniform, when they returned home after having served in the "white man's army." During the same period, lynching and white riots against Negroes took place in many cities including Chester, Pennsylvania; Philadelphia; Washington, D.C.; Omaha; Charleston; Longview, Texas; Knoxville; and Tulsa. The number of riots is too extensive for further review; the reader can find additional historical detail in the Kerner Commission report.

The main purpose of this discussion is to support the argument that violence, particularly racial violence, has been going on for centuries in America. Levy (1969) sampled newspapers from 1819 to 1968 and complied statistics on violent incidents decade by decade. He found that the number of violent events has increased in recent years; however, if adjustments are made for population growth, the trend disappears. Moreover, the number of deaths and injuries due to political violence is lower now than in previous periods, although some violence, such as racial violence, has been consistently high over the entire 150 years.

The Dynamics of Urban Riots

The riots of the mid-20th century have followed the pattern of those in previous eras, except that now the blacks rather than the whites tend to riot. There were major riots in Detroit in 1943 and in Harlem in both 1935 and 1943. In every case the riot began with a racial incident followed by rumors and inflamed passions which led to massive violence (Lieberson and Silverman, 1965). In 1964 there were a number of race riots across the United States, including one in Harlem that began when a 15-year-old Negro boy was shot by the police. The worst riots in recent history took place in 1967, when there were 164 disorders in 23 cities, with the most serious being in Newark and Detroit (Wolfgang and Cohen, 1970). Both of these riots accounted for 64 deaths, over 1000 injuries, and property losses of 50 million dollars.

One way to study urban riots is to investigate the psychodynamics of the individuals involved. Following the large-scale riots of 1967 in Newark and Detroit, Caplan and Paige (1968) conducted detailed interviews with 437 respondents in Detroit and 236 in Newark. The persons selected were randomly chosen from the black ghettos where the riots took place, and respondents were interviewed by other blacks. On the basis of the interviews, each person was classified as a "rioter" or "nonrioter" in the hopes of comparing the background and motives of each type.

In Detroit, 11 per cent of those interviewed turned out to have actively participated in the riots, and in Newark the figure was 45 per cent. The main purpose of the study was to test the validity of three common theories about the causes of riots: (a) the "riffraff" theory, (b) the rising expectations (or relative deprivation) theory, and (c) the blocked opportunity theory.

The riffraff theory argues that rioters are irresponsible deviates of society and they are mainly criminals, unassimilated recent migrants, or emotionally disturbed individuals frustrated because of their status at the bottom of society. In its simplest form, the riffraff theory suggests that riots are caused by troublemakers (i.e., rioters). To many people, this "theory" is the simplest and most convenient to accept, but the Caplan and Paige study fails to support it. The evidence against the riffraff theory is as follows: (a) rioters and nonrioters have about the same annual income, so that rioters are not necessarily more poverty stricken; (b) both groups have about the same rate of unemployment, so that rioters are not necessarily those who are jobless or lazy; (c) those who riot are generally better educated, not more poorly educated, so that rioting cannot be attributed to lack of education; (d) long-term residents are more likely to riot, so that the trouble can not legitimately be blamed on newcomers or outsiders; (e) both rioters and nonrioters have similar family backgrounds and do not differ markedly in personality traits; (f) both rioters and nonrioters attend church with about the same regularity; (g) both groups express a surprising faith in the Protestant ethic. When asked, "Is getting what you want out of life a matter of ability or being in the right place at the right time," 77 per cent of the rioters and 76 per cent of the nonrioters replied that it was ability.

The rising expectations theory asserts that, compared with other groups, Negroes are not improving their status fast enough. Respondents were asked if life was getting better, worse, or staying about the same, and both groups answered about the same. If anything, the rioters tended to feel that life was beginning to get somewhat better. About one-third of each group felt that the economic gap between whites and blacks was widening; however, more rioters than nonrioters noticed a widening gap between prosperous blacks and poor blacks. The rising expectations or relative deprivation theory would predict that rioting would occur when things are starting to get better, but not fast enough, rather than when they are at their worst. There is partial support for this theory, particularly when blacks compare their status with other blacks, for the rioters tended to feel that they were beginning to get ahead.

Related to the rising expectations theory is the blocked opportunity theory, which focuses on environmental rather than on personal factors. This theory holds that riots are the result of the massive discrimination against the Negro that has frozen him out of the economic and social life of America. Widespread prejudice helps maintain a stereotype of Negro inferiority and prevents social and economic mobility. This theory was tested by asking if respondents had found job obstacles and discrimination against them which blocked their goals. Significantly more rioters reported such experiences, and further probing revealed that it was not due to lack of training or education. Rioting Negroes expressed more pride in their own race, but less pride in the country as a whole. Almost twice as many rioters said that if the country engaged in a major war it would not be worth fighting to save it. In summary, it appears that the frustration resulting from the exclusion of blacks from American society is one of the most fundamental causes of riots.

Similar conclusions have come from other studies. Ransford (1968) interviewed residents of the Watts area of Los Angeles following the riots of 1965. These authors concentrated on measuring the amount of contact individuals had had with white people, their perceived powerlessness, and the racial discrimination they had perceived. They found that all three factors interacted in such a way that Negroes who are racially isolated from whites, who feel powerless to influence events, and who feel a strong dissatisfaction because of discrimination are the most volatile group, with 65 per cent expressing a willingness to resort to violence. The study suggests that there may be a distinction between educated middle class Negroes who are vocal in civil rights activities and who place great faith in the revolution of rising expectations, and the individuals interviewed in Watts. The latter group appears to be intensely disillusioned and embittered, and for the most part, many have given up any hope of improvement through normal democratic procedures such as peaceful protests or elections. A sad footnote to the riots of the 1960's is that business, community, and government leaders gathered in the aftermath and formed organizations dedicated to bringing about environmental and social changes in the ghettos, but as of 1972 most of these pledges remain empty promises.

Caplan (1970) has attempted to summarize a profile of the ghetto militant. Militancy is not limited to a deviant and irresponsible minority, but represents an almost normative approach to civil rights objectives. Most black militants are no more criminally oriented than anyone else, but they feel justified in breaking laws which serve to repress them. They have a new sense of pride in their race, if not their country. They have rejected the traditional Negro role of passive adaptation, acceptance of inferiority, and nonachievement and have replaced it with a sense of mission dedicated toward improving their quality of life. To the extent that this brings them into direct confrontation with white society, racial conflicts will probably continue.

In summary, riots are "caused" by some violent precipitating incident, but they would never occur if there were not deep underlying social and economic bitterness. The Kerner Commission singled out a number of general causes for this basic bitterness, including (a) pervasive white racism, (b) black migration and white exodus, (c) black ghettos (d) frustrated hopes, (e) the legitimizing of violence, (f) the feeling of powerlessness, (g) the encouragement of violence by extremists, (h) police power.

It is not difficult to find examples which illustrate the dynamics of social violence. Power is abused by those in authority, and individuals who are persecuted respond with contempt for the law and the social system in general. Marx (1970) points out that historically most of the casualties in riots are caused by the police and supplies quotations illustrating the bloodthirstiness of some police. At the Democratic National Convention in Chicago in 1968, many of Mayor Daley's police went berserk in what official reports later termed a police riot. In response, militant groups glorified the killing of any policeman as a symbol of white power. It is interesting to note that in recent years there have been over 100 civil rights murders, but almost no murders of white racists (Marx, 1970). In the South, crimes of whites against blacks are frequently condoned, causing widespread disrespect of the law. Blacks, on the other hand, are severely punished for even trivial offenses. For serious crimes, blacks are much more likely to be sentenced to death than are whites (Clark, 1970).

Defenders of the present system of "law and order" sometimes accuse their critics of being "paranoids" in search of a conspiracy. But only a blind person could fail to see how social justice is routinely compromised by those in authority, whether they be FBI agents, generals, local police, or politicians. Attorney General Mitchell has fought long and hard to get provisions making it possible for police to break and enter without a warrant, to jail people without charges, and to use legal harassment to crush political dissent. Numerous government agencies keep detailed dossiers on millions of American citizens because of their political beliefs or social attitudes. Stories continue to leak out about how law enforcement agencies deliberately plan violence and riots

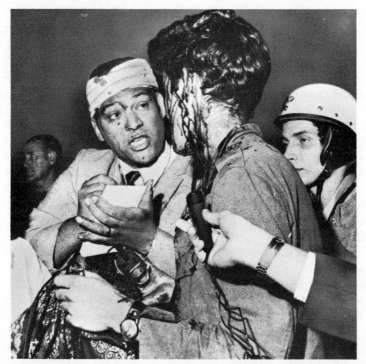

Figure 35.   *When the forces of law and order commit crimes, citizens have little recourse and democracy becomes a mockery. At the 1968 Democratic convention, Chicago police rioted and brutally beat many innocent people. NBC newsman John Evans (left) and photographer Dan Morrill were both victims of police attacks. (Courtesy of Wide World Photos.)*

to gain an excuse to arrest individuals or groups of which they disapprove (Ripley, 1971; Roberts, 1971).

On October 19, 1971 Sen. Edward Kennedy made a speech in which he argued that the misuse of law and authority endangered basic Constitutional freedoms more than any radical group (Kennedy, 1971). As an example, he pointed to the speedy and vigorous prosecution of Dr. Daniel Ellsberg, who released the Pentagon Papers. These "secret" papers in fact contained no secrets other than those revealing how government officials had deceived the public for years about the war in Viet Nam. In contrast, when National Guardsmen at Kent State fired directly into groups of unarmed students, killing four of them, law enforcement agencies dragged their feet for fifteen months, and then decided to condemn the students and drop the case.

Is this paranoia? On the same day that Senator Kennedy spoke, the following events took place: A guard was indicted for killing a prisoner by kicking him to death in a shower (Kaplan, 1971). Twenty-three Memphis policemen were suspended after they reportedly murdered a black youth and faked the evidence to make it look like an accident (Tennessee.. , 1971). And while H. Rap Brown, a black left-wing militant, was put on bail for a quarter of a million dollars following an alleged armed robbery, all charges were dropped against a right-wing militant group which had organized a fire-bombing of political opponents (Kihss, 1971). In the latter case, a Minuteman group had been caught with 125 rifles, 10 pipe bombs, five mortars, a dozen machine guns, a bazooka, three grenade launchers, and a million rounds of ammunition. In making their defense they claimed only to be peaceful collectors of guns. In addition, on the same day, the Knapp Commission began hearings on New York City police corruption (Knapp hearings, 1971). One patrolman testified that during 14 years on the force he had never heard of or known of a policeman in a gambling enforcement unit who did *not* take bribes. A gambler stated that continual police graft made it possible for him to stay in operation for 40 years. Another patrolman testified that, of over 70 policemen in his precinct, only two were honest and refused to take payoffs. If such allegations are true, and if this was a typical day, then society is faced not with a few rotten apples in the barrel, but a lot of rotten barrels.

Social violence is a paradox in a democracy, for the democratic process is supposed to avoid and correct legitimate grievances (Iglitzin, 1970). The presence of riots would seem to suggest the absence of real democracy, for riots are like instrumental acts performed in the pursuit of goals which are unobtainable by other means. The fact that a society responds more to physical force than to moral force reveals something about that society, and it makes us wonder why there have not been more riots. As one Negro said on Independence Day:

> The Fourth of July is *yours*, not mine. *You* may rejoice, *I* must mourn. To drag a man into the grand illuminated temple of liberty, and call upon him to join you in joyous anthems, is inhuman mockery and sacrilegious irony.... Fellow citizens, above your national tumultuous joy, I hear the mournful wail of millions, whose chains, heavy and grievous yesterday, are today rendered more intolerable by the jubilant shouts that reach them....

These words were spoken in 1852 (Kerner, et al., 1968), and unfortunately they remain relevant today.

WAR

Probably the oldest and simplest explanation of war is that it is a reflection of man's basic nature. Countries engage in war because their people are warlike. Because warfare has been so ubiquitous throughout human history some have argued that it fulfills a basic human need (Storr, 1964). In Freudian terminology, war is caused by the death instinct. The idea that man has a fundamental lust for killing and destruction is often portrayed with a romantic touch, as in the following passage which describes the feelings of a German soldier in World War I:*

> The great moment had come. The curtain of fire lifted from the trenches. We stood up.
>
> With a mixture of feelings, evoked by bloodthirstiness, rage, and intoxication, we moved in step, ponderously but irresistibly toward the enemy lines. I was well ahead of the company, followed by Vinke and a one-year veteran named Haake. My right hand embraced the shaft of my pistol, my left a riding stick of bamboo cane. I was boiling with mad rage, which had taken hold of me and all the others in an incomprehensible fashion. The overwhelming wish to kill gave wings to my feet. Rage pressed bitter tears from my eyes.
>
> The monstrous desire for annihilation, which hovered over the battlefield, thickened with the brains of the men and submerged them in a red fog. We called to each other in sobs and stammered disconnected sentences. A neutral observer might have perhaps believed that we were seized by an excess of happiness.
>
> ERNST JÜNGER

This soldier did not start World War I, but if all Germans (and all Frenchmen, Englishmen, Americans, and so on) were equally bloodthirsty it might be easier to explain why societies go to war. Such an explanation attempts to account for international conflict on the basis of individual motivation, and as was pointed out at the beginning of this chapter there is little reason for accepting this view. There may have been a time when warfare was highly personalized, involving face-to-face encounters in which one individual actually fought with another individual and became so angry that he enjoyed killing. But that day is over. Warfare is the result of carefully calculated political activity carried out by governments (Holloway, 1967). It is institutional behavior and

---

*Ernst Jünger, as quoted in J. G. Gray, *The Warriors.* New York, Harper and Row, 1967. Used by permission of the author.

must be analyzed in terms of these institutions rather than in terms of generalities about individual motivation. But individual motivation is not irrelevant, for it forms the basis of the political and economic institutions which draw a society into warfare.

Sometimes attempts are made to explain warfare on the basis of generalizations about animal behavior (Lorenz, 1966; Tinbergen, 1968). It was noted in Chapter 1 that most animals which developed deadly weapons also evolved with strong inhibitions against using them against conspecifics. When fighting does take place, it is usually ritualized so that injury seldom results. Animals may threaten an opponent, but if the opponent makes a gesture of appeasement or submission, attack is inhibited. In the case of humans, we have no deadly fangs or horns, and it has been suggested that this may explain our failure to develop inhibitions against killing other humans. Our deadliness has come from our technology, and this technology has developed so rapidly that evolutionary adaptations and inhibitions have not been able to keep pace. But this argument stresses man's similarities to other animals rather than his differences. Many species from ants to monkeys participate in group conflict, but there is really nothing comparable to human warfare in any other animal society (Scott, 1962b). What separates man from all other animals is his language and his technology. Technology could be used to satisfy human needs so that warfare would become unnecessary. Language, the most sophisticated ritual of all, could provide a basis for culture through which we would appreciate and prevent the horrors of war.

Thus, simple generalizations from animal behavior offer little in the way of understanding human warfare. But some analogies remain relevant. If baby rats are sprayed with a foreign odor (such as Dior perfume), their mother is likely to kill them because they have been "de-ratized." Likewise, killing is made easier in humans if the opponent is first dehumanized. In fact, such dehumanization provides a strong defense against the emotional revulsion of killing (Bernard, Ottenberg, and Redl, 1971). It is easier to kill if one is convinced that the enemy is subhuman or is somehow fundamentally evil or dispensable. Accordingly, racism often provides a justification of intergroup conflict. Some people believe that orientals ("gooks") do not value life and are not really like people. Others consider blacks ("niggers") fundamentally inferior. Still others see Russians ("Commies") as evil atheists.

Religion also may provide a rationale for hatred, as in the current disputes between Catholics and Protestants in Northern Ireland, between the Israelis and Arabs in the Middle East, and between the Moslems and Hindus in Pakistan. In Pakistan, hundreds of thousands have been killed and atrocities rival those committed by the Nazis. Reporters discovered that a common practice among Moslem soldiers in East Pakistan has been to rip away a man's *lungi* (sarong) to see if he is circumcised. Those who are not are likely to be Hindus, and they are usually executed (Pakistan, 1971). But violence breeds more violence, and the Bengali soldiers respond with atrocities of their own (Fig. 36).

Perhaps the best (or worst) example of dehumanization is that perpetrated on the Jews by the Nazis, a persecution in which a great many Germans participated. At first Jews were deprived of citizenship and later they lost all civil rights. They were placed in concentration camps and treated like animals. Jews were stripped naked, tatooed, numbered, shipped in cattle cars, fed animal food, and sprayed with insecticide. Abused, starving, and disease-ridden, the helpless prisoners looked and acted less than human, all of which made it easier to execute them.

Thus, dehumanization helps to legitimize killing, and some

Figure 36. *The bloody civil war in Pakistan led to numerous atrocities on both sides. Here a Bengali rebel triumphantly displays the head of a federal soldier. (Courtesy of UPI.)*

individuals even come to think they are performing a humanitarian service. Such brutalization is often aided by propaganda which glorifies warfare, makes suffering remote, and portrays the enemy as the embodiment of evil. Courage, bravery, and self-sacrifice are praised as contributing toward honor, patriotism, and God (each camp always has God on its side). Propagandists crank out hostile caricatures of the enemy calculated to make him as repulsive and insidious as possible. In many Hollywood movies, the Comanche chief or the Japanese general is cruel, humorless, and blood-thirsty. German U-boat commanders get special attention, for they are shown peering through the periscope waiting for an un-witting hospital ship that they can blow up. John Wayne, on the other hand, represents the force of good fighting the evil of the world. To enemies of the United States, Uncle Sam is portrayed as the Devil himself, complete with a forked tail, horns, and money stuffed in every pocket.

Another way killing is made acceptable is to make it remote. It is reported that even the war criminal Adolf Eichmann was sickened by the Nazi death camps, so he stayed away and concen-trated on pushing papers behind a desk (Milgram, 1967). Modern warfare has eliminated much of the feedback of an opponent's suffering, and this makes it easier to continue attacking. Fighter pilots engaged in a dogfight think that they are shooting at a machine and not at a person. A bombardier releases bombs by pushing a button, but he never sees all the people who are killed and maimed. Sometimes pilots later see destroyed homes and crippled children as a result of bombing, and only then suffer severe psychological and emotional effects. It is for this reason that American pilots in Viet Nam have usually been sent to Hong Kong or to Japan on leave rather than to other parts of Viet Nam, where they could see the results of their bombing.

When suffering is remote, responsibility is also remote. Today, warfare is much more attractive because the men who direct it never do any fighting themselves but instead delegate others to do it. Or, as Senator McGovern said recently:

> Very frankly, any senator who talks about sending American forces into Cambodia ought to lead the charge himself. I'm fed up with old men dreaming up wars for young men to die in, particularly stupid wars of this kind that add nothing to our security.

Through language and technology, militarism has become a respectable abstraction. Policies leading to war are made in the seclusion of conference rooms, and technology has automated fighting to make it more sanitary. Jargon is invented so that strategists can talk about killing without sounding bloodthirsty. No one authorizes the killing of civilians, but many approve of "free fire zones" which means that civilians can be killed. When aerial bombardment was first invented many people considered it a form of atrocity. Bombing is still not a pleasant thought, and so Secretary of Defense Melvin Laird invented the term "protective reaction." Killing is made impersonal, and by making it impersonal, individual responsibility is diminished and suffering is remote.

The remoteness of war is seen by the fact that many people contribute by reading instruments, pushing buttons, programming computers, and manufacturing weapons. Even the combat foot soldier rarely sees the enemy and depends on machines and firepower. Future wars may be even more abstract, with few decisions left to anyone. The dynamics of thermonuclear warfare require instant decisions so that heavy reliance must be placed upon electronic detection and computerized decisions. Theoretically, someone (the President) is "in charge" of the use of nuclear weapons, but in fact all the commands have been locked into computers so that warfare can take place almost automatically. Certainly there will be little time for thinking, and the computers will execute any program, no matter how suicidal. Sometimes it is suggested that we build a doomsday machine so that all humanity can be eliminated if anyone dares to start a war. This could be done by burying an enormous nuclear bomb — one large enough to blow up the world — deep in the earth, perhaps under New York City. It could be wired to heat sensors so that if the temperature ever reached thousands of degrees (i.e., from a nuclear attack), the doomsday bomb would explode, destroying everyone.

A reasonable person might not be surprised that population masses can be duped by propaganda and simple conformist ideas. But it is both surprising and dangerous if national leaders and policy-makers fall into the same trap. In the long run such leaders decide issues of war and peace, and it is often assumed that major decisions are the rational work of one man (i.e., the President or Prime Minister). More sober analyses often reveal that important policy decisions may be the result of consensus by a small group of individuals, what Janis (1971) calls "groupthink." It has been noted that when a group of policy-makers gathers to discuss issues, the atmosphere and dynamics may resemble that found in any small group trying to reach a decision. In an effort to maintain cohesiveness, the group exerts pressures for social conformity by trying to bring dissenters around to the majority view. If this fails the dissenters are usually ostracized. Such an atmosphere limits opportunities for independent thinking and objective criticism, and the group tends to gravitate toward a common denominator and premature consensus. Views which do not bolster group cohesiveness are likely to be rejected. Some of the observers who sat in on discussions regarding the bombing of North Viet Nam observed such "groupthink" behavior, and were amazed at the uncritical acceptance of slogans and stereotypes about the enemy. Many alternatives were excluded because the problems often tended to be formulated in terms of game theory and military jargon. And at many times the moral and philosophical considerations were secondary to economic motives.

The Military-Industrial-Congressional Complex

Early in 1971 the Columbia Broadcasting System televised a documentary entitled "The Selling of the Pentagon" which dealt with the mammoth advertising and public relations efforts by the military. The controversial program was quickly attacked by the Pentagon, and many congressmen called for a censure of CBS. Most of the criticisms, however, were aimed at editing details rather than the substance of the report. It revealed that the Pentagon is estimated to spend more money on public relations than the combined total budgets of all the major television networks. For example, about 6.5 million is spent each year grinding out propaganda movies such as "Red Nightmare," "Why Vietnam," and "The Road to War." Hollywood movie stars such as Jack Webb often narrate these films which practically equate Communism with slavery. The Pentagon distributes millions of public relations releases for newspapers and employs high-ranking military officers to tour the country giving lectures on foreign policy and promoting the interests of the military. Millions of dollars are spent each year on air shows and weaponry displays.

It is little wonder that the Pentagon mounts such a staggering public relations campaign, for how else could they convince the public that it should spend more money on a single aircraft carrier than on all primary and secondary education? Wars which were clearly in the public interest did not need advertising campaigns to keep them popular, but Viet Nam has been a different story. Few can explain why the United States has pursued the Vietnamese War with such ferocity, spending over 400 billion dollars and dropping over two and a half times as many bombs as in all of World War II. Over a million and a half people have been killed in Vietnam, most of them by American firepower. At least 100,000 of the dead have been women and young children.

To maintain such policies the Pentagon needs many strong supporters, and such support has been forthcoming from Congress and the business community. This is not surprising, because the arms industry is a profitable business. Fighting foreign wars can be made remote, but politics and the pocketbook are close to home. Between 1964 and 1970 the world has spent over a trillion dollars on arms. Since World War II the United States alone has devoted *eleven hundred billion dollars* for military purposes (Melman, 1970). This trend is increasing, not decreasing, and today many of the emerging nations of Asia, Africa, and Latin America are diverting more and more of their wealth into arms (Hess, 1970). When President Eisenhower left office in 1961 he warned of a giant military establishment which we now call the Military-Industrial-Congressional Complex. Because of its vast power and wealth, it has a strong influence on all foreign and domestic policy in the United States, and it represents a threat because it is essentially unregulated and self-perpetuating. By extracting the majority of every tax dollar the military establishment can finance almost any venture and hide behind the sacred shield of "national defense." Abroad it attempts to police the world with 3401 overseas military bases. It undermines some governments through political intrigue, and props up others with free arms (McGaffin and Knoll, 1969). At home, the Pentagon is deeply involved in almost every phase of life, from banking to education. For example, in 1969, the Massachusetts Institute of Technology was the 10th largest of all Pentagon contractors. In order to influence public policy, the military maintains hundreds of full-time lawyers, lobbyists and secret agents. Only recently has it been disclosed that the military employs a network of agents who spy on civilians, particularly those whose political views conflict with those of the military (Halloran, 1971).

Under such pressure it is little wonder that enormous sums have been squandered to strengthen the military, often without strengthening the national defense. In 1967 Secretary of Defense Robert McNamara testified before the House Appropriations Committee that the United States had spent 50 billion dollars since World War II to defend against a conventional bomber attack from the Soviet Union, even though their bomber force was very small and vastly overrated. In the 1960's the Pentagon turned to making missiles, and by its own admission 23 billion dollars was spent on missiles which proved unworkable or obsolete (McGaffin and Knoll, 1969). The current project of major interest to the Pentagon is the ABM (anti-ballistic missile) which many experts maintain cannot possibly work effectively and may jeopardize rather than maintain peace. The bill supporting development of the ABM passed in the Senate by only one vote, even though it may eventually cost the country hundreds of billions of dollars.

How does the Pentagon get such blank checks from Congress? In 1969, Congressman Richard McCarthy observed, "When you look at the composition of the Armed Services Committee and the Defense Appropriations Subcommittee in the House, you find that some members tend to ignore public opinion. Faced with a choice, they would rather cut education and Medicaid, they would rather close hospitals, than reduce military spending." A good example of this type of member is the late Mendel Rivers, Chairman of the House Armed Services Committee and a Democrat from the First Congressional District of South Carolina. Congressman Rivers was re-elected year after year on the slogan, "Rivers delivers," and his local popularity led citizens to name Route 52 through his district "Rivers Avenue." It is no small coincidence that his district and the immediate surroundings contained the following installations: the Charlestown Naval Shipyard, a Polaris submarine base, the Parris Island Marine training camp, a Marine air station, an Army supply depot, two Navy hospitals, an Atomic Energy plant which manufactures nuclear weapons, and plants built by Lockheed, McDonnell, Avco, and General Electric. No wonder he was popular. By being from a "safe" district and taking advantage of the seniority system, he rose to power and devoted his career to spending as much money as possible for the military, particularly in his home district.

Civilian businessmen are enthusiastic about military spending because it is immensely profitable. In the Nike missile system, the prime contractor (Western Electric) made a profit of 6684 per cent and the Douglas Corporation made a 36,000 per cent profit (36,000 per cent . . . , 1969). Such profits, of course, are unusual, but government hearings on the subject have revealed that major defense contractors earn profits about 70 per cent higher than firms engaged in nondefense work (McGaffin and Knoll, 1969). A more recent investigation by the GAO (General Accounting Office) revealed that military contractors realized profits almost three times as high as most other manufacturing concerns (Shabecoff, 1970). The cozy relationship between the Pentagon and large businesses is partly maintained by many high-ranking military officers who retire and immediately go to work for defense-related industries. A Department of Defense study released in 1969 reported that there were 2072 high-ranking former military officers employed by the 100 top Pentagon contractors.

Financial support for the military machine even comes from

America's churches. A recent study (Robinson, 1972) found that
ten major Protestant denominations have invested over 1.5 billion
dollars in the arms industry. The United Methodist Church, for
example, invests 14.1 per cent of its worth in military stocks
(59,751,899 dollars at 1970 market value). Not everyone, of course,
supports the military establishment, not even all military officers.
General David M. Shoup, retired commandant of the Marine Corps,
has said that

> civilians can scarcely understand or even believe that many
> ambitious military professionals truly yearn for wars and the
> opportunities for glory and distinction afforded only in combat.
> A career of peacetime duty is a dull and frustrating prospect
> for the normal regular officer to contemplate.... America has
> become a militaristic and aggressive nation.

No wonder it is commonly remarked that wars are too important
to be left to the generals.

Obedient Aggression

It may be easy to explain why politicians make belligerent
pronouncements and why businessmen are eager to get military
contracts. But somebody must do the killing, and it is harder to
explain why individuals participate, particularly when the killing
involves obvious atrocities. For insights on this we may return to
laboratory studies with the "aggression machine" and ask why
anyone even goes through with such experiments. When these
studies first appeared, Milgram (1963; 1965) doubted that anyone
would participate. He asked college students and faculty members
if they thought subjects would agree to administer severe electric
shock to a stranger. The general consensus was that most people
would not. So Milgram put this question to test by instructing
subjects that it was their job to teach someone else to memorize
a list of words, and if mistakes were made electric shock should
be administered as punishment. (The subjects were led to believe
that they were participating in an experiment testing the effects
of punishment on learning.) A conspicuous shock generator had
a master dial with 30 voltage levels from 15 to 450 volts with
corresponding labels ranging from "Slight Shock" to "Danger;
Severe Shock." The learner, of course, was a stooge who was
strapped with electrodes but was never actually shocked. His
task was to deliberately make mistakes at specified intervals and
fake pain as the shock level was turned higher and higher. At first
he was to moan and protest, then he was to pound on the wall,

and finally he would scream. At higher intensities he would demand to be let out of the experiment and would claim a heart condition. The experiment was to continue until the teacher refused to go on, or until the maximum shock level was reached. Strangely enough, most subjects remained obedient and continued to turn up the shock dial even though they thought the learner was in severe agony. The subjects were 40 males of various occupations, and 26 of the 40 went all the way to the limit of 450 volts. The other 14 defied their instructions to continue, but only after they had reached the 300-volt mark. Similar findings have been reported in other experiments, which tend to confirm the fact that people will engage in such aggression if they think that others expect them to.

The sad fact is that history is full of atrocities committed by people who were only "doing their duty." Obedience to authority has long been praised as a virtue, particularly by those who hold power. As Milgram (1967) points out, conservatives have argued for centuries that the very fabric of society is threatened by disobedience, and that it is better to obey evil commands than undermine the structure of authority. An example of obedience to criminal orders was the Nazi extermination of Jews during World War II. These atrocities were particularly criminal because of (a) the sheer number of victims, estimated at over six million people; (b) the fact that many of the victims were women and children and had no combatant status; (c) the victims were executed without a trial and were innocent by any standard of justice; and (d) the extermination was not an impulsive act but a calculated and highly organized enterprise methodically carried out over a period of years. The Germans who brought the Jews to prison camps did not feel responsible, nor did those who constructed the ovens. Even those who put the Cyclon-B into the gas chambers probably felt they were only doing their duty and obeying someone else's orders. In this way, everyone passed on the responsibility until eventually it was so diffuse and remote that no one felt responsible.

Similar arguments were heard in the My Lai trials in which American soldiers were convicted of killing a number of unarmed, unresisting civilians, including women and babies. Most of the victims were pushed into a ditch and executed while others were shot in the head at pointblank range. The public reaction to these trials was strangely mixed, for some tried to deny that the events occurred while others tried to justify them. Opton (1971) points out that a surprising number tried to mix these arguments (i.e., "It never happened, and besides, they deserved it."). Many

Americans did not want to think about it any more than the Germans like rehashing old Nazi crimes. But many of those who accepted the facts and did think about it searched for justifications. The most common justification was none other than obedience to authority: a soldier's duty is to follow orders. Some looked for more far-reaching justifications, such as the fact that "war is hell" and that war crimes are commonplace. Others placed the blame squarely on the generals and politicians who pursued the war in such a way that such atrocities were an inevitable extension of official policy.

In summary, warfare is like many other forms of large-scale social conflict. The causes are embedded in the momentum of institutions which reflect but far outweigh the motivation of individuals. Firearms, alcohol, television violence, and prisons are tolerated at enormous social cost. No one seems able to change this, no matter how rational his argument. No one really likes warfare, but many people like to get elected to office or to be awarded fat defense contracts. Because institutions can create their own ethics and can perpetuate themselves with their power, they have great capacity for destruction. In the long run modern society may suffer more from too much organization than not enough organization. Anarchists have long pointed out that institutional evil is by far the most dangerous form of evil (Milgram, 1970). The goal of anarchy is not violence and destruction, but a disruption of institutions so that perhaps large-scale destruction could be reduced to lesser forms of social upheaval. It is unfortunate that events in recent years have shown that institutions do indeed sometimes become reckless, resorting to unnecessary violence and brutality in their efforts to maintain controls. One need only examine the convention riots in Chicago in 1968, along with the massacres at My Lai, Kent State, and Attica prison, in order to realize that some of the highest officials continue to believe that the solution for violence is more violence.

But neither wars nor corrupt institutions are inevitable. Such modern industrial nations as Switzerland, Sweden, Denmark, and Norway have engaged in no wars in over a century. And while some countries in Latin America seem eternally embroiled in internal revolution, they rarely participate in foreign wars. Andreski (1964) points out that for three centuries before World War I, Britain was involved in dozens of wars. But less than one per cent of the population actually participated in these wars, and relatively little time was spent actually fighting. Livingstone (1967) reviews a number of cross-cultural studies estimating the percentage of warfare casualties in other cultures and reports that in many wars 20 to 30 per cent of the population have been killed. Such figures seem astronomical compared to wars in Western Civilization. Of course we have reached the point where one more major war could kill nearly everyone. But we have also reached the point where peace movements are gaining in popularity and in political power. More and more people are becoming convinced that foreign wars based on traditional motives of power, territory, prestige, and ideology are fundamentally a waste of human resources. There seems to be at least as much reason for hope as for despair.

7   THE CONTROL OF AGGRESSION

Scientists are often criticized for studying a problem to death without actually doing anything about it. At the opening of this book it was remarked that man has more than a detached, scholarly interest in aggression. If this is so, scientists should not be content merely to analyze aggression and to criticize society, but they should also offer constructive suggestions. But as we have seen, aggression is not a unitary process, and, accordingly, there are no simple, unitary solutions. As Feshbach (1971) has pointed out, scientists cannot yet offer definitive statements about the nature of aggression, nor can scientific evidence alone provide the basis for moral evaluation of behavior. But scientists do have educated guesses which are more than mere opinions, and it would be foolish to ignore what we have learned. We recognize that not all aggressive behavior is "bad" or maladaptive, but some clearly destructive forms can be controlled or prevented. The following is a brief summary of some of the major theoretical positions and their possible practical application.

INSTINCT THEORIES

Inventing instincts to explain motivated behavior has been a popular pastime ever since the days of Aristotle. Maternal behavior has been explained by the presence of a maternal instinct, self-preservation by an instinct for self-preservation, and aggression by an aggressive instinct. In the early part of the 20th century scientists engaged in bitter disputes about how many instincts there were or whether they existed at all. Such "theorizing" became so discredited that scientists soon completely gave up using the term instinct altogether, and they found that little was lost. Laymen, on the other hand, continue to use the term with abandon although they almost never know what they mean by it. The term instinct has almost no *explanatory* power; however, it does have a certain amount of *descriptive* utility when referring to complex, adaptive, and stereotyped behavior which is species-typical and is present at birth.

Because of the confusion created by the use of the term instinctual, ethologists such as Lorenz (1965; 1966) have placed more emphasis on terms like "innate" and "phylogenetically adapted." Lorenz sees aggression as an unlearned biological drive which evolved because of its adaptive value to the species. Thus, aggression is not necessarily a destructive force, although Lorenz feels that in man's case aggressive energy has been distorted into maladaptive behavior. Since aggression is an innate force we cannot "control" it by getting rid of it, but rather we must displace this energy into socially constructive outlets such as athletic competition or artistic expression. This view is not new and was expressed over one-half century ago by William James in an essay entitled "The Moral Equivalent of War." James argued that aggressive urges should be sublimated into morally useful substitutes to keep them from finding expression in wars.

Certainly aggressive behavior in any living animal is phylogenetically adaptive, for those animals in which it was maladaptive are no longer with us. Of course, what may be adaptive for the survival of the species may not be adaptive to the survival of an individual. Male spiders would be much smarter if they stayed away from females, but if their ancestors had had such wisdom there wouldn't be any spiders. But even phylogenetic adaptations may be of little relevance to the contemporary behavior of man, for our language and our technology dominate man's social behavior. While it may be safe to say that some aggressive behavior in some species is strongly influenced by innate components, it is incorrect to say that aggression in general is innate. Other kinds of aggressive behavior in other species are more strongly influenced by social and environmental experience. But probably most species, including man, have some sort of genetically-determined pre-wiring in their nervous system which gives individuals the capacity for organized violent and destructive behavior independent of any experience. Except in the case of the malfunctioning of a nervous system influenced by brain disease or drugs, the control of the expression of aggression is largely influenced by social and cultural factors, particularly in man.

Lorenz and Ardrey and other instinct theorists may be partly right in that the mammalian brain probably has an innate neurological substrate for organized attack and killing behavior. But there are at least three major flaws in their position. The first is that they have not developed any systematic theory. Their "theorizing" involves journalistic and poetic expressions full of undefined concepts and poorly-chosen terms which offend the scientist. No one really knows exactly what they mean nor is it clear that they themselves know. Second, instinct theorists have chosen to ignore the bulk of the scientific literature on aggression, either by choice or out of ignorance. One need only glance at the reference section of a book like *On Aggression* (Lorenz, 1966) to see that the evidence cited is very limited. It is not even a good sampling of the scientific literature on animal aggression. In addition, much of the "evidence" is of questionable value, particularly that which relies on anecdotes and unsophisticated observation. This should not be taken as a criticism of modern ethologists who have developed sophisticated procedures for making objective observations in natural settings.

Third, it is probably a mistake to consider aggression analogous to other biological drives such as hunger, a mistake which psychoanalysts also make. If we are deprived of food we get increasingly hungry. But if we are deprived of aggression we do not necessarily become more aggressive. This may be illustrated by several simple animal experiments. Van Hemel and Myer (1970) placed rats in an operant chamber in which responses were reinforced by presentation of a mouse which was promptly killed. Rats were first satiated to mouse killing and then "deprived" of mice for one, two, or four days. Their killing behavior was again measured following deprivation, and it was found that the rate of killing was unrelated to the amount of deprivation. In another experiment (Johnson, 1972), Siamese fighting fish were allowed to view conspecifics for six hours, after which they were isolated for 1, 12, or 30 hours. At the end of this deprivation period they were given the opportunity to perform a response (swimming through a hoop) which allowed them to engage in threat displays with their own mirror image. Again, it turned out that the strength of their instrumental behavior bore no relation to the length of deprivation (they actually performed the response less often rather than more often after the longest period of deprivation).

Both the Freudian and Lorenzian notions of aggressive drive are based on a kind of hydraulic model sometimes irreverently referred to as the "flush-toilet model." While this model is quaint, there is little convincing evidence to support it, and some which opposes it. At the human level, research offers little comfort for the notion of catharsis (Bandura, 1965b; Berkowitz, 1969a; Hokanson, 1970). Aggression does not build up like urine in the bladder until it finally has to be released. Encouraging the "flushing out" of hostility, as in cathartic therapy, may do little good and in fact may provide a negative model for maintaining or increasing deviant behavior.

Freud's views on aggression, of course, are considerably more complex than can be described in a brief summary. But part of the problem with psychoanalytic theory is that Freud was inconsistent in his views. At first aggression played only a minor role in his theorizing. As he grew older and more pessimistic about mankind, he finally gave it a primary role in order to help explain the sadistic and masochistic behavior he found so widespread in Europe around the time of the World Wars. Freud broadly conceived of motivating forces as being governed by the life instinct, Eros, or the death instinct, Thanatos. The death instinct has been widely criticized and rejected, even by most other psychoanalysts. Some, such as Adler, spoke of lust for power and striving for superiority as a reflection of aggressive instincts. Like other instinct theorists, Freud placed heavy emphasis on these underlying biological forces. But Freud conceived of aggression as a destructive urge while Lorenz viewed it as an adaptive instinct. In addition, Freud injected much more romance into his ideas by dwelling on the deep, dark, mysterious motivating forces which he carelessly labeled with exotic names. The death instinct, of course, is not a scientific concept and therefore it can never be proved or disproved. Nevertheless Freud and others used it to explain other concepts, and it has received a surprising amount of uncritical acceptance. For example, one author (Strachey, 1957) attempts to explain war in terms of the death instinct. Another (Abrahamson, 1970) describes the case of a man who committed several murders, which are "explained" as follows: The man had unresolved conflicts with his mother, and killed as an act of revenge because of her rejection of him. Furthermore, the shooting of his victims was a symbolic substitute for ejaculation. While this kind of analysis may or may not be meaningful to other psychoanalysts, it is of dubious value to anyone else and certainly adds little to the scientific understanding of aggressive behavior.

Unlike the ethologically-oriented instinct theorists, Freud emphasized the role of social experience, particularly in childhood. He sometimes explained aggressiveness as a result of childhood traumas, sexual conflicts, and repressed wishes. If Freudian theory were correct, aggression could be controlled but not gotten rid of by providing acceptable outlets for aggressive drive. But aggression is not simply a matter of fixed amounts of energy which are stored up, released, displaced, converted, and so on. Such views have contributed little to the solution of man's problems.

LEARNING THEORIES

Staub (1971) has pointed out that because much aggression is learned it can also be unlearned or reconditioned. We can encourage assertiveness and discourage aggressiveness. We can teach prosocial values and punish antisocial behavior. We can modify stimulus situations and reinforcement strategies. Much of this we already do without being aware of it, and learning theory provides a more rational basis for modifying behavior when that appears desirable. For example, if we were convinced that there were an invariant relationship between frustration and aggression, or between pain and aggression, we could decrease aggressiveness by decreasing frustration or pain. It is doubtful that much human aggression can be controlled so simply, but we may find many instances where modification of stimulus situations may reduce aggressiveness. For example, situational cues and environmental stimuli may function to intensify certain forms of aggressiveness; therefore, it would be prudent to minimize exposure to such instigating stimuli.

From learning theory we have also come to appreciate the fact that much aggression is instrumentally learned. Such behavior is influenced by positive and negative reinforcement, and our knowledge of instrumental conditioning allows us to view it in terms of principles of acquisition, extinction, generalization, and discrimination. We can fail to reward aggressiveness or punish it if necessary. We can reward alternative behavior incompatible with aggression. We can teach individuals to discriminate situations when aggression is unjustified. We can also increase inhibitions, decrease instigations, and assist in cognitive clarification. Such behavior modification procedures are commonly applied to normal children in the home, but they can also be formalized in the laboratory to treat more severe forms of destructiveness. Agras (1967) selected chronic schizophrenic patients who repeatedly tried to smash windows or any other glass they found. This behavior necessitated having them restrained. In a series of counterconditioning sessions these patients were instructed to visualize breaking glass, and whenever they did so they were punished with electric shock. Eventually they lost their urge to smash windows, and follow up studies revealed little subsequent tendency to revert to their previous destructive behavior.

Behavior modification can also be used to reinforce competing behavior. Staats and Butterfield (1965) described the case of an unusually destructive 14-year-old boy who repeatedly failed in school and was considered incorrigible and mentally retarded. With the help of a probation officer and 20 dollars in reward money, the boy was taught to read by reinforcing him for correct reading responses with tokens which could be exchanged for money. At the end of four and a half months his reading ability had leaped dramatically and he began to receive passing grades for the first time in his life. By selectively reinforcing this competing behavior, he not only improved in his studies, but his aggressive behavior sharply declined and he became much more cooperative.

There is nothing new about using instrumental conditioning to control behavior. The only thing which is new is its deliberate application in new situations where the conditions are controlled and manipulated to gain maximum efficiency. As previously pointed out, we already practice behavior modification without knowing it, sometimes for the worse. We put petty criminals in prison, teach them to hate society, and turn them into hardened criminals. A parent may think he is teaching a lesson by punishing his child, but the lesson the child may learn is to mistrust the parent, to perform the act somewhere else, or to be punitive toward others. Since behavior modification is constantly taking place through contingencies of reward and punishment, it would seem wise to strive for beneficial rather than haphazard results.

Another principle of learning, originally described by Pavlov, is that of passive inhibition. Scott (1958a) points out that resorting to fighting can be habit forming, but practicing *not* fighting can also be habit forming. Rosenberg (1970) has suggested that one way to minimize aggression is to emphasize nonaggression and to stress the more positive aspects of human behavior. The most dramatic application of this is Mahatma Gandhi's principle of nonviolence, which was also successfully used by the late Rev. Martin Luther King in the United States. By practicing nonviolence it was hoped that an example for positive behavior would be set and all the consequences of the use of force rejected.

SOCIAL AND DEVELOPMENTAL THEORIES

In many respects social and developmental theories are extensions of learning theory. For example, Bandura (1965b) considers modeling behavior to be complex associative learning based on vicarious representational processes (although not necessarily built up by repeated trials). Modeling influences, whether live or film-mediated, can clearly affect the social behavior of children and even adults. This provides a positive alternative to antisocial behavior, for parents, teachers, and other models can have great influence through moral leadership, particularly if they are practicing what they preach. Bandura (1969) reviews a number of experiments which show that positive models can change behavior by getting others to volunteer their services, perform altruistic acts, pledge themselves to social action, assist persons in distress, and seek out information relevant to the solution of a problem.

Correspondingly, negative models can have antisocial influences, and one way to control destructive violence is to limit exposure to such models. Children grow up surrounded by negative models: the glamour associated with cowboy guns, war heroes, and shoot-'em-ups on television. As they grow older they may discover that the procedures involved in being hired for a job or being accepted into college are something less than democratic. Often society provides models of hypocrisy and corruption rather than of justice.

The fact that social influences begin operating very early in life suggests that special attention be focused on the developmental process. Moral values, social attitudes, and emotional stability can be affected by early social experience (or lack of it). Studies of the authoritarian personality (Adorno, et al., 1950) suggest that lack of love is a fundamental cause of aggression and that the authoritarian personality syndrome is a product of the pressures of our society. But as Sanford (1971) points out, we do not want our children to be incapable of fear, or unable to express anger and outrage. Rather, we should help them to attain the capability of distinguishing when to react and when not to react. But many parents are not really qualified for this kind of leadership, and a reasonable goal might be to help parents do a better job in raising their children:*

> ... A vast American literature on child development, much of it addressed directly to parents, goes far beyond cautions about authoritarianism in setting forth general conditions for healthy development. It is possible to summarize much of this literature by saying that children need to be brought up in an atmosphere of trust, love, justice, freedom, and truth. Trust in someone is absolutely necessary if the child is to learn the most elementary facts about the social world and to establish those stable relationships upon which basic inner stability depends. The child must be loved if he is to develop the self-esteem and sense of identity that enable him to love others in a genuine way. Justice is the cornerstone of faith in the human community; its denial to a child is a major stimulus for aggression and unbridled self-seeking. If a child or young person does not feel that he is justly treated he does not care about freedom; and he must have freedom, in amounts suited to his stage of

---

*From Sanford, N. Going beyond prevention. *In* N. Sanford and C. Comstock (Eds.), *Sanctions for Evil*. San Francisco, Jossey-Bass, 1971.

development, if he is to experience making choices. This experience is requisite to his becoming an autonomous person. Truth is the overriding value. The child must learn to appreciate it and live according to it if he is to gain any understanding of and therefore some control over himself and if he is to work with others in gaining control over his environment. He can be taught only by example.

How these values can guide the day-to-day behavior of parents toward their children has been the subject of innumerable books, pamphlets, articles, and newspaper columns. The great trouble is that everything that can be specifically recommended has the aspect of being more easily said than done. Parents have problems of their own which stand in the way of giving their children what they need. Many parents are highly authoritarian and bring to their relations with their children the same moralistically punitive attitudes that they express toward out-groups and toward their own impulses. And these attitudes are constantly reinforced by the culture in which they live. Many parents are so taken up with getting love or justice or freedom for themselves that they have neither the inclination nor the ability to give these things to their children; others are capable of love and know what they should do but are prevented by the pressures of everyday life in our society — to get money, status, respectability — from taking effective action.

Further research is needed on the entire socialization process, from parental attitudes and child rearing practices to peer influences during development. An enlightened understanding of these complex influences will at least reduce the unwitting teaching of aggressive behavior. A recognition of the importance of early experience on later aggressive behavior may serve to stimulate society's interest in seeing to the needs of children.

Racial prejudice is a socially learned form of aggression, and as the Kerner report showed, it is one of the most fundamental causes of social violence. Studies have revealed that racial prejudice is learned at an early age, and children often adopt the racial hostilities of the adults around them. But manipulation of the social environment can reduce the development of intergroup hostility. Deutsch and Collins (1951) studied black-white relations in four new housing projects, two of them segregated and two integrated. Housewives were interviewed about their attitudes before they moved in and again after they had lived there for a while. Those who moved into the integrated housing naturally had more interactions with blacks than those who lived in segregated apartments. It was found that those who experienced more interactions with blacks showed a significant decrease in their racial prejudices, and this change could not be explained by attitudes existing before moving in. Another experiment (Harding and Hogrefe, 1952) found that white department store employees who had never worked on an equal status with Negroes were reluctant to do so, but those with previous integrated experience expressed no such fear.

These studies and others like them indicate that racial hostility can be decreased by social contact, particularly if contact takes place under favorable conditions. But increased contact under unfavorable conditions may have the opposite effect and increase intergroup tension and prejudice (Amir, 1969). Unfavorable conditions are of course fostered by segregation whether it is due to ghettos in the city or snob zoning in the suburbs. Society pays a high price for tolerating any form of discrimination, for this provides a sure formula for social strife.

Similar analogies can be made at the international level. Cultural, scientific, diplomatic, and tourist exchanges reduce international tensions. Little can be gained by building real or psychological walls, whether a society is closed from within or isolated from without, and much can be resolved by negotiation rather than war. Studies of conflict resolution suggest that there may be conceptual similarities in bargaining procedures either between individuals or between nations (Deutsch, 1969). Terms such as threat, deterrence, cooperation, competition, and credibility apply to both, and what we learn in the laboratory may help us to improve international relations.

PHYSIOLOGICAL THEORIES

Some of the most fruitful research on aggression control in recent years has come from studies of brain function. McNeil (1959) pointed out that chemical or neural malfunction can override any rational state, just as rabies does when it attacks the limbic system. If everyone had a completely normal nervous system we might not be so concerned. But there is evidence to suggest that 10 to 15 million Americans have some kind of organic brain disease (Mark and Ervin, 1970). While much of this results in cerebral palsy, mental retardation, convulsive disorders, and hyperkinetic behavior disorders, there is without question a significant percentage of individuals whose repeated personal violence is a direct result of brain dysfunction. As was pointed out in Chapter 3, genetic and physiological abnormalities are usually caused early in life, often before birth. Others are caused later in life, but regardless of the timing there are many kinds of behavior disorders which cannot be successfully treated by any type of behavior therapy or psychiatric care. Many of these cases could be prevented in the first place by better nutritional habits (particularly during pregnancy), better maternity practices, improved child and adult health care and diagnosis of disease, and a reduction in radiation exposure and chemical poisoning from industrial wastes. For those now suffering from severe dysfunctions of the nervous system, brain surgery and certain drug treatments offer new hope. Certainly there are many ethical questions which need to be considered before resorting to brain surgery, but they need to be weighed against the morality of letting people rot in prison.

The judicious use of certain drugs also offers hope to certain individuals, although we are far from discovering any wonder drug to prevent violence. Tranquilizing drugs such as Thorazine (chlorpromazine) tend to reduce violent outbursts in psychotic patients while not preventing them from engaging in normal activities. But some drugs which are effective with assaultive psychotics may not be effective with violence-prone normal people (Tinklenberg and Stillman, 1970). Non-phenothiazine–type tranquilizers and sedative-hypnotic drugs are of limited use, for near anesthetic doses may be necessary to eliminate violence. Drugs and gases intended to curb riots by central nervous system action have been designed to be dispensed with aerosol cans and dart guns, but these devices are hazardous. No dosage can be obtained which is both safe and effective for all individuals. The dangers of new drugs may be greater than their benefits, for they are often misused by doctors. In some mental hospitals patients are kept sedated with medications which make it easier for the staff to carry out custodial duties. But some of the newest drugs, such as Lithium, are effective in treating mood disorders and in quieting manic-depressive psychotics without sedating them (Gattozzi, 1970). Unfortunately it is too early to judge the usefulness of Lithium in treating violence in normal people. Some recent investigations indicate that Lithium reduces or abolishes intraspecific aggression in Siamese fighting fish, hamsters, and mice (Weischer, 1969).

The use of drugs to treat violent individuals is not new, for as long ago as 1941 Dunn used synthetic female hormones (stilbestrol) on convicted criminals and reported a significant reduction in aggressive behavior without major adverse side effects. Hormone therapy is still being evaluated and many new hormone and nonhormone drugs are being tested each year. But as yet there are no magic drugs which prevent assaultive behavior without also affecting other psychological systems (Tinklenberg and Stillman, 1970). There may never be a single, general "cure" for aggressive behavior, for it has been stressed repeatedly that aggression has a diversity of causes which cannot be treated in a unitary fashion. Moyer (1969b) reviews some of the current research on drugs and aggression and reports that different drugs have been successful for different kinds of problems, ranging from hostile feelings to psychotic rampages. In his laboratory, Moyer keeps small quantities of tasteless diazepam, a centrally-acting skeletal muscle relaxant, in the milk of vicious monkeys and finds that these animals become tame and friendly with no apparent sedation or other side effects. Who knows what would happen if such drugs were introduced into cow milk? Similar suggestions have already been made by Kenneth Clark, president of the American Psychological Association (Clark, 1971). Clark has suggested that at some future time society may want to apply the findings of psychotechnology to its leaders by placing them under medication as a condition of office. Presumably, drugs that reduce hostility and aggressiveness may provide a form of "psychological disarmament" which would reduce the likelihood of war. Abhorrent as it may sound, a humane psychotechnology may be preferable in the long run to a nuclear holocaust.

CULTURAL THEORIES

Bandura and Walters (1963b) have noted that children growing up among the culture of the head-hunting Iatmul are surrounded by aggressive models, and it is not surprising that the expression of aggressive behavior acquires normative proportions. Boys are rewarded for reproducing the aggressive behavior of adults and negatively reinforced for more tranquil behavior. In contrast, the Hutterites stress pacifism as a style of life and children grow up rarely displaying any interpersonal aggression.

Western civilization also has its norms, and these norms change with time. Only a few centuries ago in England there were over 200 separate crimes which were punishable by death (Mulvihill and Tumin, 1969). Today, capital punishment is generally outlawed completely or else is used only rarely for the very worst crimes. Compared to homicides, twice as many people die from suicides and five times as many from car accidents, yet there is grave concern about murders and relatively little about suicides and automobile deaths. In America, girls are usually protected and scolded for aggressive behavior while boys are openly encouraged to be aggressive. Enormous social destruction results from white collar crime, corporate crime, and organized crime, yet the public is much more concerned with petty crime in the streets or protest marches on college campuses.

But in addition to variability from culture to culture, there is also considerable variability within cultures. For example, polls taken for the National Commission on the Causes and Prevention of Violence indicate that about half of the respondents consider it perfectly acceptable for the police to physically beat unarmed citizens who are rude. On racial matters, responses indicate that about half of the country has not yet accepted the idea of an integrated society. The war in Viet Nam is another issue which has polarized the nation. A great many peace demonstrations and protests have indicated massive opposition to the war. But there has also been strong support for the war, as is illustrated by the 19-year-old soldier who told a reporter (The Day..., 1969).

I think someone ought to kill those long-haired, queer bastards back in the world. Anyone who demonstrates against the war ought to be lined up and killed, just like any other gook here.

But even soldiers do not always agree. Following reports of Americans executing prisoners of war, one platoon sergeant said the following:

I see these little skinny fellows, with their AK-47, their 50 rounds of ammunition and their bag of rice going against all our firepower, and man, I have to admire them. I can't hate a man like that! If he became my prisoner, I would respect him.

(SHABECOFF, 1970)

But another commented:

If only I could get that gook alone for five minutes!

More detailed analyses of cultural differences in aggression can be made along the lines of unicentric versus multicentric forms of social organization (Mulvihill and Tumin, 1969). Law might be diffuse or absent, as in the case of frontier justice or ghetto police protection, or it might be highly centralized and strictly enforced as in a police state. But the amount of overt conflict may not be an indication of the amount of violence in a society, for a noisy democracy involves much less suffering than a quiet police state. In a culturally diversified nation the task of finding norms acceptable to all is especially difficult, for there is always the danger that minority interests will get trampled by the majority. If a harmonious society is the ultimate goal it is imperative that the social rights of every individual be assiduously defended.

ENVIRONMENTAL THEORIES

A recent political cartoon by Tom Darcy pictured a moon in the sky and a quotation of one of the Apollo astronauts describing his impressions: "It's a vast, lonely, forbidding... expanse of nothing and doesn't appear to be a very inviting place to live and work.... It's essentially gray, no color.... It makes you realize just what you have back on earth." In the foreground of the cartoon is a city slum, and the reader is quickly struck by the fact that in many respects the desolation on earth rivals that on the moon. Such urban desolation is not new to man:

> Lack of street lighting provided an environment conducive to frequent night attacks on those brave souls who ventured from the security of their homes. Life expectancy was considerably reduced by the seriousness with which personal and family feuds were kept alive. Life in the [city] was far from safe, white-collar crime was not uncommon and games of chance often provided a dangerous pastime for those who participated. Plagues, wars, and political upheavals usually produced social conditions favorable to crime and general immorality as they were then interpreted.

This is not New York City, but Renaissance Florence (Wolfgang, 1956). Even the earliest civilizations had problems with crime in their cities; Hebrew, Greek, Roman, and Chinese cities used some form of police protection (Mulvihill and Tumin, 1969). Today, crime rates are disproportionately high for the young, the poor, and those in minority groups, all of whom are concentrated in the decaying cities. In Chicago, the chances of a resident being assaulted in a Negro ghetto are 1 in 77, while in an upper middle class suburban neighborhood there is a comfortable 1 in 10,000 chance. Children brought up in the inner cities are more likely to be socialized into a world of every kind of "violence": disease, poverty, sickness, malnutrition, poor education, lack of jobs, and racial discrimination. Among the blacks who do manage to find jobs, salaries on the average are 39 per cent lower than for whites (Rosenthal, 1971). The social problems created by slum environments adversely affect everyone, and the failure of society to deal with the problems of the cities is a false economy. Instead of improving the environment, massive sums are spent on superhighways, supersonic transport planes, and nuclear missiles, all of which damage and degrade the environment.

No one argues that violence and aggression would disappear if we eliminated poverty and urban decay, and many people throughout the world get along peacefully even though they live in squalor. At the same time no one contests the fact that crime could be reduced sharply by dealing directly with sociological problems. Crime will not be ended by beefing up the police force, but rather by eradicating the breeding ground for crime and replacing it with an environment conducive to normal human development. The idea that a favorable environment can reduce antisocial behavior is illustrated by milieu therapy with psychopathic boys who might otherwise end up in reformatories (McCord and McCord, 1956). Instead of placing hyperaggressive boys on aversive control based on punishment they were given the positive reinforcement of friendship, understanding, and a certain amount of permissiveness. By controlling the entire social environment and by encouraging a sense of conscience, aggressive behavior was noticeably reduced.

Is there any way the *milieu* of society as a whole can be changed? McNeil (1959) discusses radical social and cultural innovations such as deliberately creating a well-policed subculture or a colony of highly aggressive individuals that will exist separate from the rest of society. If this is not to be simply a prison, the problem of deciding whom to "commit" would be staggering. In recent years clinical tests have increased in sophistication, but as yet there is none which can adequately *post*dict violent behavior, let alone *pre*dict it (Megargee, 1970). Other suggestions include massive anti-aggression therapy for the public, or perhaps having compulsory therapy for all national leaders. Simpler (but fundamentally more radical) approaches have traditionally been more popular, particularly those which harp on law and order:

> The streets of our country are in turmoil. The universities are filled with students rebelling and rioting. Communists are seeking to destroy our country. Russia is threatening us with her might. The republic is in danger. Yes, danger from within and without. We need law and order. Yes, without law and order our nation cannot survive.... We shall restore law and order.

Law and order means power, and power means control; that is why Adolf Hitler made this statement. It is ironic that even today there are political leaders in America who have made their fame and fortune by calling for bigger jails and more repressive laws. The formula of appealing to authority while crushing dissent is a familiar pattern which helps ruthless politicians gain power at the expense of the freedom of the people. This raises the question of whether civil disobedience or violence can be justified under some circumstances, a question which political scientists have debated for centuries.

POLITICAL THEORIES

In Sophocles' *Oedipus* trilogy, written about 440 B.C., Antigone, daughter of Oedipus, was forbidden by King Creon to bury her brother Polyneices, who had been killed in an effort to gain rule of the city of Thebes. But Antigone followed her conscience and disobeyed the king, and as a result Creon walled her up in a tomb.

Frankel (1964) has observed that individuals who break laws on the basis of some principle are usually either saints or madmen. Should we assume that every law that exists is a just law, or that a greater wrong is always done by breaking the law? Does obedience to evil laws cause more social violence than illegal acts?

Smith and Deutsch (1972) have summarized some of the traditional views of political philosophy regarding civil obligation and disobedience. *Ethical naturalists* such as Sophocles, Thomas Aquinas, and Martin Luther King have argued that man is morally obliged to obey just authority because the state serves as a means for fulfilling man's nature. If the state is unjust, however, legitimacy is lost and there is no longer a moral obligation to obey its laws. *Organicists* such as Rousseau, Hegel, and Mussolini have regarded the state as a higher entity than any individual: people should be motivated by what they ought to do for the good of the superior state rather than what they want to do as individuals. The ideas of the *Social contract theory* originated with Plato, and reached a peak of popularity with Thomas Hobbes and John Locke in the 17th and 18th centuries. The contract doctrine is based on an analogy between relationships of individuals and relationships of individuals to governments and individuals to previous and future generations. According to this theory, a contract with the state is binding and imposes moral obligations on individuals to obey its terms (the laws of the land); however, if the state breaks the contract, so may the individuals. *Utilitarians* such as Bentham rejected attempts to deify the state and substituted the utility of the greatest good as a pragmatic justification for political obligation. If the state provides a way of fulfilling human happiness, it should be obeyed. If it does not, individuals are duty-bound to revolt, providing that revolution will bring greater benefits.

Perhaps most relevant to the 20th century is political *anarchism,* although this theory can be traced to ancient Chinese philosophers. The popular stereotype of the anarchist is someone who worships destruction of social order for its own sake. This distortion, however, is little more than a convenient image advanced by those in power. Most anarchists share the conviction that principles of individual conscience transcend any political authority or human law. What is moral or right is determined by conscience rather than any kind of legal force. To the extent that the state is perpetuated by coercive uniformity, it corrupts everyone. The beliefs of one of the greatest American writers of the 19th century, Henry David Thoreau, exemplify the anarchist philosophy. Thoreau believed that every individual has a moral obligation to disobey laws which violate individual conscience.

Many of these political theories surface from time to time, usually to justify some cause. For example, opponents of the Viet Nam War have used civil disobedience and overt disruption in an effort to change governmental policy. Those in power, naturally, argue that all laws should be obeyed, right or wrong. A curious contradiction of this is the government trials related to the My Lai massacre in 1968. The government has argued that individuals have a moral obligation to disobey immoral orders. Perhaps this was an attempt to legitimize the morality of the war or to exonerate higher officials. According to the standards of justice imposed by the United States on government officials of Germany and Japan at the end of World War II, many of the high ranking Americans ultimately responsible for My Lai would be executed as war criminals.

DEMOCRACY AND SOCIAL CHANGE

With regard to civil disobedience, President Nixon has popularized the views of Sidney Hook (Hook, 1969), who argues that disobedience threatens the democratic system. Individuals should not be allowed to decide which laws to obey, according to Hook, for in a democracy the majority is just and binding and in the long run we must rely on authority. Unfortunately, majority rule may be legally binding, but this does not necessarily make it just. It is easy to confuse the ideals of democracy with its actual accomplishments, as Hook does. In a perfect democracy the majority will should be binding because it would be just. But a perfect democracy does not yet exist; and those accused of trying to destroy democracy may be trying to get rid of imperfections and not democracy itself. Many years ago de Tocqueville warned of the "tyranny of the majority" which might lead to legitimized oppression of minorities. Today we find that substantial numbers of Americans are unwilling to share social and economic rights with minority groups, and according to nearly all of the commission reports this is one of the most important causes of social violence in the United States. There is an urgent need to rebuild ghettos, yet instead we are pouring money into the ABM. At a rally opposing the multibillion dollar ABM, John Lindsay remarked:

I come here, fundamentally, to speak of a city that has felt the full crippling impact of military force; a city that suffers each day destruction from our armed might. That city is not Berlin. It is not Hiroshima. It is not Hanoi. That city is New York.

Frankel (1964) points out that civil disobedience may strengthen rather than weaken democracy. A minority may use disobedience to dramatize injustice, as the early Christians did, and through suffering themselves they may eventually change and improve the entire system. Blind observation of every law does not automatically strengthen the law, for laws are in need of constant revision. The observing of laws which are convenient to some at the expense of others undermines the entire system, including those laws that are just. Many laws are passed with the aid of special interest lobbies, but few people, if any, lobby for the poor or for the average consumer. The books are full of laws passed, not by the pressure of the voters, but by the pressure of wealthy businessmen, powerful labor unions, and influential politicians. This often results in social injustice, and such injustice is clearly a form of violence.

Figure 37. *Tolerating racism and social injustice is very costly for society in the long run, for it encourages the formation of revolutionary groups which seek to destroy society's institutions. (Courtesy of G. Cole, in Wallace, J. Psychology: A Social Science. Philadelphia, W. B. Saunders, 1971.)*

Injustice may not be considered violent in the ordinary sense, for it is not necessarily motivated by a desire for destruction. But some of the worst social destruction which occurs is a result of symbols or social-legal arrangements (Sanford and Comstock, 1971). When a society tolerates ghettos, the destructiveness caused within such conditions far outweighs the violence to outsiders.

It can be pointed out that American pluralism has much to be proud of, for it has given opportunity to more people than any other country. It can also be argued that the normal democratic machinery provides remedies for injustices, and time rather than civil disobedience will improve society. But such observations may be used as excuses for maintaining the status quo. In some areas blacks have been voting regularly in the democratic system for over two centuries and yet they still live in poverty, just like their ancestors. Social change is normal and healthy in a democracy, and empty rhetoric is no substitute. America has always been a revolutionary country, for it was born out of a desire for justice and equality, not out of a desire for order. Anyone who has forgotten this should study the Declaration of Independence, which advocates overthrowing any form of government which violates the rights of the people. Those who support corruption and oppose social change probably contribute the most toward the tearing down of society's institutions. As Aristotle remarked in *Poetics,* the greatest crimes are caused by excess and not by necessity.

The planet Earth is getting psychologically smaller and smaller, and man is building walls where he should be tearing them down. The greatest natural calamity of the 20th century occurred in November, 1970, when a cyclone hit East Pakistan, killing an estimated half-million people. This disaster received only passing notice throughout the world, and the unwillingness to help led to much unnecessary suffering. The United States, for example, was in a position to quickly mobilize thousands of airplanes, as it has done regularly in Viet Nam. Yet an entire week passed before two helicopters were finally contributed.

Today, there is a staggering inequality of wealth throughout the world, and man's long-range hope for peace and survival may depend on the willingness of those with wealth and power to give some of it up and share it. Two-thirds of the world's population exists on an average annual per capita income of less than 300 dollars, an amount that G.M. board chairmen earn in less than an hour. In the coming decades it is likely that the majority of human beings will exist at the margin of subsistence (Simpson, 1968). At least one-third to one-half of the world's population suffers from hunger or malnutrition. There are 100 million more illiterates today than there were 20 years ago. Infant mortality is four times as high in poor countries as in rich countries. One-fifth of all males in poor countries cannot find any employment. The industrial giants spend over 200 billion dollars each year for weapons of destruction while devoting only seven billion to helping the poor countries (Reston, 1969; 1971). The United States holds six per cent of the world's population but consumes 60 per cent of its resources. Sometimes the wealthy are so busy maintaining the system that only the poor and uneducated really understand what is happening. How long can we expect the have-nots to suffer in silence?

In a report to the United Nations, Lester Pearson of Canada stated:

> A planet cannot, any more than a country, survive half-slave and half-free, half engulfed in misery, half careening along toward the supposed joys of almost unlimited consumption.

Also addressing the same group, Robert McNamara, head of the World Bank, commented about the concentration of wealth in the hands of a few:

> In that direction lies disaster, yet that is our direction today unless we are prepared to change course, and do so in time.... There are really no material obstacles to a sane, manageable and progressive response to the world's development needs. The obstacles lie in the minds of men.

So far, civilization has been relatively lucky, for world revolution has not yet broken out. Gurr (1969) points out that in the United States intense discontent has resulted only in riots and not in any concerted revolutionary activity. Many other countries with the same internal and external problems have ended up in violent political revolution. *The violence and hatred seen in many other countries throughout history makes contemporary America seem tame by comparison.* Nevertheless, Americans should take this as an urgent warning rather than as a note of relief, for there still may be time to eliminate the causes of violence rather than treating the symptoms. The UNESCO (United Nations Educational, Scientific, and Cultural Organization) constitution states that since men used their brains to invent war, they must also construct a defense for peace with the same powerful weapon. The National Commission on the Causes and Prevention of Violence has compiled a list of recommendations for positive social reconstruction, and they are worth summarizing here.

1. A reduction in economic deprivation and degradation through increased job opportunities, income-supplementation, and better housing.

2. A reduction in political alienation by giving citizens more participation in government and creating better channels of communication between government and the poor, the under-privileged, and the unorganized.

3. The reduction of pathologies in child development through better family service programs.

4. The improvement of educational opportunities for every child.

5. The creation of new and useful roles for youth.

6. The reduction and elimination of discrimination and prejudice.

7. Better help for family problems to reduce violence among intimates.

8. A more effective and sensitive approach to drug problems.

9. A reduction of violence by the law.

10. A better way of dealing with social problems caused by alcohol.

11. A more comprehensive program of suicide prevention.

12. Reforms in the corrections system.

13. Reforms in juvenile justice.

14. Reforms in the police system.

15. Better control of organized crime.

16. Compensation to victims of major violent crimes.

17. Expanded and coordinated research on all aspects of violent behavior.

None of these recommendations is by any means utopian. Society now spends enormous sums of money on social control and on an almost pathological concern for defense (Comstock, 1971). If we are going to concentrate on defense, we should be defending ourselves from the zealous war planner as well as the dope peddler and thief. Or, better yet, we might, as a society, sponsor an Institute for Peace, as Scott (1970) proposed. We could easily obtain more order, security, and stability if we relied on coercion and suppression of freedom. The task of maintaining order is complicated by the fact that we expect it to be done democratically. Democracy is probably the most complex form of government, and it is based on the assumption that justice is much more important than efficiency (Turk, 1971). It is also based on an enlightened concern for the welfare of others. We must be guided by positive values and the kind of principles that democracy has espoused for centuries. We do not need new principles, but rather a fresh commitment to the old ones.

REFERENCES

Abrahamsen, D. *Our Violent Society*. New York, Funk and Wagnalls, 1970.

Adams, D., and Flynn, J. P. Transfer of an escape response from tail shock to brain-stimulated attack behavior. *J. exper. anal. Behav.*, 1966, 9, 401–408.

Ader, R. Effects of early experience and differential housing on behavior and susceptibility to gastric erosions in the rat. *J. comp. physiol. Psychol.*, 1965, 60, 233–238.

Adler, N., and Hogan, J. A. Classical conditioning and punishment of an instinctive response in *Betta splendens. Anim. Behav.*, 1963, 11, 351–354.

Adorno, T. W., Frenkel-Brunswik, E., Levinson, D. J., and Sanford, N. *The Authoritarian Personality*. New York, Harper and Row, 1950.

Agras, W. S. Behavior therapy in the management of chronic schizophrenia. *Amer. J. Psychiat.*, 1967, 124, 240–243.

Albrecht, H. von. Freiwasserbeobachtungen an Tilapien *(Pisces, Cichlidae)* in ostrafrika. Zeitschrift für Tierpsychologie, 1968, 25, 377–394.

Allee, W. C., Collias, N., and Lutherman, C. Z. Modification of the social order among flocks of hens by injection of testosterone propionate. *Physiol. Zool.*, 1939, 12, 412–420.

Altman, J. *Organic Foundations of Animal Behavior*. New York, Holt, Rinehart and Winston, 1966.

American Rifleman. Articles from a series, February through May, 1968.

Amir, Y. Contact hypothesis in ethnic relations. *Psychol. Bull.*, 1969, 71, 319–342.

Amsel, A. The role of frustrative non-reward in non-continuous reward situations. *Psychol. Bull.*, 1958, 55, 102–119.

Andreski, S. Origins of war. *In* J. D. Carthy and F. J. Ebling (Eds.), *The Natural History of Aggression*. London, Academic Press, 1964.

Archer, J. Effects of population density on behavior in rodents. *In* J. H. Crooke (Ed.), *Social Behavior in Birds and Mammals*. New York, Academic Press, 1970.

Ardrey, R. *The Territorial Imperative*. New York, Atheneum, 1966.

Ardrey, R. *The Social Contact*. New York, Atheneum, 1970.

Azrin, N. H., Hutchinson, R. R., and Hake, D. F. Extinction-induced aggression. *J. exper. anal. Behav.*, 1966, 9, 191–204.

Azrin, N. H., Hutchinson, R. R., and McLaughlin, R. The opportunity for aggression as an operant reinforcer during aversive stimulation. *J. exper. anal. Behav.*, 1965, 8, 171–180.

Azrin, N. H., Hutchinson, R. R., and Sallery, R. D. Pain aggression toward inanimate objects. *J. exper. anal. Behav.*, 1964, 7, 223–227.

Baenninger, L. P. The reliability of dominance orders in rats. *Anim. Behav.*, 1966, 14, 367–371.

Baenninger, L. P. Interspecific aggression in wild mice. Paper presented at the Eastern Psychological Association, New York, Apr., 1971.

Baenninger, L. P., and Baenninger, R. "Spontaneous" fighting and mouse-killing by rats. *Psychon. Sci.*, 1970, 19, 161.

Baenninger, R. Visual reinforcement, habituation, and prior social experience of the Siamese fighting fish. *J. comp. physiol. Psychol.*, 1970, 71, 1–5.

Baenninger, R., and Grossman, J. C. Some effects of punishment on pain-elicited aggression. *J. exper. anal. Behav.*, 1969, 12, 1017–1022.

229

Baenninger, R., and Ulm, R. R. Overcoming the effects of prior punishment on inter-species aggression in the rat. *J. comp. physiol. Psychol.*, 1969, 69, 628–635.

Baker, R. K., and Ball, S. J. *Mass media and violence*, Vol. IX. Washington, D. C., U. S. Government Printing Office, 1969.

Bandler, R. J., Jr. Facilitation of aggressive behaviour in the rat by direct cholinergic stimulation of the hypothalamus. *Nature*, 1969, 224, 1035–1036.

Bandura, A. Social learning through imitation. *In* M. R. Jones (Ed.), *Nebraska Symposium on Motivation*. Lincoln, University of Nebraska Press, 1962.

Bandura, A. Influence of model's reinforcement contingencies on the acquisition of imitative responses. *J. per. soc. Psychol.*, 1965a, 1, 589–595.

Bandura, A. Vicarious processes: a case of no-trial learning. *In* L. Berkowitz (Ed.), *Advances in Experimental Social Psychology*, Vol. II. New York, Academic Press, 1965b.

Bandura, A. *Principles of Behavior Modification*. New York, Holt, Rinehart and Winston, 1969.

Bandura, A. Analysis of modeling processes. *In* A. Bandura (Ed.), *Theories of Modeling*. New York, Atherton, 1970.

Bandura, A., Grusec, J. E., and Menlove, F. L. Observational learning as a function of symbolization of incentive set. *Child Devel.*, 1966, 37, 499–506.

Bandura, A., and Huston, A. C. Identification as a process of incidental learning. *J. abnorm. soc. Psychol.*, 1961, 63, 311–318.

Bandura, A., Ross, D., and Ross, S. A. Transmission of aggression through imitation of aggressive models. *J. abnorm. soc. Psychol.*, 1961, 63, 575–582.

Bandura, A., Ross, D., and Ross, S. A. Imitation of film-mediated aggressive models. *J. abnorm. soc. Psychol.*, 1963a, 66, 3–11.

Bandura, A., Ross, D., and Ross, S. A. A comparative test of the status envy, social power and secondary reinforcement theories of identificatory learning. *J. abnorm. soc. Psychol.*, 1963b, 67, 527–534.

Bandura, A., and Walters, R. H. *Adolescent aggression,* New York, Ronald Press, 1959.

Bandura, A., and Walters, R. H. Aggression. *In* National Society for the Study of Education, *Child Psychology*. Chicago, 1963a.

Bandura, A., and Walters, R. H. *The Social Learning of Deviant Behavior: A Behavioristic Approach to Socialization*. New York, Holt, Rinehart and Winston, 1963b.

Banks, E. M., and Fox, S. F. Relative aggression of two sympatric rodents: a preliminary report. *Comm. Behav. Biol.*, 1968, 2, 51–58.

Baran, D., and Glickman, S. E. "Territorial marking" in the mongolian gerbil: a study of sensory control and function. *J. comp. physiol. Psychol.*, 1970, 71, 237–245.

Barclay, A. M. The effect of hostility on physiological and fantasy responses. *J. Personality*, 1969, 37, 651–667.

Barclay, A. M., and Haber, R. N. The relation of aggressive to sexual motivation. *J. Personality*, 1965, 33, 462–475.

Bard, P., and Mountcastle, V. B. Some forebrain mechanisms involved in expression of rage with special reference to suppression of angry behavior. *Res. Publ. Assoc. Res. Nervous Mental Disease*, 1948, 27, 362–404.

Barfield, R. J., and Sachs, B. D. Sexual behavior: stimulation by painful electric shock to skin of male rats. *Science*, 1968, 161, 392–395.

Barfield, R. J., and Sachs, B. D. Effect of shock on copulatory behavior in castrate male rats. *Hormones and Behavior*, 1970, 1, 247–253.

Barker, R. G., Dembo, T., and Lewin, K. Frustration and regression: an experiment with young children. *University of Iowa Studies in Child Welfare*, 1941, 18, 1–314.

Barlow, G. W. Ethology of the Asian teleost, *Badis badis*. IV. Sexual behavior. *Copeia*, 1962, 2, 346–360.

Barnett, S. A. *The Rat: A Study in Behavior*. Chicago, Aldine, 1963.

Baron, A., Brookshire, K. H., and Littman, R. A. Effects of infantile and adult shock-trauma upon learning in the adult white rat. *J. comp. physiol. Psychol.*, 1957, 50, 530–534.

Bartholomew, A. A., and Sutherland, G. A defense of insanity and the extra Y chromosome, R. v. Hannel. *Australian and New Zealand J. Criminology,* 1969, 2, 29–37.

Bartholomew, G. Reproductive and social behavior of the northern elephant seal. *Univ. Calif. Publ. Zool.,* 1952, 47, 369–472.

Baumhart, R. C. How ethical are businessmen? In G. Geis (Ed.), *White-Collar Criminal.* New York, Atherton, 1968.

Beach, F. A. The snark was a boojum. *Amer. Psychol.,* 1950, 5, 115–124.

Beeman, E. A. The effect of male hormone on aggressive behavior in mice. *Physiol. Zool.,* 1947, 20, 373–405.

Benedict, R. *Patterns of Culture.* New York, Mentor Books, 1934.

Bennett, M. A. Social hierarchy in ring doves. II. The effects of treatment with testosterone propionate. *Ecology,* 1940, 21, 148–165.

Berkowitz, L. The expression and reduction of hostility. *Psychol. Bull.,* 1958, 65, 257–283.

Berkowitz, L. *Aggression: A Social Psychological Analysis.* New York, McGraw-Hill, 1962.

Berkowitz, L. *The Development of Motives and Values in the Child.* New York, Basic Books, 1964.

Berkowitz, L. Some aspects of observed aggression. *J. per. soc. Psychol.,* 1965, 2, 359–369.

Berkowitz, L. Experiments in automatism and intent in human aggression. *In* C. D. Clemente and D. B. Lindsley (Eds.), *Aggression and Defense. Brain Function,* Vol. 5. Berkeley, University of California Press, 1967.

Berkowitz, L. Control of aggression. In P. M. Caldwell and H. Ricciuti (Eds.), *Review of Child Development Research,* Vol. 3. New York, Russell Sage Foundation, 1969a.

Berkowitz, L. *Roots of Aggression.* New York, Atherton, 1969b.

Berkowitz, L. The contagion of violence: an S-R mediational analysis of some effects of observed aggression. *In* W. J. Arnold and M. M. Page (Eds.), *Nebraska Symposium on Motivation.* Lincoln, University of Nebraska Press, 1970.

Berkowitz, L., and Geen, R. G. Film violence and the cue properties of available targets. *J. per. soc. Psychol.,* 1966, 3, 525–530.

Berkowitz, L., and Knurek, D. A. Label-mediated hostility generalization. *J. per. soc. Psychol.,* 1969, 13, 200–206.

Berkowitz, L., and LePage, A. Weapons as aggression-eliciting stimuli. *J. per. soc. Psychol.,* 1967, 7, 202–207.

Bernard, V. W., Ottenberg, P., and Redl, F. Dehumanization. *In* N. Sanford and C. Comstock (Eds.), *Sanctions for Evil.* San Francisco, Jossey-Bass, 1971.

Bernstein, H., and Moyer, K. E. Aggressive behavior in the rat: effects of isolation, and olfactory-bulb lesions. *Brain Research,* 1970, 20, 75–84.

Bevan, W., Daves, W. F., and Levy, G. W., The relation of castration, androgen therapy, and pre-test fighting experience to competitive aggression in male C57BL/10 mice. *Anim. Behav.,* 1960, 8, 6–12.

Billingslea, F. Y. The relationship between emotionality and various other salients of behavior in the rat. *J. Comp. Psychol.,* 1941, 31, 69–77.

Bitterman, M. E. Toward a comparative psychology of learning. *Amer. Psychol.,* 1960, 15, 704–712.

Block, H. A., and Geis, G. *Man, Crime and Society: The Forms of Criminal Behavior.* New York, Random House, 1962.

Boice, R. Social behaviors and hierarchies in box turtles *(Terrapene). Proceedings, 78th Annual Convention, American Psychological Association,* 1970a, 5, 229–230.

Boice, R. Competition in captive anurans: aggression or misdirected feeding? Paper presented at the Psychonomic Society, San Antonio, Texas, Nov. 5–7, 1970b.

Bourlière, F. *The Natural History of Mammals.* New York, Knopf, 1954.

Bowlby, J. A note on mother-child separation as a mental health hazard. *Brit. J. Med. Psychol.,* 1958, 30, 230–240.

Bowlby, J. *Attachment and Loss.* Vol. 1, *Attachment.* New York, Basic Books, 1969.

Bowlby, J., Ainsworth, M., Boston, M., and Rosenbluth, D. The effects of mother-child separation: a follow-up study. *Brit. J. Med. Psychol.*, 1956, *29*, 211–247.

Braddock, J. C., and Braddock, Z. I. Aggressive behaviour among females of the Siamese fighting fish, *Betta splendens*. *Physiol. Zool.* 1955, *28*, 152–172.

Braddock, J. C., and Braddock, Z. I. Effects of isolation and social contact upon development of aggressive behavior in the Siamese fighting fish *(Betta splendens)*. *Anim. Behav.*, 1958, *6*, 249. (abstract)

Bramel, D., Taub, B., and Blum, B. An observer's reaction to the suffering of his enemy. *J. per. soc. Psychol.*, 1968, *8*, 384–392.

Brawn, V. M. Aggressive behavior in the cod, *(Gadus callarias L.) Behaviour*, 1961, *18*, 107–147.

Bronson, F. H., and Desjardins, C. Aggression in adult mice: modification by neonatal injections of gonadal hormone. *Science*, 1968, *161*, 705–706.

Bronson, F. H., and Eleftheriou, B. E. Relative effects of fighting on bound and unbound corticosterone in mice. *Proc. Soc. Exper. Biol. Med.*, 1965, *118*, 146–149.

Brower, L. P. Ecological chemistry. *Sci. Amer.*, 1969, *220*, 22–29.

Brown, J. S., and Farber, I. E. Emotions conceptualized as intervening variables with suggestions toward a theory of frustration. *Psychol. Bull.*, 1951, *48*, 465–495.

Brown, R. Z. Social behavior, reproduction and population changes in the house mouse *(Mus musculus L.)*. *Ecol. Monog.*, 1953, *23*, 217–240.

Bryan, J. H., and Schwartz, T. Effects of film material upon children's behavior. *Psychol. Bull.*, 1971, *75*, 50–59.

Buss, A. H. *The Psychology of Aggression*. New York, Wiley, 1961.

Buss, A. H. Aggression pays. *In* J. L. Singer (Ed.), *The Control of Aggression and Violence*. New York, Academic Press, 1971.

Butcher, J. Manifest aggression: MMPI correlates in normal boys. *J. consult. Psychol.*, 1965, *29*, 446–454.

Butler, R. A. Incentive conditions which influence visual exploration. *J. exper. Psychol.*, 1954, *48*, 19–23.

Butterfield, P. A. The pair bond in the zebra finch. *In* J. H. Crook (Ed.), *Social Behaviour in Birds and Mammals*. New York, Academic Press, 1970.

Caggiula, A. R., and Eibergen, R. Copulation of virgin male rats evoked by painful peripheral stimulation. *J. comp. physiol. Psychol.*, 1969, *69*, 414–419.

Cairns, R. B. Social behavior changes by cross-species rearing. *Amer. Psychol.*, 1964, *19*, 484. (abstract)

Cairns, R. B. Attachment behavior of mammals. *Psychol. Rev.*, 1966a, *73*, 409–426.

Cairns, R. B. Development, maintenance and extinction of social attachment behavior in sheep. *J. comp. physiol. Psychol.*, 1966b, *62*, 298–306.

Cahoon, D. D., Crosby, R. M., Dunn, S., Herrin, M. S., Hill, C. C., and McGinnis, M. The effect of food deprivation on shock-elicited aggression in rats. *Psychon. Sci.*, 1971, *22*, 43–44.

Calhoun, J. B. Mortality and movement of brown rats *(Rattus norvegicus)* in artificially supersaturated populations. *J. Wildlife Mgmt.*, 1948, *12*, 167–172.

Calhoun, J. B. The study of wild animals under controlled conditions. *Anns. N. Y. Acad. Sci.*, 1950, *51*, 1113–1122.

Calhoun, J. B. Population density and social pathology. *Sci. Amer.*, 1962, *206*, 139–146.

Calhoun, J. B., and Webb, W. L. Induced emigrations among small mammals. *Science*, 1953, *117*, 358–360.

Campbell, J. S., and Shoham, S. The family and violence. *In* Report of the Task Force in Law and Law Enforcement to the National Commission on the Causes and Prevention of Violence, *Law and Order Reconsidered*. New York, Bantam Books, 1970.

Candland, D. K., and Bloomquist, D. W. Interspecies comparisons of the reliability of dominance orders. *J. comp. physiol. Psychol.*, 1965, *59*, 135–137.

Caplan, N. The new ghetto man: a review of recent empirical studies. *J. Soc. Issues*, 1970, *26*, 59–74.

Caplan, N., and Paige, J. M. A study of ghetto rioters. *Sci. Amer.*, 1968, *219*, 15–21.

Carthy, J. D., and Ebling, F. J. Prologue and epilogue. In J. D. Carthy and F. J. Ebling (Eds.), *The Natural History of Aggression*. New York, Academic Press, 1964.

Casler, L. The effects of extra tactile stimulation on a group of institutionalized infants. *Genet. Psychol. Monog.*, 1965, *71*, 137–175.

Casler, L. Perceptual deprivation in institutional settings. In G. Newton and S. Levine (Eds.), *Early Experience and Behavior*. Springfield, Ill., Charles C Thomas, 1968.

Challenge of Crime in a Free Society: A Report of the President's Commission on Law Enforcement and Administration of Justice. Washington, D. C., U.S. Government Printing Office, 1967.

Chester, P. Maternal influences in learning by observation in kittens. *Science*, 1969, *166*, 901–903.

Christian, J. J. Effect of population size on the adrenal glands and reproductive organs of male mice in populations of fixed size. *Amer. J. Physiol.*, 1955, *182*, 292–300.

Clark, K. B. The pathos of power. Presidential address to the American Psychological Association, Washington, D. C., Sept., 1971.

Clark, R. *Crime in America*. New York, Simon and Schuster, 1970.

Clark, R. A. The projective measurement of experimentally induced levels of sexual motivation. *J. exper. Psychol.*, 1952, *44*, 391–399.

Clark, R. A., and Sensibar, M. R. The relationship between symbolic and manifest projections of sexuality with some incidental correlates. *J. abnorm. soc. Psychol.*, 1955, *50*, 327–334.

Clayton, F. L., and Hinde, R. A. The habituation and recovery of aggressive display in *Betta splendens*. *Behaviour*, 1968, *30*, 96–106.

Cloudsley-Thompson, J. L. *Animal Conflict and Adaptation*. London, G. T. Foules and Co., 1965.

Coale, A. J. Man and his environment. *Science*, 1970, *170*, 132–136.

Commission on Obscenity and Pornography. Washington, D. C., U. S. Government Printing Office, 1970.

Comstock, C. Avoiding the pathologies of defense. In N. Sanford and C. Comstock (Eds.), *Sanctions for Evil*, San Francisco, Jossey-Bass, 1971.

Conner, R. L., and Levine, S. Hormonal influences on aggressive behaviour. In S. Garattini and E. B. Sigg, *Aggressive Behaviour*. New York, Wiley, 1969.

Conner, R. L., Stolk, J. M., Barchas, J. D., Dement, W. C., and Levine, S. The effect of parachlorophenylalanine (PCPA) on shock-induced fighting behavior in rats. *Physiol. Behav.*, 1970, *5*, 1221–1224.

Cook, R. F., and Fosen, R. H. Pornography and the sex offender: patterns of exposure and immediate arousal effects of pornographic stimuli. *Technical reports of the Commission on Obscenity and Pornography*, Vol. 7, Washington, D. C., U. S. Government Printing Office, 1970.

Court-Brown, W. M. *Human Population Cytogenetics*. New York, Wiley, 1967.

Cowden, J. Adventures with South Africa's black eagles. *Nat. Geog.*, 1969, *136*, 533–551.

Craig, W. Why do animals fight? *Int. J. Ethics*, 1928, *31*, 264–278.

Crimes of Violence. A staff report submitted to the National Commission on the Causes and Prevention of Violence, Washington, D. C., U. S. Government Printing Office, 1969.

Crook, J. H. The socio-ecology of primates. In J. H. Crook (Ed.), *Social Behaviour in Birds and Mammals*. New York, Academic Press, 1970.

Crook, J. H., and Butterfield, P. A. Gender role in the social system of Quelea. In J. H. Crook (Ed.), *Social Behaviour in Birds and Mammals*. New York, Academic Press, 1970.

Crook, J. H., and Gartlan, J. S. Evolution of primate societies. *Nature*, 1966, *210*, 1200–1203.

Cross, H. A., and Harlow, H. F. Prolonged and progressive effects of partial isolation on the behavior of macaque monkeys. *J. exp. res. Pers.*, 1965, *1*, 39–49.

Dalton, K. *The Premenstrual Syndrome.* Springfield, Ill., Charles C Thomas, 1964.

Daly, R. F. Mental illness and patterns of behavior in 10 XYY males. *J. Nerv. Ment. Dis.*, 1969, *149*, 318–327.

Daniels, D. N., Trickett, E. J., Shapiro, M. M., Tinklenberg, J. R., and Jackman, J. M. The gun law controversy: issues, arguments and speculations concerning firearms legislation. *In* D. N. Daniels, M. F. Gilula, and F. M. Ochberg (Eds.), *Violence and the Struggle for Existence.* Boston, Little, Brown and Co., 1970.

Darwin, C. *The Expression of the Emotions in Man and the Animals.* London, John Murray, 1872.

Davenport, R. K., and Menzel, E. W., Jr. Stereotyped behavior of the infant chimpanzee. *Arch. Gen. Psychiat.*, 1963, *8*, 99–104.

David, M., and Appell, G. Mother-child interaction and its impact on the child. *In* A. Ambrose (Ed.), *Stimulation in Early Infancy.* New York, Academic Press, 1969.

Davis, K. Extreme social isolation of a child. *Amer. J. Sociol.*, 1940, *45*, 554–565.

Davis, K. Final note on a case of extreme social isolation. *Amer. J. Sociol.*, 1947, *52*, 432–437.

The day the war become a personal theory. *San Francisco Examiner and Chronicler*, Nov. 23, 1969.

Delgado, J. M. R. Discussion. *In* C. D. Clemente and D. B. Lindsley (Eds.), *Aggression and Defense.* Los Angeles, University of California Press, 1967 (p. 24).

Delgado, J. M. R. *Physical Control of the Mind.* New York, Harper and Row, 1969a.

Delgado, J. M. R. Radio stimulation of the brain in primates and man. *J. International Anesthesia Research Society*, 1969b, *48*, 529–542.

Denenberg, V. H. Early experience and emotional development. *Sci. Amer.*, 1963, *208*, 138–246.

Denenberg, V. H. Critical periods, stimulus input and emotional reactivity: a theory of infantile stimulation. *Psychol. Rev.*, 1964, *71*, 335–351.

Denenberg, V. H. Stimulation in infancy: emotional reactivity and exploratory behavior. *In* D. C. Glass (Ed.), *Neurophysiology and Emotion.* New York, Russell Sage Foundation, 1967.

Denenberg, V. H. The effects of early experience. *In* E. S. E. Hafez (Ed.), *The Behavior of Domestic Animals.* London, Tindall and Cox, 1969.

Denenberg, V. H., Brumaghim, J. T., Haltmeyer, G. C., and Zarrow, M. X. Increased adrenocortical activity in the neonatal rat following handling. *Endocrinol.*, 1967, *81*, 1047–1052.

Denenberg, V. H., Hudgens, G. A., and Zarrow, M. X. Mice reared with rats: modification of behavior by early experience with another species. *Science*, 1964, *143*, 380–381.

Denenberg, V. H., Paschke, R., Zarrow, M. X., and Rosenberg, K. Mice reared with rats: elimination of odors, vision and audition as significant stimulus sources. *Devel. Psychobiol.*, 1969, *2*, 26–33.

Denenberg, V. H., and Rosenberg, K. M. Nongenetic transmission of information. *Nature*, 1967, *216*, 549–550.

Denenberg, V. H., Rosenberg, K. M., Paschke, R. E., Hess, J. L., Zarrow, M. X., and Levine, S. Plasma corticosterone levels as a function of cross-species fostering and species differences. *Endocrinol;* 1968, *83*, 900–902.

Denenberg, V. H., Rosenberg, K. M., Paschke, R., and Zarrow, M. X. Mice reared with rat aunts: effects on plasma corticosterone and open field activity. *Nature*, 1969, *221*, 73–74.

Denenberg, V. H., and Whimbey, A. E. Behavior of adult rats is modified by the experiences their mothers had as infants. *Science*, 1963, *142*, 1192–1193.

Denenberg, V. H., and Zarrow, M. X. Rat pax. *Psychology Today*, 1970, *3*, 45–47 and 66–67.

Denenberg, V. H. Developmental factors in aggression. Paper presented at a symposium at the State University of Iowa, May, 1971.

Denny, M. R., and Ratner, S. C. *Comparative Psychology.* Homewood, Ill., Dorsey Press, 1970.

DeSisto, M. J. Hypothalamic mechanisms of killing behavior in the rat. Doctoral thesis, Tufts University, 1970.

DeSisto, M. J. and Huston, J. P. Effect of territory on frog-killing by rats. *J. Gen. Psychol.*, 1970, 83, 179–184.

Deutsch, M. Socially relevant science: reflections on some studies of interpersonal conflict. *Amer. Psychol.*, 1969, 24, 1076–1092.

Deutsch, M., and Collins, M. E. *Interracial housing: a psychological evaluation of a social experiment.* Minneapolis, University of Minnesota Press, 1951.

Dicks, D., Myers, R. K., and Kling, A. Uncus and amygdala lesions: effects on social behavior in the free ranging rhesus monkey. *Science*, 1969, 165, 69–71.

Dickson, D. P., Barr, G. R., and Wieckert, D. A. Social relationship of dairy cows in a feed lot. *Behaviour*, 1967, 29, 195–203.

Dittman, A., and Goodrich, D. A comparison of social behavior in normal and hyper-aggressive preadolescent boys. *Child Devel.*, 1961, 32, 315–327.

Dollard, J. C., Doob, L., Miller, N., Mowrer, O., and Sears, R. *Frustration and Aggression.* New Haven, Yale University Press, 1939.

Dosey, M. A., and Meisels, M. Personal space and self-protection. *J. per. soc. Psychol.*, 1969, 11, 93–97.

Dreyer, P. I., and Church, R. W. Reinforcement of shock-induced fighting. *Psychon. Sci.*, 1970, 18, 147–148.

Dunn, G. W. Stilbestrol induced testicular degeneration in hyper-sexual males. *J. Clin. Endocrinol.*, 1941, 1, 643–648.

Dunning, D. C. Warning sounds of moths. *Zeitschrift für Tierpsychologie*, 1968, 25, 9–138.

Edwards, D. A. Mice; fighting by neonatally androgenized females. *Science*, 1968, 161, 1027–1028.

Edwards, D. A., and Herndon, J. Neonatal estrogen stimulation and aggressive behavior in female mice. *Physiol. Behav.*, 1970, 5, 993–995.

Egger, M. D., and Flynn, J. P. Effect of electrical stimulation of the amygdala on hypothalamically elicited attack behavior in cats. *J. Neurophysiol.*, 1963, 26, 705–720.

Egger, M. D., and Flynn, J. P. Further studies on the effects of amygdaloid stimulation and ablation on hypothalamically elicited attack behavior in cats. *In* W. R. Adey and T. Tokizane (Eds.), *Structure and Function of the Limbic System.* Amsterdam, Elsevier, 1967.

Ehrlich, P., and Freedman, J. Population, crowding and human behavior. *New Scientist and Science J.*, Apr. 1, 1971, 10–14.

Eibl-Eibesfeldt, I. The fighting behavior of animals. *Sci. Amer.*, 1961, 205, 112–122.

Eibl-Eibesfeldt, I. *Ethology.* New York, Holt, Rinehart, and Winston, 1970.

Eibl-Eibesfeldt, I., and Wickler, W. Die ethologische Deutung einiger Wächter-figuren auf Bali. *Zeitschrift für Tierpsychologie*, 1968, 25, 719–726.

Ellison, G. D., and Flynn, J. P. Organized aggressive behavior in cats after surgical isolation of the hypothalamus. *Arch. Ital. Biol.*, 1968, 106, 1–20.

Emlen, S. T. Territoriality in the bullfrog, *Rana catesbeiana. Copeia*, 1968, 2, 240–423.

Emmerich, W. Continuity and stability in early social development: II. Teacher ratings. *Child Devel.*, 1966, 37, 17–28.

Endo, G. T. Social drive or arousal: a test of two theories of social isolation. *J. exper. child Psychol.*, 1968, 6, 61–74.

Eron, L. Relationship of TV viewing habits and aggressive behavior in children. *J. abnorm. soc. Psychol.*, 1963, 67, 193–196.

Ervin, F. R., Mark, V. H., and Stevens, J. Behavioral and affective responses to brain stimulation in man. *In* J. Zubin and C. Shograss (Eds.), *Neurobiological Aspects of Psychopathology.* New York, Grune and Stratton, 1969.

Estes, R. D. The comparative behavior of Grant's and Thomson's gazelles. *J. Mammalogy*, 1967, 48, 189–209.

Estes, R. D. Territorial behavior of the wildebeest *(Connochaetes taurinus* Burchell) 1923. *Zeitschrift für Tierpsychologie*, 1969, 26, 284–370.

Etkin, W. Cooperation and competition in social behavior. In W. Etkin (Ed.), *Social Behavior and Organization Among Vetebrates.* Chicago, University of Chicago Press, 1964.

Etkin, W., and Freedman, D. G. *Social Behavior from Fish to Man.* Chicago, University of Chicago Press, 1964.

F. A. A. asks TV outlets to bar bomb-hoax film. *New York Times,* Aug. 11, 1971.

Faris, R. E. L. *Social Disorganization.* New York, Ronald Press, 1955.

Feierabend, I. K., and Feierabend, R. L. Aggressive behaviors within politics, 1948–1962: a cross-national study. *J. Conflict Resolution,* 1966, *10,* 249–272.

Felipe, N. J., and Sommer, R. Invasions of personal space. *Social Problems,* 1966, *14,* 206–214.

Ferguson, J., Henriksen, S., Cohen, H., Mitchell, G., Barchas, J., and Dement, W. "Hypersexuality" and behavioral change in cats caused by administration of p-Chlorophenylalanine. *Science,* 1970, *168,* 499–500.

Feshbach, N., and Feshbach, S. Personality and political values: a study of reactions to two accused assassins. *In* B. S. Greenberg and E. B. Parker (Eds.), *The Kennedy Assassination and the American Public.* Stanford, Stanford University Press, 1965.

Feshbach, S. The stimulating vs. cathartic effects of vicarious aggressive activity. *J. abnorm. soc. Psychol.,* 1961, *63,* 381–385.

Feshbach, S. The function of aggression and the regulation of aggressive drive. *Psychol. Rev.,* 1964, *71,* 257–272.

Feshbach, S. Effects of exposure to aggressive content in television upon aggression in boys. *Proceedings of XVI International Congress of Applied Psychology,* Copenhagen, 1968, 669–672.

Feshbach, S. Aggression. *In* P. H. Mussen (Ed.), *Carmichael's Manual of Child Psychology,* Vol. II. New York, Wiley, 1970.

Feshbach, S. Dynamics of morality of violence and aggression: some psychological considerations. *Amer. Psychol.,* 1971, *26,* 281–291.

Feshbach, S., and Jaffee, W. Effects of inhibition of aggression upon sexual arousal. Preliminary Report, 1970.

Feshbach S., and Singer, R. D. *Television and Aggression.* San Francisco, Jossey-Bass, 1971.

Feshbach, S., Stiles, W. B., and Bitter, E. Reinforcing effect of witnessing aggression. *J. exper. res. Pers.,* 1967, *2,* 133–139.

Fisher, A. E. The effects of differential early treatment on the social and exploratory behavior of puppies. Unpublished doctoral dissertation, Pennsylvania State University, 1955.

Fisher, A. E. Effects of stimulus variation on sexual satiation in the male rat. *J. comp. physiol. Psychol.,* 1962, *55,* 614–620.

Fisher, D. G., Kelm, H., and Rose, A. Knives as aggression-eliciting stimuli. *Psychol. Rep.,* 1969, *24,* 755–760.

Fisher, J. Interspecific aggression. *In* J. D. Carthy and F. J. Ebling (Eds.), *The Natural History of Aggression.* New York, Academic Press, 1964.

Flanders, J. P. A review of research on imitative behavior. *Psychol. Bull.,* 1968, *69,* 316–337.

Flynn, J. P. The neural basis of aggression in cats. *In* D. C. Glass (Ed.), *Neurophysiology and Emotion.* New York, Rockefeller University Press and Russell Sage Foundation, 1967.

Flynn, J. P., Vanegas, H., Foote, W., and Edwards, S. Neural mechanisms involved in a cat's attack on a rat. *In* R. E. Whalen, R. F. Thompson, M. Verzeano, and N. M. Weinberger (Eds.), *The Neural Control of Behavior.* New York, Academic Press, 1970.

Ford, C. S., and Beach, F. A. *Patterns of Sexual Behavior.* New York, Harper and Row, 1951.

Fort, J. *The Pleasure Seekers.* New York, Bobbs Merrill, 1969.

Fowler, H., and Whalen, R. E. Variation in incentive stimulus and sexual behavior in the male rat. *J. comp. physiol. Psychol.,* 1961, *54,* 68–71.

Fox, M. W. Aggression: its adaptive and maladaptive significance in man and animals. *In* M. W. Fox (Ed.), *Abnormal Behavior in Animals*. Philadelphia, W. B. Saunders, 1968.

Francoeur, R. T. *Utopian Motherhood: New Trends in Human Reproduction.* Garden City, Doubleday, 1970.

Frankel, C. Is it ever right to break the law? *New York Times Magazine*, Jan. 12, 1964.

Free, J. B., Weinberg, I., and Whiten, A. The egg eating behaviour of *Bombus lapidarius* L. *Behaviour*, 1970, *36*, 313–317.

Freedman, D. A. The influence of congenital and perinatal sensory deprivation on later development. *Psychosomatics*, 1968, *9*, 272–277.

Freedman, D. A. Congenital and perinatal sensory deprivation: some studies in early development. *Amer. J. Psychiat.*, 1971, *127*, 1539–1545.

Freedman, D. G. Constitutional and environmental interactions in rearing of four breeds of dogs. *Science*, 1958, *127*, 585–586.

Fuller, J. L. Experiential deprivation and later behavior. *Science*, 1967, *158*, 1648–1652.

Fuller, J. L., and Clark, L. D. Genetic and treatment factors modifying the post-isolation syndrome in dogs. *J. comp. physiol. Psychol.*, 1966, *61*, 251–257.

Funkenstein, D. H., The physiology of fear and anger. *Sci. Amer.*, 1955, *192*, 74–80.

Galef, B. G., Jr. Aggression and timidity, responses to novelty in feral Norway rats. *J. comp. physiol. Psychol.*, 1970a, *70*, 370–381.

Galef, B. G., Jr. Target novelty elicits and directs shock-associated aggression in wild rats. *J. comp. physiol. Psychol.*, 1970b, *71*, 87–91.

Garattini, S., and Sigg, E. B. (Eds.). *Aggressive Behavior*. New York, Wiley Inter-science, 1969.

Garcia, J., Ervin, F. R., and Koelling, R. A. Learning with prolonged delay of re-inforcement. *Psychon. Sci.*, 1966, *5*, 121–122.

Gardner, J. W. Moral decay and renewal. *Saturday Review*, Dec. 14, 1963.

Garn, S. M., and Block, W. D. The limited nutritional value of cannibalism. *Amer. Anthropol.*, 1970, *72*, 106.

Gattozzi, A. A. Lithium in the treatment of mood disorders. U. S. Dept. of Health, Education and Welfare, Washington, D. C., U. S. Government Printing Office, 1970.

Gebhard, P. H., Gagnon, J. H., Pomeroy, W. B., and Christenson, C. V. *Sex Offenders: An Analysis of Types*. New York, Harper and Row, 1965.

Geen, R. G., and O'Neal, E. C. Activation of cue-elicited aggression by general arousal. *J. per. soc. Psychol.*, 1969, *11*, 289–292.

Geen, R. G., and Pigg, R. Acquisition of an aggressive response and its generaliza-tion to verbal behavior. *J. per. soc. Psychol.*, 1970, *15*, 165–170.

Geis, G. The heavy electrical equipment antitrust cases of 1961. *In* G. Geis (Ed.), *White-Collar Criminal*, New York, Atherton, 1968.

Gerber, M. The psychomotor development of African children in the first year and the influence of maternal behavior. *J. per. soc. Psychol.*, 1958, *47*, 185–195.

Gilliland, A. R. A revision and some results with the Moore-Gilliland aggressiveness test. *J. appl. Psychol.*, 1926, *10*, 143–150.

Gillin, J. C., and Ochberg, F. M. Firearms control and violence. *In* D. N. Daniels, M. F. Gilula, and F. M. Ochberg (Eds.), *Violence and the Struggle for Existence*. Boston, Little, Brown and Co., 1970.

Ginsburg, B. E. Genetic parameters in behavioral research. *In* J. Hirsch (Ed.), *Behavior: Genetic Analysis*. New York, McGraw-Hill, 1967.

Ginsburg, B. E. Wolf social behavior. Paper presented at the New England Psycho-logical Association, Boston, Mass., Nov. 13, 1970.

Ginsburg, B. E., and Allee, W. C. Some effects of conditioning on social dominance and subordination in inbred strains of mice. *Physiol. Zool.*, 1942, *15*, 485–506.

Glickman, S. E., and Schiff, B. A biological theory of reinforcement. *Psychol. Rev.*, 1967, *74*, 81–109.

Glueck, S., and Glueck, E. *Unraveling Juvenile Delinquency*. Cambridge, Harvard University Press, 1950.

Goldfarb, R. L. The horror of prisons. *New York Times*, Oct. 28, 1970.

Goldstein, M. J., Kant, H. S., Judd, L. L., Rice, C. J., and Green, R. Exposure to pornography and sexual behavior in deviant and normal groups. *Technical Reports of the Commission on Obscenity and Pornography.* Washington, D. C., U. S. Government Printing Office, 1970.

Gonzalez, R. C. Frustrative non-reward in fish. Paper presented at the Psychonomic Society, San Antonio, Texas, Nov. 5–7, 1970.

Goransen, R. E. The catharsis effect: two opposing views. *In* R. K. Baker and J. J. Ball (Eds.), *Mass Media and Violence,* Vol IX. Washington, D. C., U. S. Government Printing Office, 1969.

Goransen, R. E. Media violence and aggressive behavior; a review of experimental research. *In* L. Berkowitz (Ed.), *Advances in Experimental Social Psychology.* New York, Academic Press, 1970.

Gorer, G. Man has no "killer" instinct. *New York Times Magazine,* November 27, 1966.

Goss-Custard, J. D. Feeding dispersion in some over-wintering wading birds. *In* J. H. Crook (Ed.), *Social Behaviour in Birds and Mammals.* New York, Academic Press, 1970.

Gould, J. T.V.: A bomb backfires. *New York Times,* December 16, 1966.

Gould, J. U.S. aide accused on TV violence. *New York Times,* January 12, 1972.

Goy, R. W., and Phoenix, C. H. Hypothalamic regulation of female sexual behavior: establishment of behavioral oestrus in spayed guinea pigs following hypothalamic lesions. *J. Reprod. Fert.,* 1963, 5, 23–40.

Goy, R. W. Early hormonal influences on the development of sexual and sex-related behavior. *In* F. O. Schmitt (Ed.), *The Neurosciences.* New York, Rockefeller University Press, 1970.

Grabowski, J., and Thompson, T. Effects of visual reinforcer brightness and color on operant behavior of the Siamese fighting fish. *Psychon. Sci.,* 1968, *11,* 111.

Grant, E. C., and Chance, M. R. A. Rank order in caged rats. *Anim. Behav.,* 1958, 6, 183–194.

Gray, J. G. *The Warriors.* New York, Harper and Row, 1967.

Gray, P. H. Evidence that retinal flicker is not a necessary condition of imprinting. *Science,* 1960, *132,* 1834–1835.

Greene, J. T. Altruistic behavior in the albino rat. *Psychon. Sci.,* 1969, *14,* 47–48.

Grunt, J. A., and Young, W. C. Psychological modification of fatigue following orgasm (ejaculation) in the male guinea pig. *J. comp. physiol. Psychol.,* 1952, 45, 508–510.

Guhl, A. M. The social order of chickens. *Sci. Amer.,* 1956, *194,* 42–46.

Gulevich, G. D., and Bourne, P. G. Mental illness and violence. *In* D. N. Daniels, M. F. Gilula, and F. M. Ochberg (Eds.), *Violence and the Struggle for Existence.* Boston, Little, Brown and Co., 1970.

Gurr, T. R. A comparative study of civil strife. *In* H. D. Graham and T. R. Gurr (Eds.), *Violence in America.* A report submitted to the National Commission on the Causes and Prevention of Violence. New York, Bantam Books, 1969.

Hagen, K. S. Following the ladybug home. *Nat. Geog.,* 1970, *137,* 543–553.

Hall, C. S. The inheritance of emotionality. *Sigma Xi Quart.,* 1938, *26,* 17–27.

Hall, C. S., and Klein, S. J. Individual differences in aggressiveness in rats. *J. comp. physiol. Psychol.,* 1942, *33,* 371–383.

Hall, C. S., and Whiteman, P. H. The effects of infantile stimulation upon later emotional stability in the mouse. *J. comp. physiol. Psychol.,* 1951, *44,* 61–66.

Hall, E. T. *The Hidden Dimension.* Garden City, N. Y., Doubleday, 1966.

Hall, K. R. L. Aggression in monkey and ape societies. *In* J. D. Carthy and F. J. Ebling (Eds.), *The Natural History of Aggression.* London, Academic Press, 1964.

Hall, K. R. L., and DeVore, I. Baboon social behavior. *In* I. DeVore (Ed.), *Primate Behavior: Field Studies of Monkeys and Apes.* New York, Holt, Rinehart and Winston, 1965.

Halleck, S. American psychiatry and the criminal. *Amer. J. Psychiat.,* 1965, *14,* 773–780.

Halloran, R. Army spied on 1800 Cubans in 2 year operation. *New York Times,* Jan. 18, 1971.

Halloran, R. Crime in Tokyo a minor problem. *New York Times*, Oct. 3, 1971.

Hamburg, D. A. Effects of progesterone on behavior. *In* R. Levine (Ed.), *Endocrines and the Central Nervous System*. Baltimore, Williams and Wilkins, 1966.

Hamburg, D. A., Moos, R. H., and Yalom, I. D. Studies of distress in the menstrual cycle and the postpartum period. *In* R. P. Michael (Ed.), *Endocrinology and Human Behaviour*. London, Oxford University Press, 1968.

Hamby, W., and Cahoon, D. D. The effect of water deprivation upon shock-elicited aggression in the white rat. *Psychon. Sci.*, 1971, *23*, 52.

Hampson, J. L. Determinants of psychosexual orientation. *In* F. A. Beach (Ed.), *Sex and Behavior*. New York, Wiley, 1965.

Haner, C. F., and Brown, P. A. Clarification of the instigation to action concept in the frustration-aggression hypothesis. *J. abnorm. soc. Psychol.*, 1955, *51*, 204–206.

Harding, J., and Hogrefe, R. Attitudes of white department store employees towards Negro co-workers. *J. soc. Issues*, 1952, *8*, 18–28.

Harlow, H. F. Love in infant monkeys. *Sci. Amer.*, 1959, *200*, 68–74.

Harlow, H. F., Dodsworth, R. O., and Harlow, M. K. Total isolation in monkeys. *Proc. Nat. Acad. Sci.*, 1965, *54*, 90–97.

Harlow, H. F., and Harlow, M. K. Social deprivation in monkeys. *Sci. Amer.*, 1962, *207*,137–146.

Harlow, H. F., Harlow, M. K., and Hansen, E. W. The maternal affectional system of Rhesus monkeys. *In* H. L. Rheingold (Ed.), *Maternal Behavior in Mammals*. New York, Wiley, 1963.

Harris, R. Annals of legislation: if you love your gun. *New Yorker*, April 20, 1968, p. 56.

Hartman, D. P. Influence of symbolically modeled instrumental aggression and pain cues on aggressive behavior. *J. per. soc. Psychol.*, 1969, *11*, 280–288.

Hartmann, H., Kris, E., and Lowenstein, R. M. *Notes on the Theory of Aggression: The Psychoanalytic Study of the Child*. New York, International Universities Press, 1949.

Hatch, A., Balazs, T., Wiberg, C. S., and Grice, H. C. Long-term isolation stress in rats. *Science*, 1963, *142*, 507.

Hazlett, B. A. Size relationships and aggressive behavior in the hermit crab *Clibanarius vittatus*. *Zeitschrift für Tierpsychologie*, 1968, *25*, 608–614.

Heath, R. G. Electrical self-stimulation of the brain in man. *Amer. J. Psychiat.*, 1963, *120*, 571–577.

Hebb, D. O. *The Organization of Behavior*. New York, Wiley, 1949.

Hediger, H. Environmental factors influencing the reproduction of zoo animals. *In* F. A. Beach (Ed.), *Sex and Behavior*. New York, Wiley, 1965.

Hero Calley. *Time*, Feb. 15, 1971, p. 14.

Hess, J. L. Poor nations spend fortune on arms purchases. *New York Times*, Aug. 18, 1970.

Hess, W. R. Stammganglien-reizversuche, 10 tagung der deutschen physiologischen gesell schaft, Frankfurt am Main. *Ber. ges. Physiol.*, 1928, *42*, 554–555.

Hicks, D. J. Imitation and retention of film mediated aggressive peer and adult models. *J. per. soc. Psychol.*, 1965, *2*, 97–100.

Himmelweit, H. T., Oppenheim, A. N., and Vince, P. *Television and the Child*. London, Oxford University Press, 1958.

Hinde, R. A. Factors governing the changes in strength of a partially unborn response, as shown by the mobbing behaviour of the chaffinch *(Fringilla coelebs)*. I. The nature of the response, and an examination of its course. *Proc. Roy. Soc. Lond., B*, 1954, *142*, 306–331.

Hinde, R. A., and Spencer-Booth, Y. Individual differences in the responses of Rhesus monkeys to a period of separation from their mothers. *J. child psychol. Psychiat.*, 1970, *11*, 159–176.

Hitt, J. C., Hendricks, S. E., Ginsberg, S. I., and Lewis, J. H. Disruption of male but not female sexual behavior in rats by medial forebrain bundle stimulation. *J. comp. physiol. Psychol.*, 1970, *73*, 377–384.

Hoffman, M. Power assertion by the parent and its impact on the child. *Child Devel.*, 1960, *31*, 129–143.

Hofstadter, R. *Social Darwinism in American Thought.* Boston, Beacon Press, 1955.

Hofstadter, R., and Wallace, M. (Eds.). *American Violence.* New York, Vintage Books, 1971.

Hokanson, J. E., and Burgess, M. The effects of three types of aggression on vascular processes. *J. abnorm. soc. Psychol.,* 1962, *64,* 446–449.

Hokanson, J. E. Psychophysiological evaluation of the catharsis hypothesis. In E. I. Megargee and J. E. Hokanson (Eds.), *The Dynamics of Aggression.* New York, Harper and Row, 1970.

Hokanson, J. E., and Shelter, S. The effect of overt aggression on physiological arousal. *J. abnorm. soc. Psychol.,* 1961, *63,* 446–448.

Hollenberg, E., and Sperry, M. Some antecedents of aggression and effects on doll play. *J. Personality,* 1950, *1,* 32–34.

Holloway, R. L., Jr. Human aggression: the need for a species-specific framework. In F. Fried, M. Harris, and R. Murphy (Eds.), *War: the Anthropology of Armed Conflict and Aggression.* Garden City, N. Y., Natural History Press, 1967.

Hook, E. B., and Kim, D. Height and antisocial behavior in XY and XYY boys. *Science,* 1971, *172,* 284–286.

Hook, S. The war against the democratic process. *Atlantic,* Feb. 1969, 46–47.

Hopper, H. E., and Pinneau, S. P. Frequency of regurgitation in infancy as related to the amount of stimulation received from the mothers. *Child. Devel.,* 1957, *28,* 229–235.

Horton, D. The functions of alcohol in primitive societies: a cross cultural study. *Quart. J. Studies on Alcohol,* 1943, *4,* 199.

Hovland, C. I., and Sears, R. R. Minor studies in aggression VI: correlation of lynchings with economic indices. *J. Personality,* 1940, *9,* 301–310.

Howard, E. *Territory in Bird Life.* London, Collins, 1948.

Hudgens, G. A., Denenberg, V. H., and Zarrow, M. X. Mice reared with rats: effects of preweaning and postweaning social interactions upon adult behavior. *Behaviour,* 1968, *30,* 259–274.

Hunt, H. F., and Otis, L. S. Early "experience" and its effects on later behavioral processes in rats: Initial experiments. *Trans. N. Y. Acad. Sci.,* 1963, *25,* 858–870.

Huston, J. P., DeSisto, M. J., and Meyer, E. Frog-killing by rats as influenced by territorial variables. Paper read at the Eastern Psychological Association, Philadelphia, Apr., 1969.

Hutchinson, R. R., and Renfrew, J. W. Stalking attack and eating behavior elicited from the same sites in the hypothalamus. *J. comp. physiol. Psychol.,* 1966, *61,* 360–367.

Hutchinson, R. R., Renfrew, J. W., and Young, G. A. Effects of long-term shock and associated stimuli on aggressive and manual responses. *J. exper. anal. Behav.,* 1971, *15,* 141–166.

Igel, G. J., and Calvin, A. D. The development of affectional responses in infant dogs. *J. comp. physiol. Psychol.,* 1960, *53,* 302–305.

Iglitzin, L. B. Violence and American democracy. *J. Soc. Issues.,* 1970, *26,* 165–186.

Imes, S., and Etaugh, C. F. Emotionality in mice as a function of infantile stimulation. *Psychon. Sci.,* 1971, *22,* 19–20.

James, W. The moral equivalent of war. In W. James, *Memoirs and Studies.* London, Longmans Green and Co., 1917.

James, W. T. Social organization among dogs of different temperaments: terriers and beagles reared together. *J. comp. physiol. Psychol.,* 1951, *44,* 71–77.

Janis, I. L. Groupthink among policy makers. In N. Sanford and C. Comstock (Eds.), *Sanctions for Evil.* San Francisco, Jossey-Bass, 1971.

Jay, P. Field studies. In A. M. Schrier, H. F. Harlow, and F. Stollnitz (Eds.), *Behavior of Nonhuman Primates,* Vol. II. New York, Academic Press, 1965.

Jersild, A. T., and Markey, F. Conflicts between preschool children. *Child. Devel. Monog.,* 1935, No. 21.

Johnson, R. N. Visual reinforcement in fighting fish and paradise fish. Paper presented at the Eastern Psychological Association, New York, Apr., 1971.

Johnson, R. N. Aggression deprivation in Siamese fighting fish. 1972. In preparation.

Johnson, R. N., DeSisto, M. J., and Koenig, A. Social and developmental experience and interspecific aggression in rats. *J. comp. physiol. Psychol.,* 1972. In press.

Johnson, R. N., DeSisto, M. J., and Koenig, A. The "Kuo effect" in rats and mice. 1972.

Johnson, R. N., and Johnson, L. D. Interspecific aggression in Siamese fighting fish, *Betta splendens.* 1972. In press.

Johnson, R. N., and Johnson, L. D. Intraspecific and interspecific aggressive behavior in the Siamese fighting fish, *Betta splendens.* Paper presented at the joint meetings of the American Association for the Advancement of Science and the American Society of Zoologists, Chicago, Dec., 1970.

Johnson, R. N., Lobdell, P., and Levy, R. Intracranial self-stimulation and the rapid decline of frustrative non-reward. *Science,* 1969, *164,* 971–972.

Johnson, R. N., Reich, L., and DeSisto, M. J. Intraspecific dominance and interspecific aggression, 1972. In preparation.

Johnson, R. P., Sachs, C. A., and Boitano, J. J. The primacy of size-age dimension over familial relationships in shock-elicited aggression in rats. *Psychon. Sci.,* 1971, *23,* 71–72.

Kaada, B. Brain mechanisms related to aggressive behavior. *In* D. C. Clemente and D. B. Lindsley (Eds.), *Aggression and Defense.* Berkeley, University of California Press, 1967.

Kagan, J. Applying the infantile stimulation model to research on human infants: general discussion. *In* A. Ambrose (Ed.), *Stimulation in Early Infancy.* New York, Academic Press, 1969.

Kagan, J., and Moss, H. A. *Birth to Maturity: A Study in Psychological Development.* New York, Wiley, 1962.

Kaplan, M. Guard at hospital indicted in death of prisoner. *New York Times,* Oct. 20, 1971.

Karli, P. The Norway rat's killing response to the white mouse: an experimental analysis. *Behaviour,* 1956, *10,* 81–103.

Karli, P. Nouvelles données experimentales sur le comportement d'aggression interspécifique Rat-Souris. *J. Physiol. (Paris),* 1961, *53,* 383–384.

Kato, H., Schull, W. J., and Neel, J. V. A cohort type study of survival in the children of parents exposed to atomic bombings. *Amer. J. Human Genetics,* 1966, *18,* 339–373.

Kaufmann, H. Definitions and methodology in the study of aggression. *Psychol. Bull.,* 1965, *64,* 351–364.

Kaufmann, H. *Aggression and Altruism.* New York, Holt, Rinehart and Winston, 1970.

Katz, J. On the death of the President: President Kennedy's assassination. *Psychoan. Rev.,* 1964–1965, *51,* 661.

Keeler, C. E., and King, H. D. Multiple effects of coat color genes in the Norway rat with special reference to temperament and domestication. *J. comp. physiol. Psychol.,* 1942, *34,* 241–250.

Kennedy, E. The "burden" of the Constitution. *New York Times,* Oct. 22, 1971.

Kenney, N. T. Sharks: wolves of the sea. *Nat. Geog.,* 1968, *133,* 224–257.

Kerner, O., et al., *Report of the National Advisory Commission on Civil Disorders.* New York, Bantam Books, 1968.

Keys, A., Brozek, J., Henschel, A., Mickelsen, O., and Taylor, H. L. *The Biology of Human Starvation.* Minneapolis, University of Minnesota Press, 1950.

Kifner, J. Mystery in Illinois: millionaire aide. *New York Times,* Jan. 15, 1971.

Kihlberg, J. Head injury in automobile accidents. *In* W. F. Caveness and A. E. Walker (Eds.), *Head Injury: Conference Proceedings.* Philadelphia, Lippincott, 1966.

Kihss, P. Minutemen case is dropped here. *New York Times,* Oct. 19, 1971.

King, D. L. The effect of early experience and litter on some weight and maturational variables. *Devel. Psychol.,* 1969, *1,* 576–584.

King, D. L. Effect of early experience and litter on some emotionality variables in the rat. *J. comp. physiol. Psychol.,* 1970, *73,* 436–441.

King, H. D., and Donaldson, H. H. Life processes and size of the body and organs of the gray Norway rat during ten generations in captivity. *Amer. Anatom. Memoirs,* 1929, No. *14.*

King, J. A., and Gurney, N. L. Effect of early social experience on adult aggressive behavior in C57BL/10 mice. *J. comp. physiol. Psychol.*, 1954, *47*, 326–330.

King, M. B., and Hoebel, B. G. Killing elicited by brain stimulation in rats. *Comm. Behav. Biol.*, 1968, *2*, 173–177.

Kinsey, A. C., Pomeroy, W. B., and Martin, C. E. *Sexual Behavior in the Human Male*. Philadelphia, W. B. Saunders, 1948.

Kinsey, A. C., Pomeroy, W. B., Martin, C. E., and Gebhard, P. H. *Sexual Behavior in the Human Female*. Philadelphia, W. B. Saunders, 1953.

Kislack, J. W., and Beach, F. A. Inhibition of aggressiveness by ovarian hormones. *Endocrinol.*, 1955, *56*, 684–692.

Klapper, J. T. *The Effects of Mass Communication*. Glencoe, Ill., Free Press, 1960.

Klingel, H. von. Soziale Organisation und Verhalten freilebender Steppenzebras. *Zeitschrift für Tierpsychologie*, 1967, *24*, 580–624.

Klingel, H. von. Soziale Organisation und Verhaltensiveisen von Hartmann und Bergzebras *(Equus zebra hartmannae und E. z. zebra)*. *Zeitschrift für Tierpsychologie*, 1968, *25*, 76–88.

Klopfer, P. H. *Habitats and Territories*. New York, Basic Books, 1969.

Kluver, H., and Bucy, P. C. Psychic blindness and other symptoms following bilateral temporal lobectomy in Rhesus monkeys. *Amer. J. Physiol.*, 1937, *119*, 352–353.

Knapp hearings: how many 'rotten apples' in the barrel? *New York Times*, Oct. 24, 1971.

Kneeland, D. E. Pocketbook issues secondary in rural Iowa. *New York Times*, Oct. 18, 1968.

Kniveton, B. H., and Stephenson, G. M. The effect of pre-experience on imitation of an aggressive film model. *Brit. J. clin. Psychol.*, 1970, *9*, 31–36.

Knutson, J. F. The effects of shocking one member of a pair of rats. *Psychon. Sci.*, 1971, *22*, 265–266.

de Kock, L. L., Stoddart, D. M., and Kacher, H. Notes on behaviour and food supply of lemmings *(Lemmus lemmus L.)* during a peak density in Southern Norway, 1966/67. *Zeitschrift für Tierpsychologie*, 1969, *26*, 609–622.

Kondo, C. Y., and Lorens, S. A. Sex differences in the effects of septal lesions. *Physiol. Behav.*, 1971, *6*, 481–485.

Koppet, L. Home court: winning edge. *New York Times*, January 9, 1972.

Kuhn, D. Z., Madsen, C. H., Jr., and Becker, W. C. Effects of exposure to an aggressive model and "frustration" on childrens' aggressive behavior. *Child Devel.*, 1967, *38*, 739–745.

Kulkarni, A. S. Satiation of instinctive mouse killing in rats. *Psychol. Rev.*, 1968, *18*, 385–388.

Kummer, H. *Social Organization of Hamadrya Baboon*. Chicago, University of Chicago Press, 1968.

Kuo, Z. Y. The genesis of the cat's response toward the rat. *J. comp. Psychol.*, 1930, *11*, 1–35.

Kuo, Z. Y. *The Dynamics of Behavior Development: An Epigenetic View*. New York, Random House, 1967.

Landauer, T. K., and Whiting, J. W. M. Infantile stimulation and adult stature of human males. *Amer. Anthropol.*, 1964, *66*, 1007–1028.

Lang, P. J., Geer, J., and Hnatiow, M. Semantic generalization of conditioned autonomic responses. *J. exper. Psychol.*, 1963, *65*, 552–558.

Lavery, J. J., and Foley, P. J. Altruism or arousal in the rat? *Science*, 1963, *140*, 172–173.

Lawson, R. *Frustration: the Development of a Scientific Concept*. New York, Macmillan, 1965.

Leakey, L. S. Development of aggression as a factor in early human and pre-human evolution. *In* C. D. Clemente and D. B. Lindsley (Eds.), *Aggression and Defense*. Los Angeles, University of California Press, 1967.

Le Boeuf, B. J., and Peterson, R. S. Social status and mating activity in elephant seals. *Science*, 1969, *163*, 91–93.

Lee, C. T. Reactions of mouse fighters to male and female mice, intact or deodorized. *Amer. Zool.*, 1970, *10*, 56.

LeMaire, L. Danish experiences regarding the castration of sexual offenders. *J. Criminal Law and Criminology*, 1956, *47*, 294–310.

Lerner, I. M. *Heredity, evolution and society*. San Francisco, W. H. Freeman, 1968.

Lessac, M. S., and Solomon, R. L. Effects of early isolation on the later adaptive behavior of beagles. *Devel. Psychol.*, 1969, *1*, 14–25.

Levine, S. A further study of infantile handling and adult avoidance learning. *J. Personality*, 1956, *25*, 70–80.

Levine, S. Maternal and environmental influences on the adrenocortical response to stress in weanling rats. *Science*, 1967, *156*, 258–260.

Levine, S., Chevalier, J. A., and Korchin, S. J. The effects of shock and handling in infancy on later avoidance learning. *J. Personality*, 1956, *24*, 475–493.

Levine, S., and Lewis, G. W. The relative importance of experimenter contact in an effect produced by extra-stimulation in infancy. *J. comp. physiol. Psychol.*, 1959, *52*, 368–369.

Levison, P. K., and Flynn, J. P. The objects attacked by cats during stimulation of the hypothalamus. *Anim. Behav.*, 1965, *13*, 217–220.

Levy, D. M. *Maternal Overprotection*. New York, Columbia University Press, 1943.

Levy, I. V., and King, I. A. The effects of testosterone propionate on fighting behavior in young C57BL/10 mice. *Anat. Rec.*, 1953, *117*, 562.

Levy, S., and Kennard, M. A study of electroencephalogram as related to personality structure in a group of inmates of a state penitentiary. *Amer. J. Psychiat.*, 1953, *109*, 382–389.

Levy, S. G. A 150 year study of political violence in the U. S. *In* H. D. Graham and T. R. Gurr (Eds.), *Violence in America: Historical and Comparative Perspectives*. New York, Bantam Books, 1969.

Lieberson, S., and Silverman, A. R. The precipitants and underlying conditions of race riots. *Amer. Sociol. Rev.*, 1965, *30*, 887–898.

Lin, N. Territorial behavior in the cicada killer wasp, *Sphecius speciosus* (Drury). *Behaviour*, 1963, *20*, 113–133.

Lindner, H. Sexual responsiveness to perceptual tests in a group of sexual offenders. *J. Personality*, 1953, *21*, 364–374.

Lindzey, G., Winston, H., and Manosevitz, M. Social dominance in inbred mouse strains. *Nature*, 1961, *191*, 474–476.

Lindzey, G., Winston, H. D., and Manosevitz, M. Early experience genotype and temperament in *Mus musculus*. *J. comp. physiol. Psychol.*, 1963, *56*, 622–629.

Lion, J. R., Bach-y-Rita, G. L., and Ervin, F. R. The self-referred violent patient. *J.A.M.A.*, 1968, *205*, 503–505.

Lion, J. R., Bach-y-Rita, G. L., Ervin, F. R. Violent patients in the emergency room. *Amer. J. Psychiat.*, 1969, *125*, 12.

Lissman, H. W. Die Umwelt des Kampffisches (Betta splendens Regan). *Zeitschrift vergl. Physiol.*, 1932, *181*, 65–111.

Livingstone, F. B. The effects of warfare on the biology of the human species. *In* M. Fried, M. Harris, and R. Murphy (Eds.), *War: The Anthropology of Armed Conflict and Aggression*. Garden City, Natural History Press, 1967.

Lockard, R. B. The albino rat: a defensible choice or a bad habit? *Amer. Psychol.*, 1968, *23*, 734–742.

Lockard, R. B. Reflections on the fall of comparative psychology: is there a message for us all? *Amer. Psychol.*, 1971, *26*, 168–179.

Loew, C. A. Acquisition of a hostile attitude and its relation to aggressive behavior. *J. per. soc. Psychol.*, 1967, *65*, 552–558.

Lore, R. Pain avoidance behavior of rats reared in restricted and enriched environments. *Devel. Psychol.*, 1969, *1*, 482–484.

Lorenz, K. Ritualized fighting. *In* J. D. Carthy and F. J. Ebling (Eds.), *The Natural History of Aggression*. New York, Academic Press, 1964.

Lorenz, K. *Evolution and Modification of Behavior*. Chicago, University of Chicago Press, 1965.

Lorenz, K. *On Aggression*. New York, Harcourt, Brace, and World, 1966.

Lovaas, O. I. Effect of exposure to symbolic aggression on aggressive behavior. *Child Dev.*, 1961, *32*, 37–44.

Lubs, H. A., and Ruddle, F. H. Chromosomal abnormalities in the human population: estimation of rates on New Haven newborn study. *Science*, 1970, *169*, 495–497.

Lyons, D. O., and Ozolins, D. Pavlovian conditioning of shock-elicited aggression, a discrimination procedure. *J. exper. anal. Behav.*, 1970, *13*, 325–331.

Maccoby, E. E. (Ed.) *The Development of Sex Differences.* Stanford, Stanford University Press, 1966.

Maccoby, E. E., and Masters, J. C. Attachment and dependency. *In* P. H. Mussen (Ed.), *Carmichael's Manual of Child Psychology*, Vol. 2. New York, Wiley, 1970.

MacDonnell, M. F., and Flynn, J. P. Control of sensory fields by stimulation of the hypothalamus. *Science*, 1966a, *152*, 1406–1408.

MacDonnell, M. F., and Flynn, J. P. Sensory control of hypothalamic attack. *Anim. Behav.*, 1966b, *14*, 399–405.

MacLean, P. D., and Ploog, D. W. Cerebral representation of penile erection. *J. Neurophysiol.*, 1962, *25*, 29–55.

MacSwain, J. W. Crossroads of the insect world. *Nat. Geog.*, 1966, *130*, 844–857.

Maier, R. A., and Maier, B. M. *Comparative Animal Behavior.* Belmont, Cal., Brooks-Cole, 1970.

Mallick, S. K., and McCandless, B. R. A study of catharsis of aggression. *J. per. soc. Psychol.*, 1966, *4*, 591–596.

Marihuana and Health. Report issued by the National Institutes of Mental Health. Washington, D. C., U. S. Government Printing Office, 1971.

Mark, V. H., and Ervin, F. R. *Violence and the Brain.* New York, Harper and Row, 1970.

Markl, H. von. Das schutzverhalten eines welses *(Hassar orestis Steindachner)* gegen angriffe von piranhas *(Serrasalmus rattereri* Kner). *Zeitschrift für Tierpsychologie*, 1969, *26*, 385–389.

Marler, P. Studies of fighting in chaffinches. (1) Behaviour in relation to the social hierarchy. *Brit. J. Anim. Behav.*, 1955, *3*, 111–117.

Marler, P. Communication in monkeys and apes. *In* I. DeVore (Ed.), *Primate Behavior.* New York, Holt, Rinehart and Winston, 1965.

Marler, P. On aggression in birds. *In* V. G. Dethier (Ed.), *Topics in Animal Behavior.* New York, Harper and Row, 1971.

Marrone, R. L., Pray, S. L., and Bridges, C. C. Norepinephrine elicitation of aggressive display responses in *Betta splendens. Psychon. Sci.*, 1966, *5*, 207–208.

Martin, R. D., Reproduction and ontogeny in tree-shrews *(Tupaia belangeri)* with reference to their general behaviour and taxonomic relationships. *Zeitschrift für Tierpsychologie*, 1968, *25*, 1409–1495.

Martin, M. F., Gelfand, D. M., and Hartmann, D. P. Effects of adult and peer observers on boys' and girls' responses to an aggressive model. *Child Development*, 1972, in press.

Marx, G. T. Civil disorder and the agents of social control. *J. Soc. Issues*, 1970, *26*, 19–58.

Marx, L. American institutions and ecological ideals. *Science*, 1970, *170*, 945.

Mason, W. A. The effect of social restriction on the behavior of rhesus monkeys. I. Free social behavior. *J. comp. physiol. Psychol.*, 1960, *53*, 363–368.

Mason, W. A. The effects of environmental restriction on the social development of rhesus monkeys. *In* C. H. Southwick (Ed.), *Primate Social Behavior.* Princeton, Van Nostrand, 1963.

Mason, W. A., and Green, P. C. The effects of social restriction on the behavior of rhesus monkeys. IV. Responses to a novel environment and to an alien species. *J. comp. physiol. Psychol.*, 1962, *55*, 363–368.

Masserman, J. H. Is the hypothalamus a center of emotion? *Psychosomatic Medicine*, 1941, *3*, 3–25.

Matthews, L. H. Overt fighting in mammals. *In* J. D. Carthy and F. J. Ebling (Eds.), *The Natural History of Aggression*, New York, Academic Press, 1964.

McCord, W., and McCord, J. *Psychopathy and Delinquency.* New York, Grune and Stratton, 1956.

McCord, W., McCord, J., and Howard, A. Familial correlates of aggression in nondelinquent male children. *J. abnorm. soc. Psychol.*, 1961, *63*, 493–503.

McDougall, W., and McDougall, K. Notes on instinct and intelligence in rats and cats. *J. comp. Psychol.*, 1927, *7*, 145–175.

McGaffin, W., and Knoll, E. *Scandal in the Pentagon: A Challenge to Democracy.* Greenwich, Conn., Fawcett, 1969.

McNeil, E. B. Psychology and aggression. *J. Conflict Resolution*, 1959, *3*, 195–293.

Mead, M. Violence in the perspective of cultural history. *In* J. H. Masserman (Ed.), *Violence and War.* New York, Grune and Stratton, 1963.

Megargee, E. I. Undercontrolled and overcontrolled personality types in extreme antisocial aggression. *Psychol. Monog.*, 1966, *80*, No. 3 (whole no. 611).

Megargee, E. I. The prediction of violence with psychological tests. *In* C. D. Spielberger (Ed.), *Current Topics in Clinical and Community Psychology*, Vol. 1. New York, Academic Press, 1970.

Megargee, E. I., and Mendelsohn, G. A. A cross-validation of twelve MMPI indices of hostility and control. *J. abnorm. soc. Psychol.*, 1962, *65*, 431–438.

Melman, S. Pax Americana II: cost of militarism. *New York Times*, Nov. 3, 1970.

Melvin, K. B., and Anson, J. E. Facilitative effects of punishment and aggressive behavior in the Siamese fighting fish. *Psychon. Sci.*, 1969, *14*, 89–90.

Melzack, R., and Scott, T. H. The effects of early experience on the response to pain. *J. comp. physiol. Psychol.*, 1957, *50*, 155–161.

Menninger, K. *The Crime of Punishment.* New York, Viking Press, 1966.

Michael, R. P., Keverne, E. B., and Bonsall, R. W. Pheromones: isolation of male sex attractants from a female primate. *Science*, 1971, *172*, 946–966.

Milgram, S. Behavioral study of obedience. *J. abnorm. soc. Psychol.*, 1963, *67*, 371–378.

Milgram, S. Some conditions of obedience and disobedience to authority. *Human Relations*, 1965, *18*, 57–75.

Milgram, S. The compulsion to do evil. *Patterns of Prejudice*, 1967, *1*, 3–7.

Milgram, S. Alternatives to aggression. Discussion. New England Psychological Association, Boston, Mass, Nov. 14, 1970.

Miller, N. E. The frustration-aggression hypothesis. *Psychol. Rev.*, 1941, *48*, 337–342.

Miller, N. E. Studies of fear as an acquirable drive. I. Fear as motivation and fear reduction as reinforcement in the learning of a new response. *J. exper. Psychol.*, 1948a, 89–101.

Miller, N. E. Theory and experiment relating psychoanalytic displacement to stimulus-response generalization. *J. abnorm. soc. Psychol.*, 1948b, *43*, 155–178.

Miller, N. E., and Bugelski, R. The influence of frustrations imposed by the in-group on attitude expressed toward out-groups. *J. Psychol.* 1948, *25*, 437–442.

Miller, N. E., and Dollard, J. *Social Learning and Imitation.* New Haven, Yale University Press, 1941.

Millon, T. *Modern Psychopathology.* Philadelphia, W. B. Saunders, 1969.

Millones, P. Consumer indignation. *New York Times*, June 30, 1970.

Mintz, M., and Cohen, J. S. *America, Inc.* New York, Dial Press, 1971.

Mischel, W. Sex-typing and socialization. *In* P. H. Mussen (Ed.), *Carmichael's Manual of Child Psychology*, Vol. 2. New York, Wiley, 1970.

Mitchell, G. Abnormal behavior in primates. *In* L. A. Rosenblum (Ed.), *Primate Behavior*, Vol. 1. New York, Academic Press, 1970.

Monahan, T. P. Family status and the delinquent child: a reappraisal and some new findings. *Social Forces*, 1957, *35*, 250–258.

Money, J. Psychosexual differentiation. *In* J. Money (Ed.), *Sex Research: New Developments.* New York, Holt, Rinehart and Winston, 1965.

Montagu, M. F. A. The new litany of "innate depravity," or original sin revisited. *In* M. F. A. Montagu (Ed.), *Man and Aggression.* London, Oxford University Press, 1968.

Moore, H. T., and Gilliland, A. R. The measurement of aggression. *J. appl. Psychol.*, 1921, *5*, 97–118.

Moore, M. Aggression themes in a binocular rivalry situation. *J. per. soc. Psychol.*, 1966, *3*, 685–688.

Morris, D. *The Naked Ape.* New York, McGraw-Hill, 1967.

Mosher, D. L., and Katz, H. Pornographic films, male verbal aggression against women, and guilt. Unpublished manuscript, summarized in Commission on

Obscenity and Pornography. Washington, D. C., U. S. Government Printing Office, 1970.

Mowrer, O. H. An experimental analogue of "regression" with incidental observations on "reaction formation." *J. abnorm. soc. Psychol.*, 1940, *35*, 56–87.

Moyer, K. E. Kinds of aggression and their physiological basis. *Comm. Behav. Biol.*, 1968, *2*, 65–87.

Moyer, K. E. Internal impulses to aggression. *N. Y. Acad. Sci.*, 1969a, *31*, 104–114.

Moyer, K. E. The physiology of aggression and the implications for aggression control. Paper presented at the Symposium on Aggressive Behavior, City University of New York, 1969b.

Moyer, K. E. The physiology of affiliation and hostility. Paper presented at the University of Virginia Sesquicentennial Symposium, Oct., 1969c.

Moyer, K. E. The physiology of aggression and the implications for aggression control. *In* J. L. Singer (Ed.), *The Control of Aggression and Violence*. New York, Academic Press, 1971.

Mugford, R. A., and Nowell, N. W. The preputial glands as a source of aggression-promoting odors in mice. *Physiol. Behav.*, 1971, *6*, 247–249.

Mulvihill, D. J., and Tumin, M. M. Crimes of violence, Vol. 12. Staff report submitted to the National Commission on the Causes and Prevention of Violence. Washington, D. C., U. S. Government Printing Office, 1969.

Munn, N. L. *Handbook of Psychological Research on the Rat*. New York, Houghton Mifflin, 1950.

Murdock, G. P. World ethnographic sample. *Amer. Anthrop.*, 1957, *59*, 664–687.

Murphy, D. P. The outcome of 625 pregnancies in women subjected to pelvic radium roentgen irradiation. *Amer. J. Obstet. Gynec.*, 1929, *18*, 179–187.

Murphy, D. P. *Congenital malformation*. Philadelphia, University of Pennsylvania Press, 1957.

Murphy, M. R., and Schneider, G. E. Olfactory bulb removal eliminates mating behavior in the male golden hamster. *Science*, 1970, *167*, 302–304.

Myer, J. S. Stimulus control of mouse-killing rats. *J. comp. physiol. Psychol.*, 1964, *58*, 112–117.

Myer, J. S. Prior killing experience and the effects of punishment on the killing of mice by rats. *Anim. Behav.*, 1967, *15*, 59–61.

Myer, J. S. Early experience and the development of mouse killing by rats. *J. comp. physiol. Psychol.*, 1969, *67*, 46–49.

Myer, J. S., and Baenninger, R. Some effects of stress and punishment on mouse-killing by rats. *J. comp. physiol. Psychol.*, 1966, *62*, 292–297.

Myer, J. S., and White, R. T. Aggressive motivation in the rat. *Anim. Behav.*, 1965, *13*, 430–433.

Mykytowycz, R. Territorial marking by rabbits. *Sci. Amer.*, 1968, *218*, 116–126.

Narabayaski, H., Nagao, T., Saito, Y., Yoshida, M., and Nagahata, M. Stereotaxic amygdalotomy for behavior disorders. *Arch. Neurol.*, 1963, *9*, 1–26.

Neumeyer, K. "Copy cat" ruse in Tate slaying. *Boston Herald Traveler*, Nov. 11, 1971.

O'Connor, N. Children in restricted environments. *In* G. Newton and S. Levine (Eds.), *Early Experience and Behavior; The Psychobiology of Development*. Springfield, Ill., Charles C Thomas, 1968.

O'Kelly, L. W., and Steckle, L. C. A note on long enduring emotional responses in the rat. *J. Psychol.*, 1939, *8*, 125–131.

Olds, J. The influence of practice on the strength of approach drives. *J. Exper. Psychol.*, 1953, *46*, 232–236.

Opton, E. M., Jr. It never happened and besides they deserved it. *In* N. Sanford and C. Comstock (Eds.), *Sanctions for Evil*. San Francisco, Jossey-Bass, 1971.

Orlansky, H. Infant care and personality. *Psychol. Rev.*, 1949, *46*, 1–48.

Pakistan: The ravaging of golden Bengal. *Time*, August 2, 1971.

Panksepp, J. Aggression elicited by electrical stimulation of the hypothalamus in albino rats. *Physiol. Behav.*, 1971a, *6*, 321–329.

Panksepp, J. Drugs and "stimulus-bound" attack. *Physiol. Behav.*, 1971b, *6*, 317–320.

Panksepp, J. Effects of hypothalamic lesions on mouse-killing and shock-induced fighting in rats. *Physiol. Behav.*, 1971c, *6*, 311–316.

Pastore, N. The role of arbitrariness in the frustration-aggression hypothesis. *J. abnorm. soc. Psychol.*, 1952, *47*, 728–731.

Payne, A. P., and Swanson, H. H. Hormonal control of aggressive dominance in the female hamster. *Physiol. Behav.*, 1971, *6*, 355–357.

Peeke, H. R. S., and Peeke, S. C. Habituation of aggressive responses in the Siamese fighting fish *(Betta splendens). Behaviour*, 1970, *36*, 232–245.

Peeke, H. R. S., Wyers, E. J., and Herz, M. J. Waning of the aggressive response to male models in the three spined stickleback *(Gasterosteus aculeatus* L.). *Anim. Behav.*, 1969, *17*, 224–228.

Phoenix, C. H., Goy, R. W., Gerall, A. A., and Young, W. C. Organizing action of prenatally administered testosterone propionate on the tissues mediating mating behavior in the female guinea pig. *Endocrinol.*, 1959, *65*, 369–382.

Plotnik, R. Changes in social behavior of squirrel monkeys after anterior temporal lobectomy. *J. comp. physiol. Psychol.*, 1968, *66*, 369–377.

Plummer, G. Abnormalities occurring in children exposed in utero to the atomic bomb in Hiroshima. *Pediatrics*, 1952, *10*, 687.

Powell, D. A., and Creer, T. L. Interaction of developmental and environmental variables in shock elicited aggression. *J. comp. physiol. Psychol.*, 1969, *69*, 219–225.

President's Commission on Law Enforcement and Administration of Justice. *Drunkenness.* Task force report. Washington, D. C., U. S. Government Printing Office, 1967.

President's Commission on Law Enforcement and Administration of Justice. *Narcotics and drug abuse.* Task force report. Washington, D. C., U. S. Government Printing Office, 1967.

Price, W. H., and Whatmore, P. B. Behavior disorders and patterns of crime among XYY males identified at a maximum security hospital. *Brit. Med. J.*, 1967, *69*, 533–536.

Propper, M. M. Exposure to sexually oriented material among young male prison offenders. *Technical Reports of the Commission on Obscenity and Pornography*, Vol. 9. Washington, D. C., U. S. Government Printing Office, 1970.

Public would outlaw all pistols except for police. *Public Opinion News Service*, Sept. 4, 1959.

Ralls, K. Mammalian scent marking. *Science*, 1971, *171*, 443–449.

Ransford, H. E. Isolation, powerlessness and violence: a study of attitudes and participation in the Watts riot. *J. Sociol.*, 1968, *73*, 581–591.

Rapoport, A. Models of conflict: cataclysmic and strategic. *In* A. deReuck and J. Knight (Eds.), *Conflict in Society.* Boston, Little, Brown and Co., 1966.

Rappeport, J. R., Lassen, G., and Hay, N. B. A review of the literature on the dangerousness of the mentally ill. *In* J. R. Rappeport, Jr. (Ed.), *Clinical Evaluation of the Dangerousness of the Mentally Ill.* Springfield, Ill., Charles C Thomas, 1967.

Rasa, O. A. E. The effect of pair isolation on reproductive success in *Etroplus maculatus* (Cichlidae). *Zeitschrift für Tierpsychologie*, 1969, *26*, 846–852.

Rasa, O. A. E. Territoriality and the establishment of dominance by means of visual cues in *Pomacentrus jenkinsi* (Pisces: Pomacentridae). *Zeitschrift für Tierpsychologie*, 1969, *26*, 825–845.

Raveling, D. G. Dominance relationships and agonistic behavior of Canada geese in winter. *Behaviour*, 1970, *37*, 291–319.

Raynes, A. E., and Ryback, R. S. Effect of alcohol and congeners on aggressive response in *Betta splendens. Quart. J. Studies on Alcohol*, 1970, *5*, 130–135.

Raynes, A. E., and Ryback, R. S., and Ingle, D. The effect of alcohol on aggression in *Betta splendens. Comm. Behav. Biol.*, 1968, *2*, 141–146.

Renfrew, J. W. The intensity function and reinforcing properties of brain stimulation that elicits attack. *Physiol. Behav.*, 1969, *4*, 509–575.

Reston, J. Washington: the cost of arms and poverty. *New York Times*, Nov. 19, 1969.

Reston, J. The painless revolution. *New York Times*, Jan. 29, 1971.

Revusky, S., and Garcia, J. Learned associations over long delays. In G. H. Bower and J. T. Spence (Eds.), *The Psychology of Learning and Motivation*, Vol. 4. New York, Academic Press, 1970.

Rice, G. E., and Gainer, P. "Altruism" in the albino rat. *J. comp. physiol. Psychol.*, 1962, *55*, 123–125.

Richardson, L. F. *Statistics of deadly quarrels*. London, Stevens and Sons, 1960.

Ripley, A. Big man on the campus: police undercover agent. *New York Times*, Mar. 29, 1971.

Robber, a Negro, gets death penalty in South. *New York Times*, May 30, 1970.

Roberts, S. V. Informer says police prompt radical acts. *New York Times*, Oct. 25, 1971.

Roberts, W. W. Hypothalamic mechanisms for motivational and species-typical behavior. In R. E. Whalen, F. R. Thompson, M. Verzeano, and N. M. Weinberger (Eds.), *The Neural Control of Behavior*. New York, Academic Press, 1971.

Roberts, W. W., and Berquist, E. H. Attack elicited by hypothalamic stimulation in cats raised in social isolation. *J. comp. physiol. Psychol.*, 1968, *66*, 590–595.

Roberts, W. W., and Kiess, A. O. Motivational properties of hypothalamic aggression in cats. *J. comp. physiol. Psychol.*, 1964, *58*, 187–193.

Roberts, W. W., Steinberg, M. L., and Means, L. W. Hypothalamic mechanisms for sexual, aggressive and other motivational behaviors in the opossum, *Didelphis Virginiana*. *J. comp. physiol. Psychol.*, 1967, *64*, 1–15.

Robinson, D. Report says 10 churches abet 'immoral acts' of arms industry. *New York Times*, January 5, 1972.

Robinson, M. H., Abele, L. G., and Robinson, B. Attack autotomy: a defense against predators. *Science*, 1970, *169*, 300–301.

Roeder, K. D. *Nerve Cells and Insect Behavior*. Cambridge, Harvard University Press, 1967.

Roediger, H. L. III, and Stevens, M. C. The effects of delayed presentation of the object of aggression in pain induced fighting. *Psychon. Sci.*, 1970, *21*, 55–56.

Ropartz, P. The relation between olfactory stimulation and aggressive behaviour in mice. *Anim. Behav.*, 1968, *16*, 97–100.

Rosenbaum, M. E., and DeCharms, R. Direct and vicarious reduction of hostility. *J. abnorm. soc. Psychol.*, 1960, *60*, 105–111.

Rosenberg, B. G. The psychology of nonaggression. Paper presented to the New England Psychological Association. Boston, Mass., Nov., 1970.

Rosenthal, J. Jail census finds 52% not convicted. *New York Times*, Jan. 7, 1971.

Rosenthal, J. Census data show blacks still poor. *New York Times*, Feb. 12, 1971.

Ross, E. S. Asian insects in disguise. *Nat. Geog.*, 1965, *128*, 432–439.

Rotter, J. B. *Social Learning and Clinical Psychology*. Englewood Cliffs, N. J., Prentice-Hall, 1954.

Rovner, J. S. Territoriality in the sheet-web spider *Cinyphia triangularis* (Clerck) (araneae, Linyphiidae). *Zeitschrift für Tierpsychologie*, 1968, *25*, 232–242.

Rugaber, W. Public is found to resist prison reform proposals. *New York Times*, Oct. 25, 1971.

Rüppel, V. G. Eine, "Luge" als gerichtete Mitteilung beim Eisfuchs. *Zeitschrift für Tierpsychologie*, 1969, *26*, 371–374.

Sackett, G. P. Some persistent effects of differential rearing conditions on pre-adult social behavior of monkeys. *J. comp. physiol. Psychol.*, 1967, *64*, 363–365.

Sackett, G. P. Abnormal behavior in laboratory-reared rhesus monkeys. In M. W. Fox (Ed.), *Abnormal Behavior in Animals*. Philadelphia, W. B. Saunders, 1968.

Sackett, G. B. Unlearned response, differential rearing experiences, and the development of social attachments by rhesus monkeys. In L. A. Rosenblum (Ed.), *Primate Behavior*, Vol. I. New York, Academic Press, 1970.

Sade, D. S. Determinants of dominance in a group of free-ranging rhesus monkeys. In S. A. Altmann (Ed.), *Social Communication Among Primates*. Chicago, University of Chicago Press, 1967.

Sanford, N. Going beyond prevention. In N. Sanford and C. Comstock (Eds.), *Sanctions for Evil*. San Francisco, Jossey-Bass, 1971.

Sanford, N., and Comstock, C. *Sanctions for Evil.* San Francisco, Jossey-Bass, 1971.

Santos, M. Effects of *Cannabis sativa* (Marihuana) on the fighting behavior of mice. *Psychopharmacologia,* 1966, *8,* 437–444.

Schacter, S. *The Psychology of Affiliation.* Stanford, Stanford University Press, 1959.

Schacter, S., and Latane, B. Crime, cognition, and the autonomic nervous system. *In* D. Levine (Ed.), *Nebraska Symposium on Motivation.* Lincoln, University of Nebraska Press, 1964.

Schacter, S., and Singer, J. E. Cognitive, social and physiological determinants of emotional state. *Psych. Rev.,* 1962, *69,* 379–399.

Schaefer, T., Weingarten, F. S., and Towne, J. C. Temperature change: The basic variable in the early handling phenomenon? *Science,* 1962, *135,* 41–42.

Schaller, G. B. Life with the king of beasts. *Nat. Geog.,* 1969, *135,* 494–519.

Schein, M. W., and Fohrman, M. H. Social dominance relationships in a herd of dairy cattle. *Brit. J. anim. Behav.,* 1956, *3,* 45–55.

Schein, M. W., and Hale, E. B. Stimuli eliciting sexual behavior. *In* F. A. Beach (Ed.), *Sex and Behavior.* New York, Wiley, 1965.

Schenkel, R. Play, exploration and territoriality in the wild lion. *In* P. A. Jewell and C. Loizos (Eds.), *Play, Exploration and Territory in Mammals.* London, Academic Press, 1966.

Schleidt, W. M., Schleit, M., and Magg, M. Störung der Mutter-Kind-Beziehung bei Trüthuhnern durch Gehöverlust. *Behaviour,* 1960, *16,* 254–260.

Schreiner, L., and Kling, A. Rhinencephalon and behavior. *Am. J. Physiol.,* 1956, *184,* 486–490.

Schwab, R. S., Sweet, W. H., Mark, V. H., Kjellberg, R. N., and Ervin, F. R. Treatment of intractable temporal lobe epilepsy by stereotactic amygdala lesions. *Trans. Amer. Neurol. Assn.,* 1965, 12–19.

Scott, J. P. Genetic differences in the social behavior of inbred strains of mice. *J. Hered.,* 1942, *33,* 11–15.

Scott, J. P. *Aggression.* Chicago, University of Chicago Press, 1958a.

Scott, J. P. *Animal Behavior.* Chicago, University of Chicago Press, 1958b.

Scott, J. P. Critical periods in behavioral development. *Science,* 1962a, *138,* 949–958.

Scott, J. P. Hostility and aggression in animals. *In* E. L. Bliss (Ed.), *Roots of Behavior.* New York, Harper and Row, 1962b.

Scott, J. P. Agonistic behavior of mice and rats: a review. *Amer. Zool.,* 1966, *6,* 683–701.

Scott, J. P. *Early Experience and the Organization of Behavior.* Belmont, Cal., Brooks-Cole, 1968a.

Scott, J. P. Evolution and domestication of the dog. *Evol. Biol.,* 1968b, *2,* 244–275.

Scott, J. P. The process of primary socialization in the dog. *In* G. Newton and S. Levine (Eds.), *Early Experience and Behavior.* Springfield, Ill., Charles C Thomas, 1968c.

Scott, J. P. A proposal for peace research. *Amer. Psychol.,* 1970, *25,* 647–648.

Scott, J. P., and Frederickson, E. The causes of fighting in mice and rats. *Physiol. Zool.,* 1951, *26,* 273–309.

Scott, J. P., and Fuller, J. L. *Genetics and the Social Behavior of the Dog.* Chicago, University of Chicago Press, 1965.

Sears, P. S. Doll play aggression in normal young children: influence of sex, age, sibling status, and father's absence. *Psychol. Monog.,* 1951, *65,* 1–42.

Sears, R. R. Personality development in the family. *In* J. M. Seidman (Ed.), *The Child.* New York, Holt, Rinehart and Winston, 1958.

Sears, R. R., Development of gender role. *In* F. A. Beach, *Sex and Behavior.* New York, Wiley, 1965.

Sears, R. R., Maccoby, E., and Levin, H. *Patterns of Child Rearing.* Evanston, Ill., Row, Peterson, 1957.

Sears, R. R., Whiting, J. W. M., Nowlis, V., and Sears, P. S. Some child rearing antecedents of aggression and dependency in young children. *Genet. Psychol. Monog.,* 1953, *47,* 135–236.

Seward, J. P. Aggressive behavior in the rat. I. General characteristics, age, and sex differences. *J. comp. physiol. Psychol.,* 1945, *38,* 175.

Shabecoff, P. Prisoner killing divides soldiers. *New York Times*, Apr. 5, 1970.

Shabecoff, P. U. S. study finds wasteful costs in defense work. *New York Times*, Mar. 18, 1971.

Shah, S. A. Recent developments in human genetics and their implication for problems of social deviance. Paper presented at the American Association for the Advancement of Science, Chicago, Dec. 28, 1970a.

Shah, S. A. *Report on the XYY chromosomal abnormality.* National Institutes of Mental Health conference report. Washington, D. C., U. S. Government Printing Office, 1970b.

Shah, S. A., and Weber, G. H. *The problem of individual violence.* Report submitted to the National Commission on the Causes and Prevention of Violence, 1968.

The shame of prisons. *Time*, Jan. 18, 1971.

Sheatsley, P. B., and Feldman, J. J. The assassination of President Kennedy: a preliminary report on public reactions and behavior. *Public Opinion Quarterly*, 1964, *28*, 189.

Sidowski, J. B. Altruism, helplessness and distress: effects of physical restraint on the social and play behaviors of infant monkeys. *Proc. Amer. Psychol. Assn.*, 1970, *5*, 233–234.

Siegel, A. E. The influence of violence in the mass media upon children's role expectations. *Child Devel.*, 1958, *29*, 35.

Siegel, A. E. Violence in the mass media. *In* D. N. Daniels, M. F. Gilula, and F. M. Ochberg (Eds.), *Violence and the Struggle for Existence.* Boston, Little, Brown and Co., 1970.

Silverman, I. Crisis in social psychology: the relevance of relevance. *Amer. Psychol.*, 1971, *26*, 583–584.

Simmons, K. E. L. Ecological determinants of breeding adaptations and social behaviour in two fish-eating birds. *In* J. H. Crook (Ed.), *Social Behaviour in Birds and Mammals.* New York, Academic Press, 1970.

Simonds, P. E. The bonnet macaque in South India. *In* I. DeVore (Ed.), *Primate Social Behavior.* New York, Holt, Rinehart and Winston, 1965.

Simpson, D. The dimension of world poverty. *Sci. Amer.*, 1968, *219*, 27–35.

Simpson, M. J. A. The threat display of the Siamese fighting fish, *Betta splendens. Anim. Behav. Monog.*, 1968, *1*, 1–73.

Singer, J. J. Hypothalamic control of male and female sexual behavior in female cats. *J. comp. physiol. Psychol.*, 1968, *66*, 738–742.

Singer, J. L. The influence of violence portrayed in television or motion pictures upon overt aggressive behavior. *In* J. L. Singer (Ed.), *The Control of Aggression and Violence.* New York, Academic Press, 1971.

Smith, D. E., King, M. B., and Hoebel, B. C. Lateral hypothalamic control of killing: evidence for a cholinoceptive mechanism. *Science*, 1970, *167*, 900–901.

Smith, H. M. *The fresh water fishes of Siam or Thailand.* Washington, D. C., U. S. Government Printing Office, 1945.

Smith, M. P., and Deutsch, K. L. Perspectives on obligation and civil disobedience. *In* M. P. Smith and K. L. Deutsch (Eds.), *Political Obligation and Civil Disobedience: Essays and Readings.* New York, Thomas Y. Crowell, 1972.

Smith, R. M. World arms bill: trillion since '64. *New York Times*, Mar. 22, 1970.

Sommer, R. Small group ecology. *Psychol. Bull.*, 1967, *67*, 145–152.

Sommer, R. *Personal Space.* Englewood Cliffs, N. J., Prentice-Hall, 1969.

Sommer, R., and Becker, F. Territorial defense and the good neighbor. *J. per soc. Psychol.*, 1969, *11*, 85–92.

Southwick, C. H. An experimental study of intragroup agonistic behavior in rhesus monkeys *(Macaca mulatta). Behaviour*, 1967, *28*, 182–209.

Southwick, C. H. Effect of maternal environment on aggressive behavior of inbred mice. *Comm. Behav. Biol.*, *Part A*, 1968, *1*, 129–132.

Southwick, C. H. Aggressive behavior of rhesus monkeys in natural and captive groups. *In* S. Garattini and E. B. Sigg (Eds.), *Aggressive Behaviour.* New York, Wiley, 1969.

Southwick, C. H., and Clark, L. H. Interstrain differences in aggressive behavior and exploratory activity of inbred mice. *Comm. Behav. Biol.*, *Part A*, 1968, *1*, 49–59.

Spencer-Booth, Y., and Hinde, R. A. Effects of brief separations from mother during infancy on behaviour of rhesus monkeys 6–24 months later. 1972. In press.

Spitz, R. A. Hospitalism: an inquiry into the genesis of psychiatric conditions in early childhood. *In* O. Fenichel, et al. (Eds.), *The Psychoanalytic Study of the Child*, Vol. I. New York, International Universities Press, 1945.

Staats, A. W., and Butterfield, W. H. Treatment of nonreading in a culturally deprived juvenile delinquent: an application of reinforcement principles. *Child Devel.*, 1965, *36*, 925–942.

Staub, E. The learning and unlearning of aggression. *In* J. L. Singer (Ed.), *The Control of Aggression and Violence*. New York, Academic Press, 1971.

Storr, A. Possible substitutes for war. *In* J. D. Carthy and F. J. Ebling (Eds.), *The Natural History of Aggression*. London, Academic Press, 1964.

Storr, A. *Human Aggression*. New York, Atheneum, 1968.

Strachey, A. *The Unconscious Motives of War*. London, George Allen and Unwin, 1957.

Strongman, K., and Champness, B. G. Dominance hierarchies and conflict in eye contact. *Acta Psychol.*, 1968, *28*, 376–386.

Sutherland, E. H. *White Collar Crime*. New York, Holt, Rinehart and Winston, 1949.

Sutherland, E. H. Crime of corporations. *In* G. Geis (Ed.), *White-Collar Criminal*. New York, Atherton, 1968.

Sweet, W. H., Ervin, F., and Mark, V. H. The relationship of violent behavior to focal cerebral disease. *In* S. Garattini and E. Sigg (Eds.), *Aggressive Behaviour*. New York, Wiley, 1969.

Taylor, R. L., and Weisz, A. E. American presidential assassination. *In* D. N. Daniels, M. F. Gilula, and F. M. Ochberg (Eds.),*Violence and the Struggle for Existence*. Boston, Little, Brown and Co., 1970.

Tellegen, A., Horn, J. M., and Legrand, R. G. Opportunity for aggression as a reinforcer in mice. *Psychon. Sci.*, 1969,*14*, 104–105.

Tennessee official calls death of a Negro youth 'homicide.'*New York Times*, Oct. 20, 1971.

Test, F. H. Social aggressiveness in an amphibian. *Science*, 1954, *120*, 140–141.

Thiessen, D. D., and Rodgers, D. A. Population density and endocrine function. *Psychol. Bull.*, 1961, *58*, 441–451.

Thirty-six thousand percent is a nice profit. *Boston Globe*, May 2, 1969.

Thoman, E. B., and Levine, S. Role of maternal disturbance and temperature change in early experience studies. *Physiol. Behav.*, 1969,*4*, 143–145.

Thoman, E. B., and Levine, S. Hormonal and behavioral changes in the rat mother as a function of early experience treatments of offspring. *Physiol. Behav.*, 1970, *5*, 1417–1421.

Thompson, T. Visual reinforcement in Siamese fighting fish. *Science*, 1963, *141*, 55–57.

Thompson, T. I. Visual reinforcement in fighting cocks. *J. exper. anal. Behav.*, 1964, *7*, 45–49.

Thompson, T. I., and Sturm, T. Visual reinforcer color and operant behavior in the Siamese fighting fish. *J. exper. anal. Behav.*, 1965, *8*, 341–344.

Thompson, W. R., and Grusec, J. E. Studies of early experience. *In* P. H. Mussen (Ed.), *Carmichael's Manual of Child Psychology*, Vol. I. New York, Wiley, 1970.

Tinbergen, N. *The Study of Instinct*. Oxford, Clarendon Press, 1951.

Tinbergen, N. Derived activities: their causation, biological significance, origin and emancipation during evolution. *Quart. Rev. Biol.* 1952, *27*, 1–32.

Tinbergen, N. *Social Behavior in Animals*. Great Britain, Methuen, 1953.

Tinbergen, N. On war and peace in animals and man: an ethologist's approach to the biology of aggression. *Science*, 1968, *160*, 1411–1418.

Tinklenberg, J. R., and Stillman, R. C. Drug use and violence. *In* D. N. Daniels, M. F. Gilula, and F. M. Ochberg (Eds.), *Violence and the Struggle for Existence*. Boston, Little, Brown and Co., 1970.

Toch, H. *Violent Men*. Chicago, Aldine, 1969.

Toch, H. The social psychology of violence. *In* E. I. Megargee and J. E. Hokanson (Eds.), *The Dynamics of Aggression*. New York, Harper and Row, 1970.

Toch, H. M., and Schulte, W. H. Readiness to perceive violence as the result of police training. *Brit. J. Psychol.*, 1961, *52*, 389–394.

Turk, A. T. The mythology of crime in America. *Criminology*, 1971, *8*, 397–411.

Turpin, R., and Lejune, J. *Human Afflictions and Aberrations.* Oxford, Pergamon Press, 1969.

Ulrich, R. Pain as a cause of aggression. *Amer. Zool.*, 1966, *6*, 643–662.

Ulrich, R., and Azrin, N. H. Reflexive fighting in response to aversive stimulation. *J. exper. anal. Behav.*, 1962, *5*, 511–520.

Uniform Crime Reports. *Crime in the United States, 1969.* Washington, D. C., U. S. Government Printing Office, 1970.

Valentine, G. H. *The Chromosome Disorders.* Philadelphia, Lippincott, 1969.

Van Hemel, P. E. Aggression as an incentive: operant behavior in the mouse-killing rat. Unpublished doctoral dissertation, Johns Hopkins University, 1970.

Van Hemel, P. E., and Myer, J. S. Satiation of mouse killing by rats in an operant situation. *Psychon. Sci.*, 1970, *21*, 129–130.

Van Lawick-Goodall, J. Tool-using bird: the Egyptian vulture. *Nat. Geog.*, 1968a, *133*, 631–641.

Van Lawick-Goodall, J. The behavior of free-living chimpanzees in the Gombe Stream Reserve. *Anim. Behav. Monog.*, 1968b, *I*, part III.

Varley, M., and Symmes, D. The hierarchy of dominance in a group of macaques. *Behaviour*, 1966, *27*, 54–75.

Vergnes, M., and Karli, P. Effets de la stimulation de l'hypothalamus latéral, de l'amygdale, et de l'hippocampe sur le comportement d'aggression interspécifique Rat-Souris. *Physiol. Behav*, 1969, *4*, 889–894.

Vergnes, M., and Karli, P. Déclenchement d'un comportement d'aggression par stimulation électrique de l'hypothalamus médian chez le rat. *Physiol. Behav.*, 1970, *5*, 1427–1430.

Vernon, W., and Ulrich, R. Classical conditioning of pain-elicited aggression. *Science*, 1966, *152*, 668–669.

Viel, B. The social consequences of population growth. *In* W. Jackson (Ed.), *Man and the Environment.* Dubuque, Iowa, Wm. C. Brown, 1971.

Vine, I. Communication by facial-visual signals. *In* J. H. Crook (Ed.), *Social Behaviour in Birds and Mammals.* New York, Academic Press, 1970.

Violent Crime. Report of the National Commission on the Causes and Prevention of Violence. New York, George Braziller, 1969.

Violence and organized crime. *In* Staff Report to the National Commission on the Causes and Prevention of Violence. *Crimes of violence*, Vol. 11. Washington, D. C., U. S. Government Printing Office, 1969.

Walker, E. P. *Mammals of the World.* Baltimore, Johns Hopkins Press, 1964.

Walters, R. H., and Parke, R. D. Emotional arousal, isolation, and discrimination learning in children. *J. exp. child Psychol.*, 1964, *1*, 163–173.

Walters, R. H., Thomas, E. L., and Acker, C. W. Enhancement of punitive behavior by audiovisual displays. *Science*, 1962, *136*, 872–873.

Ward, R. W. Ethology of the paradise fish, *Macropodus opercularis.* I. Differences between domestic and wild fish. *Copeia*, 1967, *4*, 809–813.

Warner, W. L. Murngin warfare. *Oceania*, 1930, *1*, 457–494.

Washburn, S. L. Primate studies and human evolution. Unpublished manuscript, 1971.

Washburn, S. L., and DeVore I. The social life of baboons. *Sci. Amer.*, 1961, *204*, 62–71.

Washburn, S. L., and Hamburg, D. A. Aggressive behavior in old world monkeys and apes. *In* P. C. Jay (Ed.), *Primates: Studies in Adaptation and Variability.* New York, Holt, Rinehart and Winston, 1968.

Washburn, S. L., and Harding, R. S. Evolution of primate behavior. *In* F. O. Schmitt (Ed.), *The Neurosciences.* New York, Rockefeller University Press, 1970.

Wasman, M., and Flynn, J. P. Direct attack elicited from the hypothalamus. *Arch. Neurol.*, 1962, *6*, 60–67.

Weinraub, B. Stock of A-arms is termed huge. *New York Times*, Nov. 3, 1970.

Weischer, M. L. Über die antiaggressive Wirkung von Lithium. *Psychopharmacologia*, 1969, *15*, 245–254.

Welch, B. L., and Welch, A. S. Aggression and the biogenic amine neuro-humors. *In* S. Garattini and E. B. Sigg (Eds.), *Aggressive Behaviour.* New York, Wiley, 1969.

Westby, B. W. M., and Box, H. O. Prediction of dominance in social groups of the electric fish. *Psychon. Sci.,* 1970, *21,* 181–183.

White, B. L., and Castle, P. W. Visual exploratory behavior following postnatal handling of human infants. *Percept. Mot. Skills,* 1964, *18,* 497–502.

Whittaker, R. H., and Feeny, P. P. Allelochemics: chemical interactions between species. *Science,* 1971, *171,* 757–770.

Wicker, T. The animals at Attica. *New York Times,* Sept. 16, 1971.

Wickler, W. Ökologie und Stammesgeschichte von Verhaltensweisen. *Fortschritte der Zoologie,* 1961, *13,* 303–365.

Wickler, W. Ursprung und biologische Deutung des Genitalpräsentierens männlicher Primaten. *Zeitschrift für Tierpsychologie,* 1966, *23,* 422–437.

Willems, E. P., and Rausch, H. *Naturalistic Viewpoints in Psychological Research.* New York, Holt, Rinehart and Winston, 1969.

Wilson, A. P., and Boelkins, C. Evidence for seasonal variation in aggressive behaviour by *Macaca mulatta. Anim. Behav.,* 1970, *18,* 719–724.

Windle, W. F. Brain damage by asphyxia at birth. *Sci. Amer.,* 1969, *221,* 76–84.

Wilson, J. A., Kuehn, R. E., and Beach, F. A. Modification of the sexual behavior of male rats produced by changing the stimulus female. *J. comp. physiol. Psychol.,* 1963, *56,* 636–644.

Wolfe, J. L., and Summerlin, C. T. Agonistic behavior in organized and disorganized cotton rat populations. *Science,* 1968, *160,* 98–99.

Wolfgang, M. E. Socio-economic factors related to crime and punishment in Renaissance Florence. *J. Criminal Law, Criminology, and Police Science,* 1956, *47,* 311–330.

Wolfgang, M. E. Victim-precipitated criminal homicide. *J. Criminal Law, Criminology, and Police Science,* 1957, *48,* 1–11.

Wolfgang, M. E. *Patterns in Criminal Homicide.* Philadelphia, University of Pennsylvania Press, 1958.

Wolfgang, M. E. Violence and human behavior. *In* F. Korten, S. Cook, and J. Lacey, *Psychology and the Problems of Society.* Washington, D. C., American Psychological Association, 1970.

Wolfgang, M. E., and Cohen, B. *Crime and Race: conceptions and misconceptions.* New York, Institute of Human Relations Press, 1970.

Wood, J. W., Johnson, K. G., Omcri, Y., Kawamote, S., and Keehn, R. J. Mental retardation in children exposed in utero to the atomic bombs in Hiroshima and Nagasaki. *Amer. J. Pub. Health,* 1967, *57,* 1331–1338.

Woodworth, C. H. Attack elicited in rats by electrical stimulation of the lateral hypothalamus. *Physiol. Behav.,* 1971, *6,* 345–353.

Woolton, R. J. Aggression in the early phases of the reproductive cycle of the male three-spined stickleback *(Gasterosteus aculeatus). Anim. Behav.,* 1970, *18,* 740–746.

Wynne-Edwards, V. C. *Animal Dispersion in Relation to Social Behavior.* New York, Hafner, 1962.

XYY chromosome defense. *Georgetown Law Journal,* 1969, *57,* 892–922.

Yablonsky, L. *The Violent Gang.* Baltimore, Penguin Books, 1966.

Zahl, P. A. Seeking the truth about the feared piranha. *Nat. Geog.,* 1970, *138,* 714–733.

Zarrow, M. X., Haltmeyer, G. C., Denenberg, V. H., and Thatcher, J. Response of the infantile rat to stress. *Endocrinol.,* 1966, *79,* 631–634.

Zitrin, A., Beach, F. A., Barchas, J. D., and Dement, W. C. Sexual behavior of male cats after administration of parachlorophenylalanine. *Science,* 1970, *170,* 868–869.

NAME INDEX

Kislack, J. N., 102
Kjellberg, R. W., 81
Klapper, J. T., 160
Klein, S. J., 87, 118
Kling, A., 70
Klingel, H. von, 19, 47
Klopfer, P. H., 43, 47
Kluver, H., 69
Kneeland, D. E., 152
Kniveton, B. H., 159
Knoll, E., 203, 204
Knurek, D. A., 138
Knutson, J. F., 39
Kock, L. L. de, 60
Koelling, R. A., 11
Koenig, A., 110, 123
Kondo, C. Y., 103
Koppett, L., 50
Korchin, S. J., 116
Kris, E., 126
Kuehn, R. E., 95
Kuhn, D. Z., 150
Kulkarni, A. S., 142
Kummer, H., 25
Kuo, Z. Y., 110, 121, 122

Laird, M., 201
Landauer, T. K., 119
Lang, P. J., 139
Larsen, O., 162
Lassen, G., 169
Latané, B., 67
Lavery, J. J., 142
Lawson, R., 136
Leakey, L. S., 12
LeBeuf, B. J., 24, 93
Lee, C. T., 46
Legrand, R. G., 141
Lejeune, J., 87
LeMaire, L., 99
Le Page, A., 137, 159, 166
Lerner, I. M., 64, 90
Lessac, M. S., 115
Levin, H., 125, 128
Levine, S., 97, 102, 116, 117, 118
Levinson, D. J., 215
Levison, P. K., 72
Levy, D. M., 114
Levy, G. W., 108
Levy, I. V., 100
Levy, R., 135
Levy, S., 80
Levy, S. G. A., 191
Lewin, K., 134, 136
Lewis, G. W., 117
Lewis, J. H., 103
Lieberson, S., 191
Lin, N., 20, 54

Lincoln, A., 180, 188
Lindner, H., 105
Lindsay, J., 224
Lindzey, G., 86, 118
Lion, J. R., 79
Lissman, H. N., 35
Littman, R. A., 117
Livingstone, F. B., 90, 207
Lobdell, P., 135
Lockard, R. B., 91, 159
Locke, J., 223
Loew, C. A., 140
Lore, R., 111
Lorens, S. A., 103
Lorenz, K., 3, 14, 15, 16, 19, 198, 210, 211
Lovaas, C. I., 140
Lowenstein, R. M., 126
Lubs, H. A., 89
Lutherman, C. Z., 100, 101
Lyons, D. O., 40

Maccoby, E. E., 120, 121, 125, 128
MacDonnell, M. F., 74
MacLean, P. D., 69, 96
MacSwain, J. W., 13
Madsen, C. H., Jr., 150
Magg, M., 46
Maier, B. M., 11
Maier, R. A., 11
Mallick, S. K., 158
Manosevitz, M., 86
Mark, V. H., 76, 79, 80, 81, 82, 83, 84, 97, 177, 217
Markey, F., 127
Markl, H. von, 13
Marler, P., 47, 54
Marrone, R. L., 67
Martin, C. E., 95
Martin, M. F., 150
Martin, R. D., 95
Marx, G. T., 194
Mason, W. A., 110, 111, 122
Masserman, J. H., 71
Masters, J. C., 120, 121
Matthews, L. H., 19
McCandless, B. R., 158
McCarthy, R., 204
McClelland, J., 173
McCord, J., 124, 125, 222
McCord, W., 124, 125, 222
McDougall, K., 122
McDougall, W., 122
McGaffin, W., 203, 204
McGinnis, M., 40
McGovern, G., 200
McLaughlin, R., 141
McNamara, R., 203, 227

SUBJECT INDEX

Adaptation(s), evolutionary, 1, 9, 10, 41, 43, 58, 210
  behavioral, 13–15
    in humans, 15–17
  defensive, 11–13
Affectional bonds, 119–121
  mother-child, 120
Aggression, definitions of, 4–8
"Aggression machine," experimental use of, 140, 158, 159, 205. See also *Punishment.*
Agonistic behavior, in definition of aggression, 8
Alcoholic beverages, and crime, 79, 166, 169, 171, 207
  experimental use of, 67
  versus marihuana, 175, 176, 177
Altruism, 14, 142
Amphetamines, 174, 177
Amygdala, 68, 69, 70, 81, 82, 84. See also *Limbic system.*
Androgens, and aggressive behavior, 100, 102, 103. See also *Hormones, sex.*
Antelopes, 13, 32, 54, 94
Ants, 14, 198
Apes. See *Monkeys, Chimpanzees,* and other particular types.
Aphids, ecological limitations and, 60
Appeasement, as learned response, 6, 16, 115. See also *Rituals.*
Assassination, 5, 144, 167, 168
Asses, 94
Attachment behavior, 119–121
  and cross-species rearing, 121–124
  mother-child, 120
Attribution theory, and human violence, 144
Autotomy, as defense mechanism, 11

Baboons, aggressive gestures of, 6, 31
  evolutionary adaptations of, 1, 13
  intra- and interspecific fighting in, 19, 20
  mating behavior of, 95

Baboons (*Continued*)
  social dominance and, 52, 53, 54, 55, 56
Barbiturates, 174, 177
Bats, 13
Bears, 98
Bees, 19, 21, 98
Beetles, chemical defense in, 11
Behavior modification, instrumental conditioning and, 141, 214, 215
Birds, 13, 21, 24, 25, 122. See also particular species.
  mating habits of, 57, 94, 95, 96
  social organization among, 52, 53, 54
  territorial behavior among, 21, 43, 47, 50, 51, 57
Blackcaps, 21
Blue jays, predation in, 11
Brain, 66, 69, 75, 92, 118, 210
  disease of, 169–170
    causes of, 77
    incidence of, 76, 79, 80, 217
    treatment of, 79–85, 218–219
  limbic system of, 68–85. See also *Limbic system.*
  stimulation of, chemical, 73, 174–178, 218, 219
    electrical, 70, 71, 72, 74, 75, 76, 81, 83, 141
Branching, in chimpanzees, 27
Buffaloes, 54, 94
Bulls, 87, 91, 98, 99
Butterflies, 11, 20

Caffeine, 176
Camels, 93, 94
Canine teeth, 10
Cannibalism, 21–23
Castration, 99, 100, 102, 107, 108. See also *Hormones, sex.*
Catfish, 13
Catharsis, 145, 211, 212
  television violence and, 154, 156–158, 161, 162
Cats, 4, 25, 95, 97, 99, 110, 121, 122, 150

263